With the conscious awakening of the ecology movement and the emerging women's movement focusing on Goddess traditions, *The Gaia Tradition* is a most timely and important piece of work.

Women are becoming more involved in the public eye. They are re-examining the roles they are supposed to fit into: rethinking menstruation and rediscovering the roots of an ancient religion that honored and respected women. Through the chapters of this book, women can begin to discover the magic that dwells within them. As they work through the outline provided for each season, they tap into the feminine power which they naturally contain and raise that power, manifesting it. By evoking the feminine power into their lives they awaken Goddess consciousness, which is an innate aspect of every woman just as God consciousness is an innate aspect of every man.

The Gaia Tradition provides a foundation upon which women from all walks of life can stand, finding support and direction. The book provides a rich psychologically healing effect by affirming that women are divine—not evil, stimulating the provocatively political attitude embraced by women —that which is focused on saving the life of our children and future generations on this planet as well as the planet itself. Also, *The Gaia Tradition* provides an intimate manner in which women can become initiated into the life of a "spiritual woman" who wisely nurtures and cares for herself.

The Gaia Tradition is a beneficial and important book for eco-feminists, lesbians, politically active women, New Age/metaphysically oriented women, Native American and Eastern traditionalists, housewives, modern workplace women, women in academia, psychologists and forward, open-minded women of current patriarchal religions.

About the Author

Kisma K. Stepanich was born July 4, 1958, in Southern California. She has been actively involved in the Goddess community since the early 1980s. Kisma founded Women Spirit Rising of Costa Mesa, a woman's organization that provides ongoing New and Full Moon ceremonies, monthly Goddess mythology circles, seasonal celebrations and women's spirituality workshops. Of Irish and Romanian descent, Kisma proudly claims her European heritage. Having studied and undergone initiation in the Celtic and Faery Traditions, she turned her focus to the native traditions of America and has studied and undergone initiation with several Shamans of Native American traditions. Kisma works toward integrating all indigenous traditions and worldwide Goddess cultures into one unified Earth tradition which she calls the Gaia Tradition.

To Write to the Author

We cannot guarantee that every letter written to the author can be answered, but all will be forwarded. Both the author and the publisher appreciate hearing from readers, learning of your enjoyment and benefit from this book. Llewellyn also publishes a bimonthly news magazine with news and reviews of practical esoteric studies and articles helpful to the student, and some readers' questions and comments to the author may be answered through this magazine's columns if permission to do so is included in the original letter. The author sometimes participates in seminars and workshops, and dates and places are announced in the Llewellyn *New Times*. To write to the author, or to ask a question, write to:

Kisma Stepanich

c/o The Llewellyn New Times

PO Box 64383-766, St. Paul, MN 55164-0383, U.S.A.

Please enclose a self-addressed, stamped envelope for reply or $1.00 to cover costs.

Llewellyn's Women's Spirituality Series

THE GAIA TRADITION

Celebrating the Earth in Her Seasons

Kisma K. Stepanich

1991
Llewellyn Publications
St. Paul, Minnesota, 55164-0383, U.S.A.

First edition
First printing, 1991

Cover painting "The Enchanted Sea" by Carole Hoss
Goddess illustrations by Joann Powell Colbert
    (For information about these illustrations reprooduced as cards and prints, contact the artist at 1333 Lincoln St. #136, Bellingham, WA 98226)

Library of Congress Cataloging-in-Publication Data
Stepanich, Kisma K.
    The gaia tradition : celebrating the earth in her seasons / Kisma K. Stepanich.
        p. cm.—(Llewellyn's women's spirituality series)
    Includes bibliographical references (p.   ) and index.
    ISBN 0-87542-766-9 : $12.95
    1. Goddess religion. 2. Women—Religious life. 3. Seasons-
-Religious aspects. 4. Seasons—Mythology. 5. Paganism—Rituals.
I. Title. II. Series.
BL473.5S75   1991
291.3'6—dc20   91-11884
                                          CIP

Llewellyn Publications
A Division of Llewellyn Worldwide, Ltd.
PO Box 64383, St. Paul, MN 55164-0383

About Llewellyn's Women's Spirituality Series

Who is the Goddess? This is the question most often asked by women who become acquainted with women's spirituality.

Over the last 3,500 years or so, patriarchal civilizations rose up out of the steppes and deserts and annihilated or conquered existing matriarchal cultures. Through history, we can trace the desecration of woman. Clearly, women in many countries were stripped of any value, any part in life, and reduced to mere possessions. Soulless, voiceless, worthless, women became ill-tempered harridans or evil temptresses and all their wisdom and spiritual practices were devalued. This situation was exacerbated by the publication of that vicious guidebook of denial, the *Malleus Maleficarum*, which resulted in that rage against women known as the Inquisition. The *Malleus* was and remained for centuries the classic formulation of the Church's attack on witchcraft—on women.

In the last few decades women have been beginning to reclaim their divinity, affirming the woman-power, striving to complete a fragmented picture of womanhood. Throughout this process, the quiet voice of the inner Goddess is being heard.

In their search to understand who the Goddess is, women are joining together and celebrating this inner Goddess, and, in doing so, realizing that She is also part of the external world, the feminine polarity of the life force.

In this realization, women's spirituality is being reborn and with it the magick truth that the female body is an expression of the Goddess-power in the Earth—for the Earth is the Mother-power of life on our planet. Women are birthing forth a very old wisdom that speaks of partnershipping, harmony, love and right relationship with all forms of life of this planet.

Women's spirituality is the healing power, the Goddess power, the balance power, and the channel through which the new conscious attitudes of women and men working together in partnership, equality, and spirituality will be birthed—perhaps the channel through which the turning age of Pisces into Aquarius will be achieved.

Other Books by Kisma K. Stepanich

An Act of Woman Power
(Whitford Press, a division of Schiffer Publishing, Ltd., 1989)

Forthcoming Books

Sister Moon Lodge

Dedication

I would like to dedicate this book
to my father,
Al,
who taught me that touching the Earth
was nothing to be afraid of.

PERMISSIONS

Andrews, Lynn: *Medicine Woman,*
    HarperCollins Publishers, New York, NY, 1982.
Barr-Glover, Faith: Life/Death Prayer Arrow Ceremony.
Bolen, Jean Shinoda: *Goddesses in Every Woman,*
    HarperCollins Publishers, New York, NY, 1984.
Budapest, Zsuzswanna E.: *The Grandmothers of Time,*
    HarperCollins Publishers, New York, NY, 1989.
Campbell, Joseph: *The Hero With a Thousand Faces,*
    Princeton University Press, Princeton, NJ, 1949.
Gawain, Shakti: *Creative Visualization,*
    Whatever Publishing, Inc., San Rafael, CA, 1987.
Harding, M. Ester: *Women's Mysteries,*
    HerperCollins Publisher, New York, NY.
Noble, Vicki: *The Shakti Woman,* Vol. 1, Issue 1/October 31,
    1989/Hallomas, Snake Power, Oakland, CA
Robbins, *Jitterbug Perfume,*
    Bantam Books, New York, NY, 1984.
Seed, John, et. al.: *Thinking Like a Mountain: Towards a
    Council of All Beings,* New Society Publishers,
    Philadelphia, PA, and Santa Cruz, CA, 1988.
Starhawk: *Spiral Dance,*
    HarperCollins Publishers, New York, NY, 1989.
Zukav, Gary: *The Dancing Wu Li Masters,*
    William Morrow and Co., New York, NY, 1979.

SPECIAL THANKS

I would like to thank Faith (Bette) Barr-Glover for her words of wisdom resulting from personal experience and my dear friends, family, and/or apprentices who appear in the pages of this book (whether their names be real or changed as an act of privacy).

A very special thank you goes out to Gail Carr, whose support in my life path resulted in a generous gift that allowed me to purchase a personal computer on which to write this book in comfort.

I honor Joann Powell Colbert, whose artistry and depiction of women (in their goddesshood which goes beyond reality) are portrayed at the beginning of each chapter, and Nancy Mostad who midwifed my relationship with Llewellyn, and to my editor, Phyllis Galde, whose words of support and praise helped make the final stages before production flow so smoothly.

I humbly acknowledge all my teachers, on every level, of every tradition and non-tradition and send forth blessings their way.

To Goddess I have dedicated my life. She has showered me with successes I never dreamed possible—most of all the love of my life—Jack. To you, Jack, I whisper my special thanks for believing in me.

My heart is very full. Ho. Blessed Be.

Contents ─────────────────────────────

PREFACE   xv

I   THE GAIA TRADITION   1
    A Pledge to Spirituality   7
    Belief Statement   10
    Evergreen (Poem)   14
    Trust and Experience   16
    The Wheel of the Year   20
        Factual   20
            The Four Seasons   20
            The Lunar Cycle   22
            The Eight Energy Shifts   23
        Mythological   28
            The Esoteric Spirit Wheel   28
            The Esoteric Physical Wheel   31
    Invocation (Poem)   34

II SPRING: Dancing in the Air   39
    The Correspondences of Spring   41
    The Element of Spring—Air   42
    The Phases of Spring   45
        February   45
        March   50
            Vernal Equinox   51
            Demeter and Persephone Myth   52
    The Goddess Aspect of Spring—Virgin/Maiden   59
        April   73
            Tiger-eye Journey   74

III	SUMMER: A Fire Spirit of Life	79
	The Correspondences of Summer	84
	The Element of Summer—Fire	85
	The Phases of Summer	86
	May	86
	Beltane	88
	June	92
	Summer Solstice	98
	Becoming Sisters Ceremony	101
	July	105
	The Goddess Aspect of Summer—Mother	105
IV	AUTUMN: From the Water We Rise	119
	The Goddess Aspect of Autumn— Crone/Wise Woman	130
	The Correspondences of Autumn	140
	The Element of Autumn—Water	144
	The Phases of Autumn	151
	August	151
	Lammas	153
	September	161
	Autumnal Equinox	167
	October	171
	Samhain	171
V	WINTER: A Child of Earth	179
	The Correspondences of Winter	187
	The Element of Winter—Earth	187
	Earth Elemental Journey	189
	The Phases of Winter	192
	November	192
	Dream Pillows	195
	Dreaming with Crystals	199
	December	213
	Winter Solstice	216
	A Winter Meditation	217
	January	222
	The Goddess Aspect of Winter—Great Goddess	226

VI REBIRTH: Of a Living Goddess   235
    Initiation   237
    Preparation for Initiation   240
    The Initiation Ceremony   242
    Candlemas   251
    Different Aspects of Goddess Groups   258
    To Hex or Not to Hex   263
    Traditional Versus New Age   265
    Ending Persecution   266

VII CYCLES   275

NOTES   299

BIBLIOGRAPHY   301

INDEX   305

Preface

A heat wave rushed across the grass swaying fields of Irvine in early Spring. Summer was soon approaching. My mind would not settle down and do the work I was supposed to be doing, rather it wandered out in the open fields. I was lost in the rush of warm winds and golden poppies. I wanted to kick off my shoes and enjoy the Sun. I wanted to dance and sing and kneel down and touch the Mother. I hated the limitations I had to deal with, but I understood them. I wanted to know what all of this was about anyway. Work, that is. Why had we structured this environment that we hated so much? "Are we a people that truly believes in torture?" I asked myself. We must be, because remaining in an office on a day like today was pure torture.

Well.

We live.

And we learn.

Kisma K. Stepanich
May 1989

Joan the Greenwitch

Chapter One

THE GAIA TRADITION

*The mountain road curved endlessly before us. We contin-
ued driving, looking off the side of the road for the perfect place
to hold ceremony. Spirit Sister and I longed to do ritual. We
had packed up a few belongings, and our men, and headed up
to a cabin at Lake Arrowhead. The men were off doing their
own thing and we took off to do ours.*

The road ended, so we parked.

*"Let's cross and go over to that side," I said to Spirit Sister.
I pointed across the street to where the land sank, forming a
small ravine, then rose up into a lovely, pine-tree covered hill.
Spirit Sister nodded.*

*The fresh morning Sun slipped through the air and
warmed our skin. It was late January and we were ready for
the waxing Spring. Halfway into the ravine we came upon a
huge tree stump that had two giant pine cones on it.*

*I looked at Spirit Sister, smiled and said, "It looks like
we've been given gifts." We giggled and picked up the pine cones
and carried them with us up the hill.*

1

With a light sweat breaking our skin, we arrived at the top of the hill and turned to face the view. It was lovely. Surrounding mountains lingered off not too far in the distance and the sky hugged its blue body against them. The air was fresh and clean, and the spot felt right.

We unloaded our belongings and began setting up circle. A Mexican blanket went down first, then the crystals and tarot cards and last, the medicine rattles. We kicked off our shoes and stepped into the circle. We sprinkled cornmeal around the perimeter of the blanket and then sat down in the center.

I called in the elements, acknowledged Mother Earth and Father Sky, and finished by inviting Goddess into our bodies. We sang a few songs and pulled tarot cards: Emperor; and Three of Discs. We discussed the meaning of the two cards and decided we had best do a shamanic journey using the rattles.

Together we closed our eyes and began rattling. It didn't take very long for my consciousness to shift and an altered state to come in. Somewhere in the distance, I heard the voice of Spirit and began speaking with it.

"You are Her voice," it said.

"I will speak for Her," I replied.

"Be Her."

"I am."

"It is time to perform ceremony for attunement with Her."

"We will connect with Her vibration and from this day forward share that vibration, Her vibration, with others."

Silence.

The voice continued, "I am the spirit of communication. You are the spirit of communication. Spontaneity."

"Spontaneity?" I wasn't sure what Spirit meant.

Spirit laughter gurgled from the trees to my right. "Spon-ta-ne-it-y," it repeated over and over, then continued, "Your attunement ceremonies for others must come from Spontaneity. Not planned or orchestrated but from spontaneous reaction to the vibration and the need of those who come to you to experience the ceremony and the attunement to Mother Earth."

I understood. "Oh," I nodded. "Spontaneity of ceremonial

intent and content."

"Yes."

The rattling clogged my ears for a moment, reminding me that I was on a journey. I thought I had lost contact with Spirit, but quite noisily the song of a woodpecker interrupted the already noisy site. Then I heard quite distinctly, "Listen to Gaia."

The rattle dropped from my hand and I opened my eyes to see Spirit Sister watching me. Her eyes held the mysterious awe I had grown so used to seeing.

She asked, "What were you and that woodpecker talking about?"

"Woodpecker? Me and the woodpecker talking about?" I questioned her, unsure of what she was saying.

"Kisma," she smiled. "You were chirping with the woodpecker. It was as if you were having a conversation. It went on and on. When you would stop, it would peck away. When it would stop you would chirp. Sometimes you were both going at the same time, but it was definitely apparent you were having a conversation."

I laughed and glanced over to the tree that now seemed too quiet. "I thought I was talking to Spirit." I glanced at Spirit Sister. "Perhaps I was. But I know that we are Her (Gaia's) voice and that we are Her. We should be doing ceremony for attunement. Connect with Her vibration and then share it with others. We are spirits of communication and all intent and content of our ceremonies should be performed or created spontaneously."

My brain exploded, and without warning I began reciting a chant. Spirit Sister grabbed my notebook and passed it to me. After I wrote the words down, I realized I had written the words of Gaia in a chant. I titled the chant To One Gaia.

Be me and I will speak through you.
Feel me and I will feel through you.
See me and I will show you the way,
Honor me and I honor you.

Dance my dance and I dance through you.
Hold me and I hold you.
Know me and know life,
And keep the wheel turning.

There are many ways, but one Gaia.
Bring all ways to me, to one Gaia.
Connect all ways to my energy, to one Gaia.
And peace will prevail, to one Gaia.
Then life will be on its way to transcending.

To one Gaia.
To one Gaia.
To one Gaia.
To one Gaia.

We finished our ceremony that day finding a tune for the chant. Over and over we sang it, feeling the transforming effect its vibration had on us and the creatures around us. Birds swooped down in front of us and a red-tailed hawk circled over us. The Earth seemed to come back to life around us.

When we finished chanting, we turned and smiled warmly at each other.

"The Gaia Tradition is what we are all about," I told Spirit Sister. "We're not about Wicca or Native American traditions. We simply are part of the Earth Tradition without a name. So we're part of the Gaia Tradition, and Women Spirit Rising needs to begin representing the Earth Tradition."

Spirit Sister agreed.

"I was also shown what our spirit greeting should be." I scrambled onto my knees and faced her. "We take hold of both hands."

I did what I was telling her. "First kiss the left hand, then the right hand and finish by squeezing both hands. This is an acknowledgment of the sister, the bond of sisterhood and life." We performed the greeting a few times.

"The farewell is the embracing and sharing of the Sacred Kiss." I went through the motions. "We should do this as our farewell, for as we depart from each other's company our paths may not cross again. By embracing, we hold the life force of our sister. By giving the Sacred Kiss, we kiss ourselves which you, as sister, are a reflection of me. By sharing the Sacred Kiss, we leave our essence on each other."

We shared the farewell ceremony a few times. Silently we sat looking at the life around us,. thinking intimately about the Earth wisdoms received that day. Without discussing it, we stood. I thanked Goddess, Mother Earth and Father Sky and released our hold on the elemental kingdom. We gathered our belongings together. Each took one of the giant pine cones and headed down the hill.

There is a deep-seeded ecology in each of us that takes us to the very core of our consciousness, our origin. This seed often lies dormant for thousands and thousands of years, but when it finally begins to sprout and the roots emerge, the movement of these two points, the apical meristem as it climbs upward and the radicle as it pushes down, awakens a primordial part of our being that sparks an ancient fire or burst of life equivalent to the Big Bang. We are roused from slumber. We open our eyes, stretch, yawn and begin to look around us. When we first wake, we feel somewhat scattered, confused by all that we see and feel. We search our minds for some understanding, grasping for a piece of truth to which we can cling. As we become wider awake, we take in all the structure around us, the common everyday living, and shake our heads in exasperation. Something is not quite right. We realize this, yet we aren't sure why it isn't quite right. After all, isn't this life? The world we have created? Are we not supposed to fit into society, this hierarchy of living?

"Of course," we tell ourselves. "This is the way life is and we had better get into the 'groove' of things or else we'll find ourselves looking in on the mainstream while we sit alone on the perimeter."

But inside, the primordial leaves and buds are growing. The radicle cells have differentiated into a stronger taproot with lateral roots branching off it. We find ourselves taking in the state of the Earth, how broken it is and how little open land is left around the highly populated cities. We check off a list of pollutions: water, air, food, and, inside for just one moment, it feels as if that deeply plunged taproot has transformed into a fibrous root system clinging to the topsoil. We become suspiciously aware that the four billion years of evolution organic material has gone through (procaryotic to eucaryotic) could be wiped out in less than one minute of time. A sense of fear and doomsday sweeps through our blood veins (xylem), our lungs (stomates) become a bit constricted, and the contents in our stomach (phloem) flip-flop. We begin to perspire (guttate) and wonder how we ever got into this mess.

It is only when this fear and realization of extinction set in that one becomes acutely aware of the possibility that all life is one. In that moment of awareness you worry about the people first, then the animals, then the plants and finally the Earth itself. Suddenly it is no longer just the Earth but a living, breathing entity. You begin to see how all life stems from this living entity; how cyclically life births up from the soil, and you know, in your deepest core, that this entity is female—a female analogous with Mother. Now you are sitting up. Wide-eyed.

Mother Earth. How many times have you heard the Earth referred to as Mother?

"Many times," you tell yourself. Mother Earth, Mother Nature, Earth Mother—why, all mythology and folklore calls the earth a woman and a MOTHER. The connection has been made. Your brain starts to buzz and you are drawn to this concept of the Earth being Mother. After all, doesn't it make sense?

"Yes, yes it does," you whisper to yourself. The Mother of all life really, when one stops to think about it. There is a saying from the Bible: "Man was formed from the dust of the ground."[1]

"Okay, this is beginning to make sense," you tell yourself. We definitely come from the Earth; why, even God's book tells us we come from the earth. Well then, that makes the Earth our physical Mother! If the earth is our physical Mother, and all of life on the planet began from Her body, then we are part of Her and every living thing, whether it be plant, animal, mineral, land, or human, is part of Her, and that makes all of us one. We are all one. One. So, in the most abstract essence, there is only one life.

In this newfound realization, we sense it is time to begin worshipping this life that we are one with and become integrated deeper into its core. A sigh escapes your lips. In the quiet moment of understanding, the beat of your heart vibrates in your ears—the echoing of the Mother's heart? As you close your eyes and focus on this rhythm, you make up your mind to dedicate your heart to the Mother. A new journey is at hand—a journey that will take you into the very heart of *The Gaia Tradition*.

A Pledge to Spirituality

I am! In my being, I open to the energy of Spirit, my higher aspect, to guide and heal myself and others.

May I always see the duality of Nature, its diversities, wholeness and unity, and may I accept those people who differ from me by race, appearance, sex, sexual preference, culture and religion.

May I always walk in balance and use my powers wisely, never against anyone or in a manipulative manner, but always be mindful of freewill.

May I strive to be positive and use my positive power to create a positive reality.

May I take full responsibility for all my actions, whether they be negative as well as positive, and remember whatever is sent out always returns magnified to the sender.

May my strength and commitment to my spiritual path grow in understanding of the unity of all Nature so that my inner light will shine brightly against adversity and negativity directed my way, and may my power transform it into a positive lesson.

May I always remember that the Life Energy, in all forms of life on this Planet (i.e., Homo sapiens, plants, animals, minerals, elementals, spirits and other entities), is one and the same and therefore I will always act out of Love.

May I strive to fully develop my inner wisdom and understanding so that my higher self will channel Love and Light from my being rather than my ego and guide all my thoughts, feelings and actions.

May I always be grounded and centered, allowing the Goddess and God, in all their many forms, to dwell within me, reflecting their divinity through my own higher self, my Spirit.

May I always be firm in my dedication to helping other human beings connect with the heart of Mother Earth and enter into the sanctity of The Gaia Tradition.

What is it that we really believe? We wake up; we go to work; we come home; we go to sleep. We get so wrapped up in a superficial way of life that we numb ourselves to *us*! We numb ourselves to what it is we really believe in.

The first step on our journey into *The Gaia Tradition* of wakeful consciousness is introspection and evaluation of our views on life. Whether we sit down and write them out or simply meditate on them, it is extremely valuable to get a clear picture of our beliefs. Once we confirm what we believe, we gain a stronghold on further development of spiritual evolution. When we take the time to examine the way we perceive life, we get a grasp on what we understand and embrace and what we are unclear about. How can we form opinions and stand up for what we believe in if we don't know the whole picture of what it is we really do believe?

When writing my first Belief Statement, I found it to be very limited as I was unsure what a Belief Statement was. As the years passed and I turned to my Belief Statement time and time again, I found that it was constantly being revised and eventually completely rewritten. As I matured and strove to understand who I was and what my part in life was, I came face to face with morals and dogma and other concepts which I couldn't fully accept. In the process I came to see just what I would put up with and what I would not tolerate. It was a fascinating process.

My current Belief Statement came to be as I sat one day in a favorite local site. It was early Winter, on a bright Saturday morning. I was going through a transformation. Every aspect of my life seemed to be out of my control and in the clutches of change. I needed to commune with Gaia and escape from my everyday structure. Seabirds flew overhead as did an occasional airplane departing from Orange County's famous John Wayne Airport. Huge growths of pampas grass hid me from other nature lovers as they jogged by or rode bicycles along the dirt trails of the quiet and beautiful back bay.

I was involved with a coven I had founded, and I was so very unhappy with it. It was a coven devised of six including myself. The two other women of the coven were on their way in departing and the men were trying to take over by forming new rules. They were insisting that I, the founder, be initiated by one of them now that they had all been initiated by me. I was angry and insulted and quite confused. Wicca just didn't feel good anymore (at least not the wicca that was being enforced in Luna Sea Coven by the new Patriarchs)!

So out of the necessity to cure my confusion I retreated to the back bay. I sat in the warm sunlight and closed my eyes in order to feel it better on my skin. As I sat there being filled with a nonhuman warmth, I felt the stir of Gaia beneath me. Instantly my hands lowered to the Earth. I dug my fingers into the sandy soil and breathed in deep and released my breath through my fingertips to the Mother. As always, her swirling energy flowed up into my center. My heartbeat joined her rhythm and my mind raced with the vibration of words that seemed to be created by this connection. I allowed all the words to enter my mind and sat there a little while longer before opening my eyes to write them down.

Belief Statement

I believe there is One Perfect and Supreme Life Source (force, energy, power), which is both and neither female or male, but rather a unity of all existence. When the One Life Source filtered down into the physical it split, creating a basic duality of negative/positive, female/male, black/white, night/day, invisible/visible; thus becoming a Goddess and God energy. Reaching the One Perfect and Supreme Life Source requires traveling both energies of Goddess and God and becoming balanced in these energies. Unity is then achieved and the journey to the One Life Source can begin.

I believe that the Goddess Energy creates by giving birth to all life, and the God Energy empowers that life with strength. The Goddess teaches the wisdoms of time while the God teaches the endurance in the cycles of time. Both Goddess and God Energies are diversified, encompassing negative and positive traits. In this manner all aspects of life are revealed as part of the whole. This diversity of both Energies demonstrates that "choice" is freely ours.

I believe that all paths eventually lead to the One Life Source. By being given free "choice" to either elevate our Higher Self or remain ignorant, we continually strive, even if subconsciously, to raise our vibration level to join the Spirit in its ascent to the One Life Source, for we continue to experience spiritual lessons on our Earthly journey.

I believe in Karma and its product of reincarnation as the element from where our spiritual lessons are taught. The true purpose of past-life exploration is to present us with an awareness and with certain everyday (practical) tools with which we might begin to understand our current life situations; tools which will enable us to build and create a more positive future, but most importantly tools which do not give power to our fears which hinder our growth.

I believe we contain the ability to open our minds up further than we deem possible and connect with a "Universal Mind," of sorts. When connecting with this "Universal Mind" we tap into a storage cell bank that contains myriad soul-personalities. When we open to receive the information from the storage cells, we receive information on personalities that physically existed in one time sequence or another. Once we process this information neurologically, it often seems as if we have lived other lives. Whether we truly lived those former lives or not (as this is a part of life yet to be thoroughly understood), by tapping into those memories of growth and spiritual evolution we can use this spiritual wisdom contained in the common soul (Universal Mind) to aid us in acquiring even more growth activity in our present physical incarnation.

I believe that Homo sapiens *are in no way superior to other life forms—plants, animals, minerals—for each aspect of life is necessary to compliment the others by connecting, merging, forming a unity, and becoming a whole.*

I believe the other Kingdoms are present as part of our learning process, for the natural "order" is portrayed through their characteristics and the cycles of life portrayed through their existence.

I believe that the planet Earth (Gaia) is our life support system, a living, evolving organism which continually shows us the ever-turning wheel of life: birth, growth, death, rebirth. She is not the backdrop for we humans who, by continually exercising our so-called intelligence, destroy the land, water and air. It is this separation from our life support system that severs the connection from harmony, which highlights that for all our intelligence we are in fact more ignorant than Nature which is continually working in balance around us.

I believe that all Homo sapiens *are one. The life force which sparks one individual is the same life force running through the next individual, and so on. Therefore, when we harm other souls by any deceitful means (no matter how great or small), we only harm ourselves. This "ego" need of thinking we are "one of a kind" creates our biggest obstacle to overcome in order to obtain a true oneness of harmony with all of life. If we were but to stop each day and remember that when we look into another person's eyes we are not only looking into the windows of their soul but our own soul as well, we would soon realize that the life force in them is the same life force in ourselves. Perhaps then, if we were to follow this thought-form, all acts of malice would cease. This basic awareness is the formula for understanding "Unconditional Love."*

I believe that all religions and spiritual paths are valid, for as each of us are different aspects of the One Life Source, so must we walk different paths of enlightenment portraying the different perspectives of understanding in the Truth. Though we may not agree with another person's belief system, we must not create negativity by judging and condemning them. This attitude only weakens our own faith and blackens our own religious beliefs. We must continually strive to be open and allow others their own evolution of spirit, just as we were allowed ours. It is better for us to be as the "Hermit" than to be a part of society in which we are so quick to find fault with another person's religion.

I believe that female and male are equal. Each of the sexes was created equally and neither has domain over the other. The female is physiologically superior to the male, for it is she who holds the mystery of life within. It is the female who once a month sheds the lifeblood, who carries life within the womb for nine Moons and births a new soul. It is the female who spiritually carries the power of the Sun and contains it within a body ruled by the Moon. The male is physically superior to the female for it is he who by his strength controls and by his aggressive nature conquers. It is the male who spiritually carries the mystery of the Moon which is contained within a body ruled by the Sun.

I believe that bonding between woman and man is a superior unity. As is natural in all aspects of nature for the mating of the sexes, humans have the gift of knowledge, which enables them to mate for pure pleasure or as an act of procreation. I believe that sexual communication is healthy and should not be looked down upon as an evil act. It is an act which can often be the highest communion between male and female and where often, at the moment of ecstasy, the spirits join and the two truly become one.

I believe that children are not the property of the parents but are spirits who have chosen and agreed to birth into life and learn from the experiences the two (or one) parent(s) can give. Therefore, as consciously aware individuals, we should treasure the new spirit who has so graciously chosen to birth in the body of our babes of flesh and blood and strive to create harmony, teaching the three greatest truths: Unconditional Love, Wisdom and Knowledge.

I believe that dis-ease is created by a blockage of energy flow between our mind and body. As the mind dictates the function of the body, so can it dictate the state of health of the body. It is of the utmost importance to continually work on the mind/body communion by staying centered and balanced. May we ever be mindful that negativity breeds darkness (fears, illness, harmful acts), and positivity breeds light (happiness, well-being, harmony). Therefore, we must strive to condition our attitudes to the tune of the positive melody and project that positive light to create a positive song in our daily living.

I believe that each of us individually desires, more than anything else, being reunited with our personal Creatrix/ Creator/Oneness. Let us rebirth into our hearts, our minds and daily living a genuine Love for all of life and take the first step which will lead us back home.

I laid the notebook down and watched the light reflect off the water in the distance. I listened to the drone of automobiles as they curved past the back bay. A Golden retriever suddenly bounded into my circle, ran up and sniffed my little altar, sniffed me and wagged his tail hello, then ran on his way. In the distance the faint words of the dog's owner could be heard calling him to come back, just as the faint words of Gaia were calling me to come back.

I suddenly felt so very connected with the Mother and at one with the life force that seemed to be rising up through me that day.

Evergreen

*EVERGREEN is the heart that rejoices in the
 Source.
The heart of the spiraling path,
Which winds through the Kore of Gaia.*

*EVERGREEN is the mind that opens to the
 Source.
The mind of the collected dreams,
Which spill forth, forming the body of Demeter.*

*EVERGREEN are the eyes that look within the
 Source.
The eyes of the seer,
Which find wisdom in the leaf on the vine in the
 time of the Crone.*

*EVERGREEN are the lips that speak of the
 Source.
The lips singing loudly,
Which then whisper the sounds of grace.*

*EVERGREEN is the body that grows with the
 Source.
The body that dances and dances,
Which becomes quiet fulfilling the motion of life.*

(In memory of Caitlin Dunbar
and all our dreams.)

I left the back bay that day feeling very grounded and having received an abundance of wisdom. I found the clarity I required to chart my next course—a course of change.

It is important for us to remember that once we make a conscious decision to change, we must be willing to experience new things. It is the taking of chances, going beyond those comfortable surroundings and listening to the voice of the Higher Self for direction that we become transformed. We must be willing to follow those directions and extend ourselves. Trusting and experiencing are two vital keys when it comes to changing the state of affairs our lives are in. Each one of us has the potential to become a Master in our own right.

I never quite understood what "master" really meant until one day I happened across a book at my lover's house while waiting for him to get home. It was a book written by Gary Zukav about quantum physics, and although I thought the subject matter would be over my head, I was intrigued by the title, *The Dancing Wu Li Masters*. The first interesting discovery I made was that "Wu Li" was the Chinese word for physics and actually meant "patterns of organic energy," and that depending on the pronunciation, Wu Li could also be interpreted as "enlightenment." The second discovery I made was Gary Zukav's description of what a "master" was:

> A master teaches essence. When the essence is perceived,
> he teaches what is necessary to expand the perception...the
> Wu Li Master dances with his students. The Wu Li Master
> does not teach, but the student learns. The Wu Li Master
> always begins at the center, at the heart of the matter.

I knew, after reading his description, that we could all be Wu Li (enlightened) Masters if we listened to the heart—the Christ consciousness within. (For a better understanding of my interpretation of Christ consciousness, see my book *An Act of Woman Power*, Whitford Press/Schiffer Publishing, Ltd., 1989.) We all carry the Christ consciousness within us and we have the ability to become the Goddess or God force we believe in. Should we begin to worship our Goddess/Godhood instead of always deeming it to be an external concept, then the changes would happen so fast that at first we wouldn't understand what was happening.

The time of change for community is here, and it is important not only to transform individually, but as a whole. The days of hermitage have ended. It is time to crawl out of the caves and stand in the circle of life—together—to bring about the conscious evolution now required to raise the Earth's life-force vibratory rate to the level required to undergo the regenesis necessary to connect fully with our angelic-galactic counter-selves. A devotee of the Goddess Isis, Gopi Saravati, once said to me, "this...(life) is all so mystical. In order to understand it, you must see and experience it for yourself." How right she was.

When we want to understand how quickly life can change and how one can grow through this change, all one has to do is watch the children when they are encouraged to experience something new.

Trust and Experience

One day Higher Self decided to take Child to a new experience, so off they went, hand in hand. To get to the new experience Higher Self and Child had to cross through the park, where on many occasions they had spent the day. They parked in the usual parking lot and got out of the car and began walking through the park toward a big, brown, rough-looking building on the far side of the field. Child, having been in the park before, stooped to smell the flowers and touch the grass. Child rolled down the hills and ran after the familiar birds. With glee and happiness Child became absorbed in the park where Child felt comfortable. Higher Self watched as Child portrayed this comfortable attitude and tolerated the control Child was exercising over the familiar surroundings. Higher Self also became absorbed in Child's air of confidence.

Growing restless, Higher Self realized time was passing and began calling out to Child, "The building, where new experience is in, is over here," and "It is quarter past the hour. We'll be late for new experience if you don't come along."

But Child did not pay heed to Higher Self because Child knew that past experience in the park had always been nice, was nice this day and would be nice next time they came to the park. Each time the child looked toward the building where new experience was, all Child could see was a dreary, rough, brown building.

"Why," thought Child, "does Higher Self want me to go in that ugly building and leave behind the beauty of the park and the warmth of the Sun?"

Still, Higher Self was persistent in urging Child to come along. So finally Child decided to trust Higher Self and ran to catch up. Smiling, Higher Self took Child's hand and together they crossed the final stretch of park. Up the steps of the brown, rough building they climbed and entered the front doors.

Child's eyes grew open wide and exclamations of surprise escaped Child's mouth as, in awe, Child took in the new experience. For there within the rough, brown building, bright colored ribbons and balloons hung from the ceiling and on the walls. And in the middle of the room there was a colored ball as big as a coffee table. From every direction came the sound of music and laughter and everywhere Child looked Child saw other children having fun.

As Child ran off to join in this new experience, Higher Self sighed with relief knowing that each time Child finally resigned itself to trusting Higher Self, Child would always be fulfilled with an even greater experience.

(A fond thanks to Yancey and Alisha
for sharing their tale with me.)

Now we are ready to experience *The Gaia Tradition*. The first step to experiencing is the trust as we have seen above, but most importantly attuning ourselves to the natural cycles of Gaia.

Life is cyclical. We all know this to some degree. There is birth, death and rebirth. There is love, marriage and baby carriage. There is Spring, Summer, Autumn and Winter. Cycles. Night, then day. Cycles.

Contained within the cycles are the mythologies giving form to the unknowable or the inconceivable. Myth has always played an important role; it provides the linkage required for the minds of humans to understand nature. Joseph Campbell in his book *The Hero With A Thousand Faces* explains that "...when scrutinized in terms not of what is but of how it functions, of how it has served mankind in the past, of how it may serve today, mythology shows itself to be as amenable as life itself to the obsessions and requirements of the individual, the race, the age."

And so it is that we have used myths to explain how the cosmos was created, the cycles of nature, and as a record of history. All religions are based on mythologies. It is through mythologies that society becomes visible to itself as an imperishable living unit. Generations of individuals pass, like anonymous cells from a living body, through myths; the reenactment of these myths (as is done in sacred ceremonies or festivals) creates the social duties of an individual, who can then continue the lesson of the myth into normal, everyday existence. However, the myths of yesterday no longer apply to our present day, for we have become consciously awakened intellectually.

We know that the Earth does not rest on the shoulders of Atlas because we have taken pictures of the Earth from inside spacecraft on the way back after exploring space. Likewise, we have come to understand that the sacred stories one reads (such as in the Bible) are not literal life experiences, but myths used to express and retell the order of history from a political-economic perspective. We have successfully exploited our fantasies, those dreams which bound us to things beyond our control, and suffer from knowing too much and understanding too much without having created a new mythology in which we can tell our stories: the failures, the successes. And because we no longer have an applicable mythology, spiritually we are a poor society. We no longer have a religion that as a whole we believe in. We have grown beyond the tales of childhood and ignorance and now we wander lost in the wilderness not knowing what all this (life) is really about.

The greatest asset we have on our side is that we are a progressive people, continually evolving, enduring the changes of time. Although this asset has brought us to the threshold of self-righteousness—a self-righteousness based on the ability to self-annihilate or discover a new formula—it is one which will carry us through, bringing us into universal triumph that can only come about by the efforts of us all now.

The ultimate test of one's beliefs, whether they be of a religious or spiritual system, is at hand. Antagonists as well as atheists are included in this testing. No one is "left out." We are all in this together, and together we must all change.

It is easier to say "we must change" than it is to change. How well we know this, yet we dwell constantly within the womb of change. Each minute of everyday change is active. If we are so subjected to change on a continual basis, why is it so hard for us to consciously bring about change?

I believe the answer to that question has already been given and demonstrated continually for us. Let us look at the natural cycles of nature. If we were to observe it for one year and work with the natural order of change, we would gain the new (old) formula required to triumph. The answers to our questions have always been ubiquitous. Why then, for all our intelligence, have we remained so ignorant?

Let us become simple learners again, a five-year-old in kindergarten. Re-awaken the hunger to know, the desire to perpetuate life and evoke the highest power of love to heal our Mother Body/our body. Becoming a steward of the Earth does not mean we must make sacrifices and give up the level of comfort or abundance we have. Becoming an Earth Healer means becoming awake: evolving the next step spiritually, cementing our connection to all life, joining the Oneness, being a responsible benefactor, fulfilling our prelife agreements, living the highest potential of the blueprint that is you.

The school bell is ringing. Lesson One on becoming an Earth Healer is now beginning.

The Wheel of the Year

Factual

Each year we travel around an imaginary wheel consisting of 13 lunar cycles (approximately 28 days each), eight energy shifts, and four distinct seasons. The wheel begins and ends repeatedly throughout the years of our lives. It is a wheel based upon nature—the basic nature of Gaia and the heavens, not of humankind.

The Four Seasons

Each season is caused by the tilt of the Earth's axis of rotation relative to its orbital plane and by the Earth's revolution about the Sun once a year while traveling through the zodiacal celestial sphere.[2] The Earth's axis is tilted at 23.5°. In December we incline away from the Sun and toward it in June, thus marking Winter and Summer (directly due to the amount of sunlight falling on the Earth's surface. See figure 1).

The Earth's geographic equator projected onto the zodiacal celestial sphere is called the celestial equator. The celestial equator intersects the Sun's path (the ecliptic) at two points: 1) the Vernal Equinox (in the constellation of Pisces/Aries) and 2) the Autumnal Equinox (in the constellation of Libra/Virgo), thus marking Autumn and Spring.

When the Sun crosses the celestial equator from south to north at the Vernal Equinox (approximately March 21), Spring begins. Summer starts about June 21 when the Earth axis is tilted toward the Sun in the position of its maximum distance of 23.5° north of the celestial equator, marking the Solstice. Autumn begins about September 22 when the Sun crosses the celestial equator from north to south at the Equinox. Winter begins when the Earth, on its axis, inclines away from the Sun at its farthest distance south of the celestial equator by 23.5°, marking the Winter Solstice. (The above is only true for the Northern Hemisphere; it is reversed for the Southern Hemisphere).

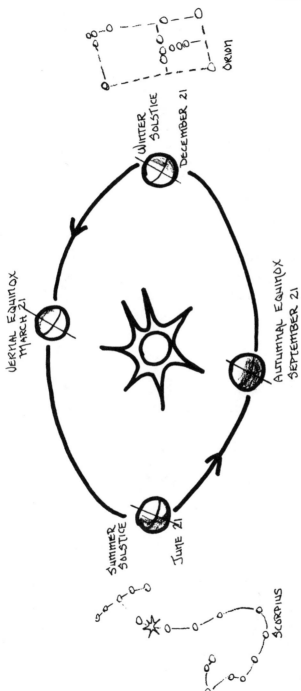

Figure 1—The Four Seasons. A diagram of the Earth's orbital plane around the Sun through the zodiacal celestial sphere marking the position of the seasons (for the northern hemisphere).

The Lunar Cycle

One lunar cycle (lunation) (Figure 2) consists of approximately 28 days, which is the amount of time it takes the Moon to complete its 360° revolution about the Earth. There are 13 lunations around the Earth during the course of one year. Because our current calendar is solar, women should learn to use the lunar calendar to chart their menstruation, as it is a much more accurate calendar.* The lunar cycle of 28 days is broken up into five phases (three major and two minor), beginning with: 1) the New, or crescent Moon, 2) the waxing phase, 3) the Full Moon, 4) the waning phase and, 5) the dark Moon (when no part of the Moon is visible).

The New or crescent Moon is seen approximately four days after the dark Moon. The waxing (increasing) Moon phase takes approximately 10 days to reach the position where we

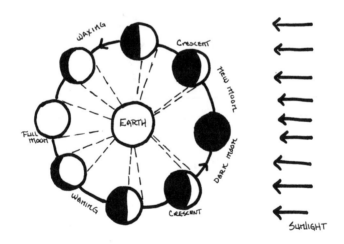

Figure 2—The Lunar Cycle. A diagram of the Moon's lunation around Earth. The lunar cycle consists of five phases: 1) the New / Crescent Moon; 2) Waxing Moon; 3) Full Moon; 4) Waning Moon, and 5) Dark Moon.

*See my book *An Act of Woman Power* (Whitford Press /Schiffer Publishing, Ltd., 1989) for a more in-depth study of the lunar calendar and women.

see a Full Moon. The Full Moon is effective for three days. Waning (decreasing) Moon phase takes about 10 days to reach the position where we no longer see any trace of the Moon in the night sky, thus taking us into the dark Moon.

Since the Moon is visible only at night, the 24-hour cycle (which we call one day) begins when the Sun sets. In other words, sunset to sunset marks one day. The days and months (as in ancient times) were tracked by the nightly position and fullness of the Moon while the seasons were tracked by the Sun's position in the sky throughout the year.

In summary, Moon tracking gives us the days/months, while the Sun tracking gives us the time of year/season.

The Eight Energy Shifts

The eight energy shifts contain the four seasons plus four additional points (figure 3). Beginning with the Spring, the eight energy shifts occur on the following dates annually.

*March 21-23	— Vernal/Spring Equinox
April 31-May	— Beltane
*June 21	— Summer Solstice/Midsummer
August 1	— Lammas/First Harvest
*September 21-23	— Autumnal Equinox
October 31	— Samhain/Hallows Eve
*December 21-23	— Winter Solstice/Yule
February 2	— Imbolg/Candlemas

Connection with the energy shifts is elevating to our spirit vibration. It allows the opportunity to become one with the elements of nature and gain a better understanding, in a basic sense, of the cycle's of nature. We become grounded in Mother Earth and our "center" opens to channel the seasonal energy.

There are many traditions worldwide, both ancient and modern, that acknowledge the eight energy shifts in some form

* Four Seasons

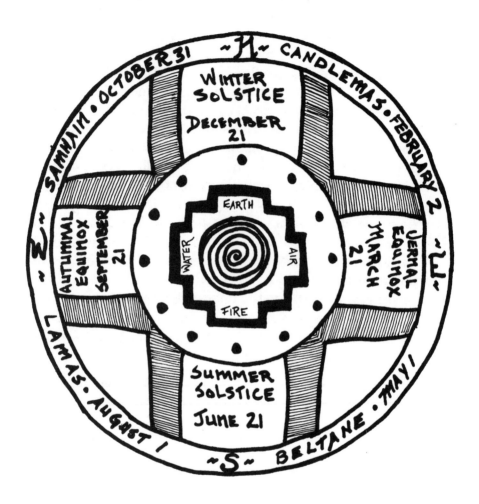

*Figure 3—The Wheel of the Year. A diagram of the eight
energy shifts which consist of the four seasons.*

of celebration. Though my experiences are colored by first the Judaeo/Christian background and then by the Faery and Celtic traditions of Old World Europe, I am choosing to travel through the wheel from as pure a universal perspective as possible.

Vernal Equinox: March 21-23

One of the four seasonal shifts is based first on the astronomical level of the Sun's ecliptic in relationship to the celestial equator of the Earth. There is complete balance on this day, as both night and day are equal in length: 12 hours each.

On Earth at this time Spring has officially begun. Green shoots spring forth, new leaves sprout on the tree branches, and the flower begins to bud. Birds return to sing us awake in the morning, and everywhere the birthing of both the animal kingdom and plant kingdom is taking place. It is the season of rebirth and new beginnings.

The energy surges forth flowing with inspiration and creativity. The intellect is sparked. Ideas are formulated. This is the energy to which the Mental Body is most sensitive and by which it is stimulated.

Beltane: April 31-May 1

This is a time of fertility. The Earth is warming again and the Sun is growing stronger. The seeds of all life are being planted for the regermination process, especially those seeds of human beings and the food crops required for our existence.

The Sun is entering the constellation of Taurus, which is the primary sign in the zodiacal celestial sphere that represents the Goddess, or Mother of Creation.

The energy shift is transformed into a receptive mode. Creativity is nurtured and the foundations, from the ideas inspired in the Mental Body during the Vernal Equinox, are being laid down. This is the energy by which the Emotional Body is most stimulated and nurtured.

Summer Solstice: June 21-23

The Sun has traveled its ecliptic to the maximum position north of the celestial equator, and the Northern Hemisphere of the Earth is receiving the fullest force of the Sun's light and energy. The daylight is at its longest duration and dominates the night at this Midsummer time.

The receptivity of the Emotional Body has nurtured the energy of Beltane and shifted into swift action, sparking the Physical Body into full force. Spirit is given the flame of life and allowed to passionately take control. This is the energy by which the Physical Body is most stimulated and activated.

Lammas: July 31-August 1

The Harvest season now begins. Fruits and vegetables from the gardens and orchards are brought in. Wild berries are picked from the vine. In days long ago the preservation of the fresh foods were begun, and storage bins of every shape and size were stocked for the coming Winter months when fresh food would not be readily available.

Together the Physical and Mental Bodies merge, allowing the thought process to flow. The energy is crackling with the bustle of physical labor and the alertness required of the mind for direction. This is the energy which allows the Physical and Mental Bodies to merge and flow.

Autumnal Equinox: September 21-23

The Sun on its ecliptic now crosses the celestial equator from north to south, beginning its journey to where the Earth will incline away from the Sun. Once again balance is achieved and day and night are of equal length: 12 hours each.

On Earth the harvest of the grain and produce has been completed and a time of thanksgiving celebrated. The physical labor required for the harvesting is now surrendered to rest. Autumn is beginning and with it the decrease in daylight. The leaves are turning various shades of yellow, orange, rust and brown and are falling to the ground.

The energetic energy of the Harvest season transforms into a rejoicing energy. The Mental Body becomes an observant witness to the land's transformation. The happiness and sharing of the thanksgiving touches the Emotional Body, allowing sincere compassion for the turning of the seasonal wheel from life toward death.

Samhain: October 31-November 1

As the wheel turns, the light continues to decline and life fades. Samhain is the third and final Harvest. It is the Harvest of the livestock, the season of the dead. The flower's bloom has faded and the petals have long since fallen. The trees stand stark against the horizon and all their leaves lie gracefully around the roots of their trunks. The land stretches barren, empty of life, faded to brown.

The energy shifts into an ultrasensitive attunement with the Spirit world, and the gateway between the land of the living and the land of the dead opens. The Spirit Body is seized and fine-tuned. All senses are turned inward. This is the energy to which the Spirit Body is most sensitive.

Winter Solstice: December 21-23

The Sun has now reached its farthest distance south of the celestial equator, and the Northern Hemisphere is inclined away from the Sun. Daylight has waned, and the night is longest at this Midwinter time. The morning will bring the birth of the "new Sun" as once again its journey into fullness begins.

All activity on Earth has slowed and a heavy silence blankets nature. Animals are in hibernation, and the wild seeds lie dormant in the ground.

The energy is laboring with the excitement of rebirthing the light of the Sun and moving through the final days of

Winter. This is the energy which the Mental Body is agitated by due to the anticipation of rebirth in all aspects of life.

Imbolg/Candlemas: February 1-2

The season of death and silence has ended. The "new Sun" that was birthed at the Winter Solstice has grown like a boy into manhood and reflects its light proudly on the Earth. Shadows stretch longer and stirrings of the animals who have been in hibernation are seen like the ground hog who meekly pokes its head above the ground.

The energy is beginning to mount as the season of Spring draws near. For the first time all Bodies (Mental, Emotional, Physical and Spiritual) merge together, filling with light while turning to nature expectantly for rebirth.

Thus the Wheel completes its cycle as the Vernal Equinox once again is celebrated.

Mythological

The mythology for the Wheel of the Year is diverse and colored by the many world traditions, but can basically be split into two levels: 1) the esoteric spirit level and 2) the esoteric physical level. Both deal with the supreme female and male deities and the life cycle of birth, death and rebirth.

The Esoteric Spirit Wheel

The Great Goddess, having created the heavens and the Earth, became lonely and desired more from life. In Her loneliness She looked into the dark void of Her heart and saw the reflection of light, and within the light She saw the face of Herself, unlike Herself. She knew it was possible to birth this other self to love and rejoice with.

Winter Solstice. In the depths of darkness the Great Goddess went into labor. The efforts of Her work shook the universe and Her moan sent forth a terrific vibration. Slowly, the Great Goddess gave birth to a "Sun" whose inner light emanated forth. The Great Goddess was overwhelmed with happiness.

Imbolg/Candlemas. As the "Sun" grew, he wandered into the universe and approached his sister, the Earth, tenderly caressing her with his long, slender rays. His light grew stronger and began reflecting off the stars and planets and moons. His spirit lit up the universe. The Great Goddess was very proud of Her "Sun's" growth.

Vernal Equinox. One day, the Great Goddess was out walking in Her garden and stopped to rest beside a pool of deep, crystal-clear water. She looked upon the smooth surface of the water and saw the reflection of light, and within the light She saw the face of Herself, unlike Herself. Looking up She beheld Her "Sun" standing before Her. He had grown beautifully into manhood and She felt love and desire surge forth within Her. The Great Goddess knew the sparking of love.

Beltane. Hand in hand the Great Goddess and the Lord of Her heart walked in the fields of flowers. Both knew joy as they had never known. Together they confessed their love for the other and vowed that love in a Holy Matrimony. The Great Goddess felt passion dance within Her.

Summer Solstice. As the wedding ceremony ended, the Great Goddess and Her Lord fell passionately embracing to the ground at the foot of a giant oak tree. Their desire was so great that all the elements of life witnessed the consummation of their marriage. As they lay exhausted from their love's labor surrounded by sweet grass, jasmine and gardenia, the Great Goddess knew fulfillment.

Lammas. Together the Great Goddess and Her Lord enjoyed life, but as the days passed the Great Goddess saw that Her Lord grew older while She remained eternally young. His youth faded and his body withered. The Great Goddess felt sadness well up within Her breast.

Autumnal Equinox. The Lord, knowing his life was waning, took the Great Goddess into his arms and held Her close to his breast.

"Lady," he told Her, "You are the greatest joy I have ever known. This day let us not think of our parting, but let us rejoice and give thanks to our days together and the great love we have shared."

In sadness and tenderness they celebrated. With feasting, singing and dancing, they gave thanks to each other. The Great Goddess understood sorrow.

Samhain. One day, as the embers glowed warm in the hearth, the Lord breathed his last breath. The Great Goddess wept for Her Lord and journeyed with his Spirit to the gateway between life and death. Sending him forth with a farewell kiss, the Great Goddess mourned Her love's death. Held deep within sorrow's clutch, the Great Goddess knew their love had been a great love and She felt the loss of this love.

Once more, the Great Goddess stood alone looking within the void of Her heart. It was then She understood that "created" life existed within a natural cycle. And so She created life on Earth and breathed the spark of Spirit into each form, designing a perpetual cycle of procreation for each species. As the cycle of birth, life and death turned, the Great Goddess' creation began to experience the emotions She too had felt. And as the wheel turned, year after year, the Great Goddess was able to re-unite with Her Lord over and over and over again through the lives of Her children on Earth.

As demonstrated above, the natural laws of nature are best understood when placed into a story form depicting human nature/relationships. Since, according to the natural laws, it is the female which gives birth to life, it is a natural inclination for the Creatrix of all life to be identified as female, which now brings us to the physical wheel.

The Esoteric Physical Wheel is the story of the relationship of the Great Goddess and Her Lord as depicted on a mortal scale while taking into consideration the seasonal energy shifts.

The Esoteric Physical Wheel

Vernal Equinox. Rebirth on Earth was beginning. Everywhere green shoots broke through the soil, flowers began budding, tiny green leaves appeared on the bough, the stream and rivers were full with melted snow. Birds returned to sing sweetly, and the Virgin ventured forth upon the land. Everywhere she went, flowers bloomed in her footprints and the animals followed after her. As she played in the meadows, life grew.

In the forest, the Lord of the Green Wood stretched his limbs, reaching out to touch the new growth with his light. Slowly he made his way out of the woods and into the meadow where the Virgin was. The Virgin and the Lord of the Green Wood found themselves face to face. Instantly they fell deeply in love.

Beltane. Together they played in the fresh, new light and felt their love grow ever stronger. They knew happiness, and the thought of life without the other was unbearable. And so the Holy Wedding was celebrated when all flowers are in bloom and the days begin turning toward the warmth of Summer. They stood in the evening light of the Moon and spoke their vows of eternal love, ending the rite with a Sacred Kiss.

Summer Solstice. Playfully the Virgin Maiden sprinted away, laughing as she ran from the Young Lord. He chased after her through the meadow and into the forest. Round and round the trunk of a giant oak tree he chased his new wife until finally she faltered in step and fell gracefully, laughing to the ground. The young Buck stood over the Maiden catching his breath. Her beauty far exceeded any that he had ever known and passionately he took his wife, consummating their marriage.

As the Summer days lazily passed and the crops planted in the Spring flourished, so the new wife's womb did grow with the seed of their union.

Lammas. Before long the Harvest season was upon them. Everywhere, the bustle of laborers gathered in the food which needed to be prepared and stored for the winter. The Mother grew heavy with child and rested as her Provider worked hard upon the land. As he brought in the food, the Mother prepared it, and soon the aroma of breads baking and sweets bubbling wafted through the air. As the storage bins of every shape and size became full, so their love became full.

Autumnal Equinox. And so the Harvest of the produce and grain was completed. Day and night equally reigned and together the Mother and her Provider gave thanksgiving for another successful Harvest year.

Samhain. Quietly the Mother prepared for the birth of her child. The Provider prepared for the third and final Harvest, that of the livestock. At the waning of the eleventh lunation, the ending of the livestock harvest was celebrated. The gateway between the land of the living and the land of the dead was open. All those who had passed that way were remembered and invited in Spirit to the feast. The veils were thin between the worlds, and communion with the ancestors was easily achieved as the night grew wild with celebration. Life was within the cycle of death, and the long Winter months were ahead. Only those blessed and strong with health would survive.

The days grew shorter and the nights longer as the deep of Winter approached. The Wise Women invited those who feared death to step forward and drink the brew of the cauldron of regeneration. The brew contained visions of future days as well as visions showing one their mistakes of the past. All knew the season of the Crone was upon them and her enforced introspection could destroy life.

Winter Solstice. When night seemed the longest, the Mother's labor was heard. Throughout the darkness, Her moans went forth, and as the longest night drew to a close, as the Earth turned and crept toward dawn, the Mother gave birth to a "Sun." Finally, the first rays of light kissed the land "good morning."

Imbolg/Candlemas. And so the Mother, the Father and their child waited out the remainder of Winter while initiating the child into life. As the nights grew shorter, the northern lights began to shine and, as the daylight grew, the ground hog finally shifted out of its burrow and there, stretched before it, lay the shadow of its body.

In celebration, the Mother lit candles for the growing light and asked that the Earth be blessed with the warmth of the Sun for the approaching rebirth of Spring.

And the wheel turned.

Before we begin to study, experience and live within the natural order of seasons upon Gaia, it is important to consider the following.

We are in the age of "anthropocentrism" (human chauvinism), the age where humans believe themselves superior over all creation. This consciousness is deeply etched in our cultures. As we embark upon our journey within the cycle of the seasons, as our attunement to Gaia begins to form, and as our connection to the life force becomes embedded within our consciousness, the layers of anthropocentrism will shed away and a beautiful spirit will begin to reveal itself, a spirit as fresh and free as the very essence of sacredness.

Our heart will beat in time with the pulse of the mystical life vibration emanating from the center of all living organisms around us. Our minds will begin to merge with a greatness beyond any conceivable imagining and so many wonderful secrets and supposed "mysteries" will be revealed. As we become stronger in our deep-seeded ecology and oneness, our very personal dance of life will suddenly flow and we will join with the purpose of creativity.

Come back to your origin, your originality, your place of birth. Come back to the state of angelic being and let your wings (which have been invisible so long) unfold out of your back. Come back to your heart and dance your spirit once more.

Invocation[3]
by John Seed

We ask for the presence of the spirit of Gaia and pray that the breath of life continues to caress this planet home.

May we grow into true understanding—a deep understanding that inspires us to protect the tree on which we bloom, and the water, soil and atmosphere without which we have no existence.

May we turn inwards and stumble upon our true roots in the intertwining biology of this exquisite planet. May nourishment and power pulse through these roots, and fierce determination to continue the billion-year dance.

May love well up and burst forth from our hearts.

May there be a new dispensation of pure and powerful consciousness and the charter to witness and facilitate the healing of the tattered biosphere.

We ask for the presence of the spirit of Gaia to be with us here, to reveal to us all that we need to see, for our own highest good and for the highest good of all.

We call upon the spirit of evolution, the miraculous force that inspires rocks and dust to weave themselves into biology. You have stood by us for millions and billions of years. Do not forsake us now. Empower us and awaken in us pure and dazzling creativity. You that can turn scales into feathers, seawater to blood, caterpillars to butterflies, metamorphose our species, awaken in us the powers that we need to survive the present crisis and evolve into more aeons of our solar journey.

Awaken in us a sense of who we truly are: tiny ephemeral

blossoms on the Tree of Life. Make the purposes and destiny of that tree our own purpose and destiny.

Fill each of us with love for our true Self, which includes all of the creatures and plants and landscapes of the world. Fill us with a powerful urge for the well-being and continual unfolding of this Self.

May we speak in all human councils on behalf of the animals and plants and landscapes of the Earth.

May we shine with a pure, inner passion that will spread rapidly through these leaden times.

May we all awaken to our true and only nature—none other than the nature of Gaia, this living planet Earth.

We call upon the power which sustains the planets in their orbits, that wheels our Milky Way in its 200-million-year spiral, to imbue our personalities and our relationships with harmony, endurance and joy. Fill us with a sense of immense time so that our brief, flickering lives may truly reflect the work of vast ages past and also the millions of years of evolution whose potential lies in our trembling hands.

O stars, lend us your burning passion.

O silence, give weight to our voice.

We ask for the presence of the spirit of Gaia.

Being connected and very much aware of the Earth's cycles is vitally important for living in a harmonious way. Today we experience never-ending trauma to the senses because we are inundated with pollutions, congestion and lack of open land (especially those of us who subject ourselves to city living). We recognize that we live in a society of modern conveniences that are not compatible with natural living.

As each age passes, we develop our lifestyles further and further away from the Earth and her cycles and closer to an environment that is confined to fluorescent lights and white concrete walls. To escape from this setup will become increasingly impossible. The end result will be a death of the natural cycles, and the survival of our species will rely on a totally manmade world. How unfortunate, for we too shall die from lack of contact to our home, the soil upon which we now so carelessly tread.

The disparity of living in the world today (a time when each moment can be our last due to the threat of nuclear warfare) makes it increasingly difficult to function in a natural way. It is so very important and relatively easy to connect with Mother Earth and her cycles. The first step is simply becoming more aware of the season, those four counterparts that equate to one year: Spring, Summer, Autumn and Winter. By witnessing the seasons first and then celebrating them on a regular annum, a chain reaction of awareness will develop. As we become more in tune with the natural energy shifts, we gain living skills that provide us with the ability to create a more balanced and harmonious environment in which to live.

When we work with the seasons, we merge with the natural order of this great planet and flow with its energy instead of against it, and in time the celebration of the seasons and Mother Earth will be brought back into the interior of our communities, providing the necessary cohesive ingredient for us to bond together and create a unity that, in our deepest sense of ecology, we recognize as missing today.

Spring Nymph

Chapter Two

SPRING ————————————————
Dancing in the Air

—————————————————————————

It is to the east I go
to see the fresh morning dawn.
As Grandfather eagle flies with the wind
my mind calls forth:
"Spirit—my friend,
Enlighten this circle I dance within!"

When was the last time you stopped and really watched the white, fluffy clouds of Spring release a light sprinkle upon the Earth or pairs of butterflies dance from flower to flower in an open field? Years? Perhaps never?

Spring is an intimate season. It reminds us of new beginnings, flower buds, a wobbly legged calf poking the underbelly of the cow in search of her teat. We're reminded that Spring fever is upon us and that love is in the air, but what we are not told is that Mother Earth is clothing herself, healing those open sores caused by the Winter cold. We are not told to take a minute or two from our busy schedules and notice the changes in the landscape. Instead, before we know it, all the flowers have bloomed, the petals already having dropped, and it's the middle of Summer. Spring is too precious to ignore and forget to join in its celebration of rebirth and new beginnings.

As with most beginnings, the pace from the starting point determines the outcome. Likewise, the starting point of Spring will determine the rest of the year. If we begin to pay attention to Spring and work with the new energy of this season, we set into motion events we desire to unfold throughout the year. And so checking our attitude becomes important at this time because it is this mind-set that will become the year's foundation. If our attitude is positive, then goals will be easier to obtain and less expenditure of energy will be required to obtain them. The possibilities for growth become infinite.

The negative attitude will set up obstacles and dissension. Although you can and probably will experience times of pleasure and happiness, the final attainment of goals will be less than if you had started out focused with a positive outlook.

We contain a power within which enables us to chart the immediate course of our lives. However, gaining control of this power is an individual choice. Becoming a responsible human being seems to be a rarity these days, especially when it comes to consciousness. Too many of us would rather be victim to life's twists and turns, sabotaging our goals and the outcome by surrendering control to circumstance.

Those of us who strive to become consciously, ecologically and spiritually minded can no longer turn our backs and be irresponsible with taking charge of our lives.

On the path of Gaia, one can no longer claim ignorance. By claiming control of our immediate destiny, we ultimately begin to chart our futures, setting up the courses of events needed in order to attain our goals instead of continually dreaming of such attainments.

We live in the industrial age, an age that has proven the capabilities of our minds and dedication toward the mind energy. In the last 50 years alone the development of technology has far exceeded that which was originally thought possible. This was not done by luck alone. It was done by taking responsibility and control, putting to use the inner power of destiny to attain desires and goals never thought possible.

When comparing conscious evolution to industrial evolution, one might ask why compare two extremes that seem to naturally cancel each other out. Using these extremes easily demonstrates the great potential we humans have: that by using our fullest potential in a conscious, ecological and spiritual way we can find these keys which will safeguard the future of this planet as well as the continued advancement for humankind in reaching new heights of humanistic purity.

We are the magic. We are the power. We matter. We can and do make a difference. This attitude begins the transformation required in creating positive effects.

Positive attitude, coupled with the fresh beginning of Spring, is a time for working miracles. The following list of correspondences are the added ingredients or tools we should use to help us focus our minds enough so that we may streamline our thoughts and gain the clarity required to begin refining our mental energies. By doing so we operate in a more constructive manner and achieve the desired results.

The Correspondences of Spring

The season of the mind/inspiration/clarity
New beginnings/birth/dawn/crescent Moon
East/sight/air/light/ yellow/white
Grandfather Eagle/sylphs/high-flying birds
Ancestors of the Asian cultures
Eggs/seeds/seedlings/rabbits

Spring is housed in the quarter of east. East is the direction we turn to when creating Sacred Space or circle, for it is the place of beginnings. East is the dawn or rebirth of the Sun. The east is connected with the mind/intellect, clarity of thought and inspirations. The mind is of a masculine gender and births the action signals required to stimulate the body into movement.

Air is the element of Spring, east and the mind. All beginnings, when first whispered, are an invisible vibration which is the very makeup of air. It is this element that lifts the wings of birds, raising them to heights were they soar above the world and use their far-seeing eyes to chart the progress of their passage. The great, high-flying birds are the rulers of sight, the sense that is activated in the east. It is the fresh new light of Spring that adds clarity to sight.

The Element of Spring—Air

I stood on a winding dirt road that snaked around the deep, brown foothills (which were mountains to me) spread before the granite peaks of the lower Sierras. The Great Grandfather Wind of the North, Eurus, was breathing his full power upon the land. It was early Spring and late Winter snow still spotted the slopes and chilled the dance of breath of white.

I had been driving southbound on Highway 395 after having spent four days up in the Sierras, when the great wind started to blow 70 miles an hour. It was difficult driving, and the local radio announcer warned truck drivers to pull over to the side of the road until the wind stopped. Though I was heading home, I was not in a hurry to get there and so, as I watched the early morning Sun reflect off the western Earth bodies, my excitement took over. I couldn't keep my attention on the road stretching endlessly before me; rather my eyes watched the light reflect off the big brown beauties until I was so mesmerized by their dance that I pulled off the highway and onto the next side road. I drove a short distance and turned off on another dirt road that snaked up the mountainside, carving a design across its brown face. As I drove further on, the road got steeper, and about three quarters of the way up I stopped the car. Bundling myself up, I forced the car door open and was almost knocked over by the force of Eurus as I stepped into the wind. Icy sharpness jabbed at my face and seemed to slice through the heavy jacket and scarf I wore. The wind caught the backside of the car door, whipped it out of my hands and slammed it shut, an indication of its power. Adrenalin shot through me. I let out a good hoot and with determination, bent my body into the wind and began walking down the road. I tried to run and laughed at the failure of my attempt. I threw my arms open wide and literally threw my body into the powerful arms of the Grandfather wind and found my body being held upright. The strength of the wind was unbelievable, the slightest relaxation of my body gave the howling, rushing invisible hands every opportunity to push me along with it or off balance. I felt as if I were dancing in the air!

Moving over to the side of the road, I sat down and huddled against the dirt wall for shelter. I studied the distant mountain ranges, the valley below and the wild, wispy cloud formations in a brilliant blue sky. A yellow Sun sat halfway between the eastern horizon and the full expanse of the sky. The dance of two birds overhead brought my attention to them. I watched their glider wings, stretched out from their bodies, effortlessly slice through the power of the wind. They tumbled and dove and circled wide expanses over me. They came closer and their red tails showed me they were hawks. I was excited and knew that I was in the middle of an outrageous ceremony. A ceremony of Spring and all her correspondences—the air in its mightiest power as wind, the rebirth of the Sun, and the dance of the high-flying bird.

It felt very sacred to me, for it is in the East where I begin casting sacred space, and so it was with reverence that I slowly stood and faced the morning Sun that early Spring day. Closing my eyes, I focused my attention on the warm light:

"Greetings Brightness,
blessed be.
Thy power unlocks the golden key.
Make this day be good for me.
As I do will, so mote it be."

As always, when I acknowledge the new Sun on any given day, his burning warmth touched me. I raised my arms to the sky and began chanting.

"Swirling Air of the fresh new dawn,
whisper into my mind.
From the east you dance and fly,
soaring high, wild and free.
Playful Sylphs touch my mind
bringing forth your inspiration
and clarity of sight!

Light the path that now begins
the Spring of my Spiritual Life!"

To complete my invocation I opened my mouth and chan-
neled the rushing air, creating sounds mixed with a "do" tone.

When I remember this day, I can't help but note the one thing
that affected me the most: the clarity. It wasn't just the clarity of
the morning Sun, or that of the clean, clarity of Spring; rather it
was a clarity of insight, of mind. For the first time I believe I saw
with the clarity of the high-flying birds. I felt as if the season and
all its energy correspondences initiated me into their interior,
and their inspiration of new beginnings and possibilities was
planted deep within each center of every cell of my body.

We can use the correspondences to help tune us into the
very special energy that is connected with the season. In doing
so we connect fully with the energy, forming a bond with the
season that allows us to access and draw upon the power, such
as the power of inspiration and clarity in the Spring, throughout the year. Although it is important for us to work intensely
with energy at its most auspicious time, so it is important for
us to be able to invoke that energy (when needed) during other
seasons, and to also be able to combine it with the highlighted
energy of another season.

In summary, the new beginning or planting of seeds in the
Spring is associated with the Mental Body—the mind or intellect—for the very reason that all action is prompted and experienced in this body first. We see with our inner eyes (inspiration) the possibilities or desires of goals and their ultimate outcome, thus using the farsightedness of Grandfather Eagle. The
element of air allows our invisible wings to be lifted high above
the plane we dwell on, taking us into the outer recesses of possibilities. The east is the place of the rising Sun, the place
where the Sun is (re)birthed each day, which understandably
marks the place of new beginnings and ties into the newness
life experiences each Spring. Yellow or white is the color of
light that is produced by the Sun, the inner light that allows

clarity into the mind.

Understanding how the correspondences connect and merge allows us to gain a deeper insight into using the power of the Spring energy to its most sensitive and exalted level, keeping in mind that there are varying degrees of the power during its cycle.

Each season contains three months and a natural cycle that consists of three phases or degrees of power: 1) a waxing phase, 2) a full phase and 3) a waning phase. The Spring months are February, March and April. February is the waxing phase. March is the full phase, and April is the waning phase. When we work magick in a given season, we can enhance the outcome of the ceremony by working during the appropriate phase for full power.

The Phases of Spring

February

The first month in the Spring season, the waxing phase of Spring. The energy at this time is one of re-awakening. This is the time of the light, the light of the future. Astrologically, Aquarius influences this time. Aquarian energy is one of freedom and magic. The water bearer pours her jugs of water out upon the Earth, but they never become depleted. The water is a symbol for the flow of life, showing infinite possibilities.

Uranus is the ruler of Aquarius. Uranian energy is that of consciousness, the re-awakening of consciousness into the light of future life.

By taking the magical freedom of the energy at this time and imbuing focused intent through ceremony, you can successfully plant seeds that will manifest themselves quickly into the physical/your life. Unlike the short-term planting of seed ceremonies performed at New Moon, the planting of seed, ceremonies performed during the waxing phase of Spring are for the germination of long-term goals (the grander, the better).

Spring is the time of self being reborn. You are "starting over" in a new cycle, a new energy cycle. Now is the most important time to evoke the highest vibration of positivity within your sacred circles. To achieve the highest vibration of clarity, the aid of meditation (to form the perfect picture of what long-term goal you wish to manifest in your life) is a very successful technique to use.

It was February 1988. As was normal in those days, my friend Kevin and I had been on a road trip and were heading home. With two more days left on our trip, we drove late into the evening and ended up camping on the shores of Lake Powell. After setting up camp, I climbed into my sleeping bag. I was exhausted from the five hours of straight driving. No sooner had my head hit the pillow than I fell into a deep sleep.

In my dream a scraggly, old, withered woman stood next to my sleeping bag. I jumped out of it and stood next to her.

"For $2, I take you there," her voice crackled. "For $2 I show you the secret, and for $2, I bring you back." I just stood there looking at her. She was a sketchy sort and I didn't feel completely comfortable with her yet, although she had a wisdom about her. Finally, I nodded my head "yes."

"Who are you?" I asked.

"Coyote Woman."

I opened my eyes and listened to the stillness of the night. The stars were a blanket above. My eyes closed.

"Let's go," she said and turned, her silver hair shinning in the night. I followed the old woman up into the canyons. She stopped before a bush and a tree, the mouth of a cave peeking out from behind the bush. Holding out her knarled hand she spoke. "$2." I reached into my pocket and put two one-dollar bills in her hand. She disappeared into the cave. I followed. Upon entering the cave blackness surrounded me. I couldn't see a thing. She grabbed hold of my hand and led me further in.

Putting her hand against my chest, stopping me in midstep, her hiss regarding the secret echoed in the darkness. Again I stuffed two dollars in her hand. A light from a torch flared. The inside of the cave was illuminated. The walls were covered with petroglyphs. Before us, sitting in a crescent circle, were old women and men. They looked like mummies, they were so leathery and wrinkled.

An old man sitting in the center opened his eyes. Life flashed out at me. "You must know this?" he half informed, half questioned me. I nodded. He motioned to the old woman sitting at the end of the crescent to his left. She rose slowly and moved back into the darkness. When she reappeared she carried a scroll. She stood between me and the crescent of ancients. Soundlessly, she unrolled the scroll, which was long. She held it up before her and it unrolled further, the weight of the paper carrying it to the ground. On the paper was a list of names.

"Look closely at the list," the old man instructed me. I moved closer and bent to see the names. Merlin Stone, Marija Gimbutas, Diane Stein, Marion Weinstein, Lynn Andrews, the Farrars, Doreen Valiente, Dion Fortune, Rolling Thunder, Starhawk and many more were listed. I was familiar with almost all the names on the list. I stood back and looked at the old man. He opened his eyes and flashed his life on me again.

"This is a blacklist," he informed me. "A list that men who sit in high places have made." I glanced back at the list.

A black list, I thought to myself. I looked at the old man, not sure I understood what he was trying to tell me. He continued. "When you publish your books, your name will be added to this list and you will become blacklisted too."

I stepped back, the full impact of what he was telling me, the force, pushing me back. The glyphs on the walls suddenly came alive and danced in the flickering of the torchlight. I looked sharply at Coyote Woman, who stood motionless holding the torch, her beady, black eyes now closed. I looked back at the woman standing before me who was still holding the list.

"Blacklisted?" I questioned. "By who?"

"By the men who govern your laws. By the men who feel you threaten the current order of government."

Silence.

"There could be another inquisition," screamed through my mind. The ancient read my thoughts.

"Yes," he sighed. "The people whose names appear on this

blacklist would suddenly disappear should the threat become real to these men in high places." The old woman dropped the scroll to the ground and returned to her sitting place. The light began to dim and flicker violently. The waving shadow and light washed over the ancients sitting before me.

"Those you come in contact with must be warned." His surprisingly blue eyes burned into mine. Suddenly blackness swallowed us. "As you have now been warned."

I heard his last words, an echo in the wind. I felt a hand on my arm. Coyote Woman felt reassuring, yet her hiss came sharply to my ear.

"Last payment," she demanded. I stuffed the final two dollars in her hand.

I opened my eyes. A faint scuffling sound breaking through the silent night moved away from the truck where I lay. I noted the stars had moved further west on their velvet backdrop. A twilight effect edged the sky/Earth border. Soon the morning Sun would wash over me.

I thought about what the old man had said, and about the book I longed to write but had never given voice to. Perhaps I was meant to write a book after all, I mused. It amazed me that I would have something to say that would bother the government and smirked at the irony of it. After all, I was the most exquisite rebel I knew forever bucking the system and society in general. I turned on my side, pulling the sleeping bag over my head. I needed to sleep.

The next morning, I knew I had to perform a Spring Ceremony, a seed planting ceremony. It was time to write that book, and why not begin creating it with the powerful energy of the waxing Spring?

I acted quickly on my decision above and, upon returning home, performed a ceremony in which I literally planted seeds in the Earth; seeds I first filled with the focused intention of writing a book. Almost immediately following the ceremony, I was relieved of employment and given five months of freedom, at which time I birthed *An Act of Woman Power* (Whitford Press, Schiffer Publishing, Ltd., 1989). Thirty days before the manuscript was completed, I sent query letters to 24 publishing houses. Nine days after I placed the final period on the last page, I received a contract for my book.

The above is an example of how powerful the waxing Spring energy can be if used.

Dates to consider, research and celebrate in the future:

February 1:   *The Lesser Eleusinan Mysteries* (Greek)
                Beginning preparation for spiritual initiation which ends at the Spring Equinox
                Wives' Feast (Irish)
                Celebration shared between wives
                Lady Day, The Lady's Sabbat, Crone Wake (Celtic)

February 2:   *Feast of Bridget* (Irish)
                The eternal Flame
                Imbolg (Celtic)
                Passage of power between the Sun and Earth, the beginning of the germination and regeneration of nature
                Candlemas (Wiccan)
                The initiation time of witches

February 3:   *Celebration of Brigantia* (Irish)
                The all-seeing eye

February 7:   *Feast of Selene* (Greek)

February 11:   *Our Lady of Lourdes* (French)
                The appearance of the Virgin Mary (1858) to Bernadette Soubirous

February 12:   *Festival of Diana* (Roman)
                Protection of wildlife (Artemis, Greek)

February 13-21: *Parentalia* (Roman)
                Celebration of the ancestors/lineage

February 14:   *Lupercalia* (Roman)
The celebration of the natural sexual "heat" of nature; today acknowledged as Valentine's Day

February 16:   *Celebration of Victoria* (Roman)
Goddess of Victory

February 17:   *Fornacalia* (Roman)
Feast of the ovens and baked foods

February 18:   *Festival of Women as Cultivators* (Persian)

February 19:   *Feralia* (Roman)
Purification ceremonies

February 22:   *Concordia* or *Caristia* (Roman)
Caristia is the divine personification of harmony

February 26:   *Hygeia's Day* (North African)
Goddess of healing and disease prevention

February 29:   *Leap Year Day*
Under the tutelage of Juno; women can propose marriage

March

The fullness of Spring surrounds us and, like the Pisces fishes, we can look in both directions with little effort. Neptune possessively presides over the energies and prods the subconscious mind with his trident, inspiring the intuitive facilities.

We can use our intuition in conjunction with the Full Moon of March and delve to depths never thought possible. Our highest ideals can be looked at and scrutinized for realistic possibilities. Mirror magic can be used to look deeply at these ideals and reflect into our consciousness the directions we must take in order to fulfill them.

The energy of Spring is swiftly changing and moving into the action of the Summer season, at which time the energies will rush around us and carry us wholly into the disposition of liveliness, the time of introspection understandably coming to a cessation. Therefore the performing of "mirror mirror on the wall" becomes more prominent, because the highest activation of spiritual intuition dominates the energy directly related to the power of Neptune and the stage upon which the Pisces influence now freely swims.

All subtle bodies (mental, emotional, spiritual) are aligned and available for accessing, waiting to be fully rebirthed at the Vernal Equinox, at which time the energy begins to shift, opening the doorway into our creative potentialities where the mental body firmly moves into full action.

Vernal Equinox (March 21-23)

The Vernal or Spring Equinox is a time of equilibrium when day and night are of equal length and the tide of the wheel of the year flows smoothly. At this time of balance, of suspended activity when human beings shift gears to a different phase and energy, life can seem rather turbulent. By becoming aware of this shift instead of allowing the turbulence to distress us, we can open and allow it to exhilarate us. Instead of falling prey to the psychic tumult, we can take a moment to acknowledge the Earth and her seasonal shift by grounding our energy deep in her core. This grounding acts as an anchor holding us firmly until the energy is moving forward once again.

The Vernal Equinox can also be understood when told through the myth of Demeter, who is the grain mother, the giver of crops, and her daughter, Kore or Persephone, who is the grain maiden, the embodiment of the new crops that was celebrated in pre-Hellenic Greece, (ancient Greece before the classical myths of Hesiod and Homer in the seventh century B.C. The classical myths were a reflection of a cultural amalgamation of three waves of barbarian invaders, the Ionians, the Achaeans and finally the Dorians, who moved into Greece from 2500 to 1000 B.C., bringing with them a patriarchal social order and their thunderbolt god, Zeus, and Ares, the god of war).[1]

Demeter and Persephone

In the beginning there was a time when life did not know the season of Winter. The cycles of nature existed; seeds germinated, sprouted and blossomed and moved through the fullness of their cycle until they naturally faded into decay and dust, spilling the seeds for rebirth to begin the cycle again.

The clan people worked together in partnership. The men of the clan trekked the land looking for game while the women and children remained behind to forage the thick growth of plants encircling their homes. Eventually the women came to know which plants birthed the foods that nourished the body. The healing arts grew as they came to understand which leaves and roots eased discomfort and banished pain and illness. The plants that contained the magical properties were also discovered.

During this beginning Demeter, the Great Earth Goddess, watched over her earthly children and rejoiced in their discoveries. But as is natural with all cycles, Demeter knew that the lives of her earthly children were difficult and their food supply seasonal. So it came to pass that the Great Earth Goddess gave to them the gift of wheat and barley. She showed them how to plant the seed, cultivate and finally harvest the wheat and grind it.

Persephone, the beautiful daughter of Demeter, roamed the land with her mother. Together the two watched over the progress of the people, their food supplies, their crops. During the sprouting of the crops, Persephone could be seen walking tenderly among them. Often she would bend over and caress the tender green shoots. It seemed as if she encouraged their growth.

As the seedlings reached maturity, Persephone would wander dreamingly off into the hills gathering flowers and playing with the animals. She would return to her mother who continued to care for the maturing crops and would place beautiful floral wreaths on Demeter's crown. Because Persephone's favorite flower was the bold red poppies, the flower crones were greatly comprised of its beauty. It was not unusual to see Demeter and Persephone decked with flowers dancing together through open fields and gently sloping valleys. When Demeter felt especially fine, tiny shoots of barley or oats would spring up in the footprints she left.

On one such afternoon, Demeter sat on a hill overlooking the wheat fields. Persephone lay on the grass with her head in Demeter's lap. As the two sat there, life on Earth began to shift.

"Mother," Persephone spoke. "As I walk in the hills I have come across spirits of those people who have died. They are very sad and seem unable to leave their earthly home. Sometimes they are still very attached to someone who still lives. I believe that mortals can see them too, when the night is very dark and Grandmother Moon hides her face. I believe that they do not mean any harm. They seem so confused.

"Once I spoke to a spirit and it said it did not understand what had happened to it and where it was supposed to dwell now." The young woman sat up and looked at her mother. "Is there no one to greet them in the underworld?"

A sigh escaped Demeter's lips. She answered very softly. "My daughter, all of this planet, and all life forms, are of my domain. From the surface soil I pull up the plants to blossom forth with flower and food. In caves and caverns the mortals know to store the seed from the harvest until the time of sowing has come. They know that the seed is stored within the Earth so that the spirits who dwell in the underworld can fertilize the seed with renewal."

Demeter looked at her daughter and brushed the bangs out of her eyes. "The realm of the dead is my domain. I am very aware of the spirits who dwell there, but, Persephone, the realm of living needs me too, and it is here that I must give my attention."

Persephone smiled at her mother and thought about the sadness that seemed to hang over the spirits she had seen.

"Mother, the spirits of the dead need us too, so perhaps I shall go and care for them."

Demeter sprang to her feet. A cold wind blew suddenly upon the land. At first she was speechless, but then quickly reminded Persephone of the beauty and life that the Earth's surface contained. She spoke of the flowers, especially the poppies. Then she told her daughter of the dark gloom of the underworld and begged her to reconsider.

Slowly, Persephone stood and placed her arms around her mother. Tears ran down her face. In silence they stood, each treasuring the presence of the other. Though unspoken, both knew that Persephone was right.

"Oh my daughter," Demeter smiled. "Your love is great, and it is true we must give to all life forms. Very well; you must go. Know this: that for every day you dwell in the underworld, my sorrow will be great and I will mourn your absence."

Turning, Demeter led Persephone to a deep chasm in the Earth. "This is where you shall enter, and where you shall emerge back to the living."

Persephone hugged her mother. She gathered three poppies and three sheaves of wheat to take with her as a reminder of the living. Finally, she turned toward the chasm, and without further delay entered the underworld. Demeter stood and watched her daughter disappear into the Earth.

As Persephone descended deeper and deeper she was concerned about the chill, but she was not afraid. Deeper and deeper into the darkness she continued, picking her way slowly along the rocky path. It seemed as if hours passed. Surrounded only by silence, she heard a low moaning sound. She followed the direction of the sound and entered a giant cavern where thousands of spirits of the dead walked aimlessly. The moaning sound came from them in their state of confusion and pain.

Persephone moved to the center of the cavern and climbed onto a large, flat rock. Standing amongst the spirits, the energy of her aura seemed to increase in brightness and in warmth. The spirits were drawn to her light. They gathered around the rock.

"I am Persephone and I have come to be your Queen. Each of you has left your earthly body and now resides in the realm of the dead. If you come to me, I will initiate you into your new world."[1]

She motioned for those close to the rock to ascend and stand next to her. She turned to each spirit and embraced it, engulfing it in her aura. Looking deeply into their eyes, she spoke:

"You have waxed into the fullness of life
And waned into darkness;
May you be renewed in tranquility and wisdom."[1]

The months passed. As Queen of the Underworld, Persephone received and renewed the dead without ever resting or even growing weary.

However, on the surface, Demeter grew very sad. She roamed the Earth hoping to find her daughter emerging. In her sorrow she forgot about the crops and the cycles of life. It seemed as if her energy were removed from the living.

Then finally one morning a beautiful red poppy pushed its way through the soil where Demeter sat. At first she was confused at this sight. She plucked the poppy from the ground and started to crush it in her hand, the reminder of Persephone too great to bear. But suddenly, a breath whispered forth on the breeze, "Persephone is here!"

Demeter leapt to her feet and ran down the hills through the fields into the forests. As she ran, her energy caused the dormant seeds to germinate and push tiny green shoots up through the soil. Birds began singing again. Animals poked their noses out from their hibernation places.

When at last Demeter reached the chasm were her daughter's descent into the underworld took place, there stood Persephone, Queen of the Underworld.

With great joy the two ran together and hugged. Their tears and laughter of happiness vibrated across the land, and the children of Earth saw the wondrous rebirth of life around them as a result of the Great Earth Goddess' happiness.

And so the seasons had come to be. Persephone's descent into the underworld was known as a time of release and all life underwent a transformation, moving into a resemblance of death. This season was known as Winter. The Spring was the time when Persephone retuned and signs of her return were witness across the land as life rebirthed into fullness.

Starhawk, in her book *The Spiral Dance* (Harper & Row,

1987), described the energies best when she wrote, "Springs return is here, a joyful time, the seed time, when life bursts forth from the Earth and the chains of Winter are broken. Light and dark are equal; it is a time of balance, when all the elements within us must be brought into a new harmony."

If we take both concepts, that of the Ascension of Persephone from the netherworld and the rebirth of nature on Earth, we can begin to understand just how intimate our celebrations can become.

If celebrating the Vernal Equinox for the first time, begin by acknowledging the new growth (rebirth) of the plant kingdom. You would plan a ceremony to be out on the land; in order to connect fully with the rebirthing energy rising up from the core (Kore, Persephone) of Mother Earth (Demeter), and honor the new life by actually planting seeds, or seedlings, into the Earth or a pot to be tended. A simple outline to follow when preparing for such a ceremony might be as follows.

I.   Find a private spot outdoors where you can hold your celebration. Create a circle, outlining it with freshly cut flowers. (I perform my celebrations in the boundary of the circle. The circle is the representative of Mother Earth, the womb, completion, continuation.) With a compass detect where each of the four directions is located and mark each quarter with a candle or a crystal. (I acknowledge the four directions, the four elements —east/air, south/fire, west/water and north/earth—because our bodies and all life is made up of these four elements. Therefore they are gateways into higher consciousness.)

II.   Acknowledge/invoke the quarters/elements:

East: *Energy of the East*
        Airy sylphs and high flying friends
        Assist us now, protect us now.
        Guide Kore (Persephone) to our circle.

South: *Energy of the South*
        Fiery salamanders and passion spirited friends

> *Assist us now, protect us now.*
> *Light the way for Kore.*

West: *Energy of the West*
      Watery undines and deep swimming friends
      Assist us now, protect us now.
      Allow your flow to carry Kore to us now.

North: *Energy of the North*
      Earthy gnomes and strong, grounded friends
      Assist us now, protect us now.
      Part the Gateway, allow Kore through.

III. Raise the energy of the circle. This is done to focus you on the intent of your celebration. In this ceremony you are focusing on the element of rebirth, new life and the underlying principle that it is the energy of Kore, Persephone, as she ascends from the depths of the netherlands that are responsible for the resurgence of new life on Earth. The "Kore Chant" (Starhawk, *The Spiral Dance*) has become a traditional chant to use as an aid in focusing attention.

> *Her name cannot be spoken,*
> *Her face was not forgotten,*
> *Her power is to open,*
> *Her promise can never be broken.*

> *All sleeping seeds She wakens,*
> *The rainbow is Her token,*
> *Now Winter's power is taken,*
> *In love, all chains are broken.*

> *She changes everything She touches, and*
> *Everything She touches, changes.*
> *Change is, touch is; Touch is, change is.*
> *Change us, touch us; Touch us, change us.*

IV. Planting of seeds. As you prepare to plant the seed or seedling, it is important you open your heart and mind to the energy of Kore to receive an affirmation or personal chant to use for the growing of your higher self during the waxing season. This chant or affirmation should be written down and used continuously until the season of release (Autumn). After completing the above, speak the words as you plant so the power of your words is imbued into the seeds or seedling.

Two chants that can be spoken over your seedling throughout the year at New Moon and Full Moon are:

New Moon: *Grow and prosper, seedling mine,*
from the beginning of ancient time.
Take the secrets, future, present and past,
root them to grow deep and fast.
Branches grow a path to find,
the passage into my inner mind.

Full Moon: *Plant of power, I nurture thee.*
Attract all power and store it for me.
By all the power of land and sea,
As I do say, so mote it be.
By all the power of Moon and Sun,
As I do will, it shall be done.

V.   Now is the time for inner journey or journal writing. If you are bold and wish to chant and raise the energy into a cone of power and release that power into the plant, now would be the time.

VI.   Give thanks to the new energy of rebirth.

VII.   Dismiss the quarters/elements:

Farewell, spirits of the East (South, West, North)
thank you for your power of air (fire, water, earth).
Peace.

VIII. Your celebration has ended.

As we work with the seasons year after year, our ceremonies will become deeper and more meaningful. We begin to
journey inward during the season of the waning (Winter) and
as Spring rebirths, we too rebirth. So, as we experience the
wheel, our Vernal Equinox eventually evolves into a celebration of our own internal aspect of Persephone rising from the
depths into the light. We begin to bring forth new life and new
energy as we celebrate our own maidenhood journey back into
the waxing season of activity.

The Goddess Aspect of Spring—Virgin / Maiden

*Hear the words of the Star Goddess, who is the beauty of the
green Earth and the white Moon among the stars and the mysteries of the waters. She who is known by many names:*

Abundantia (Roman)
Adah (Semitic)
Aderenosa (Chaldaean)
Adra Nedegra (Babylonian)
Adsullata (Celtic)
Aega (Greek)
Aegea (Danish)
Aegke (Greek)
Agatha (Greek)
Aglaia (Greek)
Agnes (Roman-Jewish)
Agrotera (Greek)
Aigle (Norse)
Akamoth (Gnostic)
Akaru-Hime (Japanese)
Akewa (Argentinan)
Akua 'ba (African)
Alaisiagae (Roman)

Albina (Tuscan)
Alcyone (Greek)
Alea (Arkadian)
Aleitheia (Gnostic)
Allat or Alilat (Arabian)
Althaea (Cretan)
Al-Uzza (Arabian)
Alys (British)
Ama No Uzume (Japanese)
Amata (Roman)
Amatsu-Otome (Japanese)
Ama Usum Gal Ana
    (Sumerian)
Amazon (Armenian)
Amtea (Greek)
Ana or Anassa (Danaan)
Anahid (Persian)
Anat or Anath (Anatolian)

Anatis (Persian)
Andarta, Andrasta or
    Adrastea (Celtic)
Andromeda (Greek)
Anesidora
    (Pre-Hellenic Greek)
Ankhet (Egyptian)
Annis (Greek)
Antheia
    (Pre-Hellenic Greek)
Anunet (Sumerian)
Aphaea or Aphaia (Greek)
Aphrodite
    (Pre-Hellenic Greek)
Aprilis (Roman)
Apsaras (Hindu)
Apt (Gnostic)
Aradia (Italian)
Arethusa (Norse)
Ariadne (Cretan)
Arianrhod (Welsh)
Aritimi (Greek)
Arsai (Canaanite)
Artemis (Greek)
Arunta, Araunta or Arunda
    (Australian)
Asha Poorna (Hindu)
Aspalis (Phthian)
Assinboin (Native American)
Astraia or Astraea (Greek)
Asva (Hindu)
Asynjor (Teutonic)
Ataensic
    (North American Indian)
Atanua (Polynesian)
Ate (Greek)
Athara (Ascalon)

Athene or Athena (Cretan)
Atlanta (Greek)
Atropos (Greek)
Attar (Arabic)
Aurora (Roman)
Ay (Turkish)

Ba' Alatu Mulki, Ba' Alatu
    Darkati or Ba' Alatu
    Samen Ramen (Canaanite)
Banana-Maiden (Celebes)
Banbha (Irish)
Bast or Bastet (Egyptian)
Basuli (Hindu)
Bathsheba (Hebrew)
Baubo (Greek)
Belisama (Roman)
Belit-Ilanit (Chaldaean)
Belit Sheri (Sumerian)
Bene (Greek)
Benten, Benzaiten or
    Benza-Tennyo (Japanese)
Bethulta (Hebrew)
Bharati (Hindu)
Bitch (Indo-European)
Black Virgin (Romanian)
Blathnat (Irish)
Blodeuwedd (Irish)
Boadicea (British)
Branwen (Irish)
Brigentis (Celtic)
Brito Martis or Britomaris
    (Crete)
Brizo (Greek)
Buffalo Woman (Kiowa),
Bunzi (Zaire)

Caksusi (Hindu)
Calliope (Greek),
Callisto (Arcadia)
Car, Ker, Q're or Caryatis
    (Greek)
Caristia (Roman)
Cecilia (Roman)
Celaeno (Greek)
Cerdo (Greek)
Chala or Chapala (Hindu)
Chandra (Indian)
Changing Woman (Navajo)
Charites (Greek)
Chasca (Incan)
Chauturopayini (Hindu)
Chibcha Huitaca (Panamanian)
Chimalmat (Mayan)
Chionia (Greek)
Clio (Greek)
Cliona (Irish)
Clotho (Greek)
Coventina (British)
Coyolaxaugui or
    Coyolxauhqui (Aztec)
Creiddylad (Welsh)
Cuna (Panamanian)
Cupra (Etruscan)
Cynthia (Greek)

Dahud (Briton)
Damara (British)
Daphne (Greek)
Dea Hammia (Syrian)
Deianeira (Greek)
Delia (Roman)
Delight (Hindu)
Delphyna (Greek)

Dennitsa (Slavic)
Deorgreine (Cretan)
Derketo (Ascalonian)
Devana (Slavic)
Dictynna or Dyktynna
    (Greek)
Diiwica (Serbian)
Dike (Greek)
Diviana (Greek)
Domina (Egyptian)
Doris (Greek)
Dryads (Greek)
Dugnai (Slavic)
Dziewona (Polish)

Eire, Erin or Eriu (Irish)
Eirere (Greek)
Elaine (British)
Elate (Greek)
Electra (Greek)
Entu (Sumerian)
Eos (Greek)
Eostara or Eostre
    (German)
Erate or Erato (Greek)
Eriu or Erin (Irish)
Erytheia (Norse)
Essyllt (Celtic)
Eunomia (Greek)
Euphrosyne (Greek)
Euripedes (Greek)
Euterpe (Greek)

Filia Vocis (Latin)
Flora (British)
Fodhla (Irish)

Frimia or Fimila (Teutonic)
Fro-Freyr (Scandinavian)

Galatea (Greek)
Gauri (Indian)
Gendenwitha (Iriquois)
Gna (Teutonic)
Goda (Saxon)
Gruagach (Scottish)
Gum Lin (Chinese)
Gungu (Hindu)
Gynacea (Greek)

Hainuwele (Indonesian)
Haltija (Finnish)
Hamadryad (Greek)
Harimella (Scottish)
Harmonia (Greek)
Hebe (Greek)
Heliades (Greek)
Hemera (Greek)
Herodias (Gaulish)
Hesperides (Norse)
Hilde (No. European)
Hina or Hine (Polynesian)
Hina-Titama (Polynesian)
Hippodamera (Greek)
Hippolyte (Greek)
Hnossa (Teutonic)
Ho Hsien-Ku (Chinese)
Huitaca (Colombian)
Hygieia (Greek)

Iamanja (Brazilian)
Iambe (Greek)
Iduna or Idun (Norse)
Imbaluris (Hittite)

Ina (Hervey Islands)
Inari (Japanese)
Iseult (Celtic)
Ishikoridome-No-Mikoto
    (Japanese)
Isolde (Celtic)
Istustaya (Anatolian)

Jotma (Indian)
Justicia (Roman)

Ka Ding (Himalayan)
Kaikilani (Polynesian)
Kallisto (Greek)
Kamikaze (Japanese)
Kamrusepa (Anatolian)
Kanya (Hindu)
Kara (Teutonic)
Ka Sngi (Himalayan)
Ka Um (Himalayan)
Kauri (Pre-Vedic)
Kebehut (Egyptian)
Kedesh (Syrian)
Khadomas (Tantric)
Khonsu (Theban)
Kichijo-Ten (Japanese)
Kima (Hebrew)
Klotho (Greek)
Kore (Greek)
Krittikas (Hindu)
Kshiti-Apsaras (Greek)
Kuan or Kwan Yin (Chinese)
Kuhu (Hindu)
Kumari (Hindu)
Kunnawarra (Aboriginal)
Kupala (Slavic)
Kurotrophis (Greek)

Kwannon (Japanese)

Lachesis (Greek)
Lahamu (Chaldaean)
Lakshmi (Indian)
Laphria (Aetolian)
Lasna (Etruscan)
Lasya or Lasema (Tibetan)
Lat (Arabic)
Latis (British)
Laudine (Arthurian)
La Virgen Morena (Spanish)
Lia (New South Wales)
Liban (Irish)
Libya (Libyan)
Li Chi (Chinese)
Limnaious (Greek)
Living Goddes, The (Nepalese)
Luna (Roman)
Lunas (Syrian)
Luned (Arthurian)

Madhurri (Hindu)
Maia (Greek)
Maira (Gnostic)
Maitri (Hindu)
Malha (Hindu)
Marian, Miriam, Mariamne,
    Myrrhine, Myrrha, Maria
    and Marina (Egyptian)
Mary-Gipsy (Egyptian)
Malinalxoch (Aztec)
Manah (Arabic)
Mare (French)
Mayavati (Hindu)
Mecha (Celtic)
Mehiti (Egyptian)

Melete (Greek)
Melita (Assyro-Babylonian)
Mella (Zimbabwean)
Melpomene (Greek)
Melusine (Greek)
Meni (Chaldaean)
Menos (Egyptian)
Merit (Egyptian)
Mermaid (Britain)
Merope (Greek)
Minerva (Roman)
Minona (W. African)
Mizunoe (Japanese)
Mneme (Greek)
Mnemosyne (Greek)
Moerae (Greek)
Molis (Assyro-Babylonian)
Morning Star (Aboriginal)
Muses (Greek)
Myestyas (Slavic)
Myrto, Myrtea or Myptoessa
    (Mediteranean)

Namagiri (Hindu)
Nanna (Danish)
Napkaia (Sicily)
Neiro (Sabine)
Nemesis (Roman)
Nereids (Greek)
Nerthus (Teutonic)
Niachero (Zaire)
Niamh (Irish)
Nidaba (Sumerian)
Nike (Pre-Hellenic Greek)
Nimue (Arthurian)
Ningyo (Japanese)
Ninmah (Sumerian)

Nisaba (Chaldaean)
Nix (Teutonic)
Nunakawa-Hime (Japanese)

Oba (Nigerian)
Oceanid (Greek)
Oenothea (Greek)
Okitsu-Hime (Japanese)
Olwyn (Welsh)
Onatha (Iroquois)
Opis or Oupis (Greek)
Oread (Greek)
Oreithuia (Greek)
Oshun (Brazilian Voodoo)
Ostara (Saxon)
Oto (Japanese)
Oya (Brazilian Voodoo)

Padma (Hindu)
Pai Mu-Tan (Chinese)
Pairikas (Persian)
Paivatar (Finno-Ugric)
Pales (Roman)
Panacea (Greek)
Panagia Arkoudiotissa
    (Anatolian)
Pandora (Pre-Hellenic Greek)
Papaya (Anatolian)
Paravati or Parvati
    (Himalayan)
Parthenos (Greek)
Pasht (Egyptian)
Pasowee (Kiowan)
Pax (Roman)
Peitho (Greek)
Peris (Persian)
Persephone (Greek)

Pheraia (Greek)
Phoebe (Greek)
Phosphoros (Greek)
Pleiades (Greek)
Pohaha (Pueblo)
Poludnista (No. Russian)
Polyhymnia (Greek)
Pressine (Greek)
Priti (Hindu)
Prorsa and Postverta
    (Etruscan)
Proserpine or Proserpina
    (Eleusian)
Proto Thronia (Amazon)
Pushepema (Tibetan)
Pythia (Greek)

Qedeshet (Egyptian)

Radha (Indian)
Rangada (Hindu)
Regina (Roman),
Renpet (Egyptian)
Rhode (Greek)
Rigantona (Welsh)
Rimmon (Irish)

Sakunadevatas (Hindu)
Salacia (Roman)
Salus (Roman)
Sarama (Vedic)
Sarasvati (Indian)
Satet (Egyptian)
Sati (Indian)
Scota (Egyptian)
Scyila (Greek)
Senjo (Japanese)

Seshat or Sefchet (Egyptian)
Sgeg-Mo-Ma (Tibetan)
Shammuramat (Jerusalem)
Shaushka (Hittite)
Sheila Na Gig (Irish)
Shina (Japanese)
Shin-Mu (Chinese)
Sin (Teutonic)
Sina (Polynesian)
Sirens (Greek)
Sjofna (Teutonic)
Sodasi (Hindu)
Sopdet (Egyptian)
Sri (Indian
Star Girl (Australoid)
Stella Maris (Greek)
Sterope (Greek)
Strenia (Roman)
Subhadra (Hindu)
Suratamangari (Hindu)
Sun Sister (Inuit)

Ta Giri Hime (Japanese)
Tagi Tsu (Japanese)
Tallai (Syrian)
Ta-Repy (Egyptian)
Tayade (Greek)
Tennin (Japanese)
Terpischore (Greek)
Teteu Innan or Teteoinan
    (Aztec)
Thalia (Greek)
Thevadas (Cambodian)
Thrud (Teutonic)
Tien Hou (Chinese)
Tui (Chinese)
Tula (Hindu)

Tuli (Polynesian)
Turan (Etruscan)
Tutela (Britain)
Tuulikki (Finno-Ugric)
Tyche (Greek)
Typhon (Greek)

Unnut (Egyptian)
Unsas (Arabian)
Urania (Greek)
Ushas (Indian)

Vac (Indian)
Vanadevatas (Hindu)
Vasanti (Hindu)
Vasudhara (Hindu)
Vechernyaya (Slavic)
Venus (Roman)
Verdandi (Teutonic)
Verthandi (Norse)
Vidyadharis (Hindu)
Vierge Noire (French)
Virgo (Greek)
Vyngwen (Celtic)

Wakahiru-Me (Japanese)
Wakasaname-No-Kami
    (Japanese)
Wenonah (Algonquin)
White Buffalo Woman (Sioux)
White Shell Woman (Pueblo)
Wudu-Maer (Old Saxon)

Xilomen (Mexican)
Xochiquetzal (Aztec)

Yakami (Buddhist)

Yakshis (Hindu)
Yami (Hindu)
Yemaya Olokun (W. African)
Yept-Hemet (Egyptian)
Yoruba (North African)

Zaliyanu (Hittite)
Zintuhi (Anatolian)
Zorya Utrennyaya (Slavic)
Zvezda Dennitsa (Slavic)

For I am the soul of nature that gives life to the universe. From me all things proceed, and unto me they must return.

The virgin of Spring is the laughing child of Mother Earth. Full of life and new hope, she dances among the wildflowers and befriends the animals of the forests and glens.

She is gentle and mischievous as the young virgin, a child girl still in adolescence.

She is wild and sexually activated as the virgin/maiden, a girl in puberty who experiences her first Moon blood.

She is powerful and protective as the maiden, a young woman who defends her ancient crown and those she loves, mercilessly.

Dr. Jean Shinoda Bolen, a Jungian analyst and Clinical Professor of Psychiatry at the University of California, San Francisco, has done extensive studies on goddess archetypes and women's personalities and has made some remarkable breakthroughs in understanding the deep-rooted goddess energy within women. Though she primarily deals with the Olympian goddesses, her work portrays thoughtful and insightful understanding into a woman's psyche.

The three virgin goddesses Dr. Bolen works with are Artemis, Goddess of the Hunt and of the Moon; Athena, Goddess of Wisdom and Crafts; and Hestia, Goddess of Hearth and Temple. She explains in her work, *Goddesses in Every Woman: A New Psychology of Women* (Harper Colophon Books, Harper & Row, Publishers, 1984), that "these three goddesses personify the independent, active, non-relationship aspects of women's psychology. All three represent inner drives in women to develop talents, pursue interests, solve problems, compete with others, express themselves articulately in words or through art forms, put their surroundings in order or lead contemplative lives. The virgin goddess aspect is that part of a woman that is unowned by or "unpenetrated" by a man—that is untouched by her need for a man or needs to be validated by him, that exists wholly separate from him, in her own right."

Esther Harding, also a Jungian analyst, further explains in her book *Woman's Mysteries* (Harper & Row, 1971) that when a virgin goddess is a dominant archetype of a woman, then she is, "one-in-herself," and "belongs to no man." She further articulates that, "A woman who is virgin, one-in-herself, does what she does—not because of any desire to please, not to be liked, or to be approved, even by herself; not because of any desire to gain power over another, to catch his interest or love, but because what she does is true. Her actions may indeed be unconventional. She may have to say no, when it would be easier, as well as more adapted, conventionally speaking, to say yes. But as virgin

Plate 1—Goddesses in Spring. Dreaming Eagle Woman grounded and centered us with drumming before our Celebraton of Easter with the Goddess. (Left to right: Jeannie, Dreaming Eagle Woman and Lisa.)

she is not influenced by the considerations that make the non-virgin woman, whether married or not, trim her sails and adapt herself to expediency."

It is the virgin/maiden's wisdom who shows us the freedom women can have. The choice we women have to bind ourselves to men or stay forever in our strength and resilience as our own commanders and caretakers. She gives the necessary strength required for a woman to enjoy her sexual freedom without shame as we have been taught to feel. Through her we understand the mighty jurisdiction we have over our bodies, the election we have to birth a child out of wedlock or to terminate a conception no matter what our marital status.

Soft and caring as she may be, if wronged the virgin transmits the essential knowledge that is mandatory to achieve the fullest aegis needed to wear as protection against the aggressor. If used through a disciplined artery, this protective energy can outwit, outmaneuver and outdo any negative and harmful attack, for by developing the skills of the virgin/maiden, we become the true warrioress or huntress. Agnes Whistling Elk (a Heyoehkah Medicine Woman Lynn Andrews apprenticed with), shares the ultimate understanding of a warrioress (as written in Lynn's first book, *Medicine Woman*, Harper & Row, 1981).

Agnes tells us that, "There are merely two choices in life. You can die like a frightened whore, or you can live like a worthy huntress and die like one. Develop hungry eyes—eyes that get hungry before your stomach. To be a huntress, you must have knowledge of what you are hunting. That's where hunting begins. As a huntress, you must never hesitate. You must analyze and then pounce, and to do that effectively you must know your own strength and weakness. The good huntress doesn't have a foolish opinion of herself. Always be sure that you are the huntress and not the hunted. The path of the hunter is sacred."

Agnes further explains, "Every woman seeks after that high warrior, that most magnificent of men within her. We seek him all our lives. If we're lucky, we conjure him in our dreams, mate with him, and become whole." This is the knowledge that the awakened virgin/maiden contains!

As we celebrate Virgin/Maiden Goddesshood in her season, the Spring, let us evoke her into our inner sanctum and deliberate upon her talents until we understand the extent of her power before ventilating it in our lives. Let us meditate upon her for one full phase of her season before claiming her. Then, at her monthly Moon time, that of the waxing silver crescent, let us begin to call to her and prepare our bodies as a vehicle for her to live through. As the wheel turns, and we return once more to her season, let us fully become the virgin/maiden, activate her energy within the electrical centers of our bodies and invoke our virgin/maiden goddess to life.

The hare, egg, flower, color white, doe, bow and arrow are but a few of the symbols connected to the virgin/maiden. She graces the Earth in the Spring and gathers her worshippers to her in the forest, where, beneath the waxing New Moon light, they come together to draw power and enlightenment from her. The virgin/maiden plunges our awareness deep into the soil we stand upon and teaches us that her altar is that of the Earth.

"Adorn my altar," she speaks to our hearts, "with the soft white cloth, woven from the soft fur of my gentle companions. Bring forth the light, white and pure as the silver crescent that rises in the night blackness. Plant the seeds to blossom forth my essence and break the egg as the sign you are rebirthed in my spirit, and vow your heart to my love. It is then I shall always dance inside you as a child, forever young, forever graceful, forever rebirthing the dance of life within you. As my playmate, I shall protect you and avenge your aggressors without hesitation."

Gray sky, moist clouds, crisp biting air hugged the morning. A scrub oak towered above, its branches spreading over us, sheltering us from the moisture that threatened to release from the clouds and pour down upon us.

The pungent scent of sage, cedar and lavender blossomed as an abalone shell with the burning mixture was passed around the circle. Next, a vial of Spring Equinox oil followed as each woman dabbed the fragrance on her wrists.

Silently we sat, each breathing in the smells of wildlife around us. We were high in the mountains on this Spring day. We had decided to celebrate the Christian Easter with the Goddess.

Eyes closed, breath relaxed, the wind rustled through the leaves above. Dreaming Eagle Woman began the soft beating of heart on a medicine drum. The sound of rattles joined (see Plate 1).

In the center of our circle, white blooms of Eostre's lily, yellow chrysanthemums, a buffalo skull from Sedona, an image of Ishtar, several crystals and a piece of lapis in the shape of an egg adorned our altar.

As the drumming and rattles stopped, Dreaming Eagle Woman called in the quarters, then had us hold hands, ending with a simple chant which we sang over and over and over:

Lady weave our circle tight,
fill us with your holy light.
Earth and air and fire and water,
bind us to you.

We rose and began circling round the altar. The beating of the drum led us on. Some of us shook our rattles while others clapped. The energy intensified. We came to a halt and stood there, eyes closed, absorbing the energy, letting it warm our bodies and take us deeper into our higher selves. Slowly, we opened our eyes and giggled at the light in each other's faces. I instructed the women to sit in a tight circle for warmth and asked them to close their eyes and feel the Goddess rising beneath us.

"Let her rise up like the green shoots," I spoke to them. "Breathe her into life. As she saturates every cell, become Maiden Goddess.

"Rebirth her. You are Maiden Goddess. Goddess of Spring. Be with your newness, your freshness, new born-ness."

We stood, at that point, and Dreaming Eagle Woman and I taught the Cherokee Dance of Life, the dance wherein we honor all life. Facing each of the directions in turn, expanding open our hearts gathering up and embracing the Earth within our arms and then bending down to touch the Earth and renew our connection with her.

The dance wherein we draw up the warm woman power of Mother Earth into our hearts and rise with it, releasing it fully up into Father Sky, and then gathering down the highest essence of male energy and pulling its coolness down into our minds and hearts to be grounded into Mother Earth.

The dance wherein we step into each of the directions, releasing our sweet medicine and gathering up the essence of the direction and bringing it through our heart to be released into its opposite direction only to be pulled back into our hearts enhanced and end by grounding the enhanced essence of the direction into our being and finally Mother Earth.

As we stood once more around the altar, ready to end our ceremony, I shared a song I had written especially for that day:

Goddesses in Spring

Goddesses in Spring, dance lightly—dance free.
Goddesses in Spring, give freely of love.

Everywhere we step, blossoms appear.
Everything we touch buds forth green life.
Anyone we hold, we fill with our peace.
Everybody knows the Goddess is here.

Goddesses in Spring, rejoice in the heart of rebirth.
Goddesses in Spring, Sister, it's you and me.

Dates to consider, research and celebrate in the future:

March 1:   Matronalia (Roman)
             Celebration of women and their power.
             Juno-Lucina, protector of

women and the family is offered prayers for a prosperous and happy wedlock.

March 2: First Festival of Vesta (Roman)
The Goddess of purifying fire
Feast of Rhiannon (Welsh)
The White Goddess as inspiration is honored.

March 3: Doll Festival/Hina Masturi
(Japanese)

March 4: Mothering Day (English)
Original Mother's Day

March 5: Festival of Isis (North African)
Ruler of safe navigation

March 8: International Women's Day
(United States) Founded in 1857

March 9: Celebration of Aphrodite and Adonis
(Near Eastern/Greek)
Celebration of lovemaking and a
successful union with your lover

March 10: Hypatia's Day (Alexandrian)
Honoring the woman, Hypatia,
who was a scholar and a divine pagan

March 11: Feast of Artemis (Greek)

March 15: Holiday of Cybele (Anatolian)
The beginning of Spring
Feast of Anna Perenna (Roman)

March 17: Liberalia (Roman)
Celebration of freedom
Festival of Astarte (Canaanite)
The celebration of the fe/male
energies coming together

March 19: Quintaria (Greek)
Feast of Athena (Minerva, Roman)

March 20: Spring Festival

March 21: Spring Equinox

March 22/23: Festival of Minerva (Roman)
Goddess of arts and science
(Athena, Greek)

March 25:   Hilaria (Roman)
             Laughing day
March 30:   Feast of Eostara (German)
             Goddess of rebirth
March 31:   Feast of the Moon Goddess (Roman)
             Honor of Luna

April

The third and final month of Spring. The waning energy of Spring. The energy of April is a contradiction to the term "waning" because we are moving into the most active season of the year. In essence, April is the darkness before the dawn.

Ruled by the ram and Mars, there is a burst of action, a sense of strength. The Vernal Equinox has kick-started the mental faculties and we are ready to get going. The emphasis at this time, however, is on "self"-identity. Being in the season of Spring and re-birth, renewal etc., we can use this cycle to evaluate our current status and comprehension of "self" and map out the transformation we wish to indulge. The usage of tiger-eye can be very beneficial.

Tiger-eye is a mineral called crocidolite and is originally blue. The golden-brown stone we know as tiger-eye is the result of oxidation. The reason this stone is important to use at this time is that it is a stone ever-changing within itself. When we observe the stone, its appearance changes depending on the angle we view it in. It is called the "mind's eye" or "all-seeing eye" and is especially intense when used as a focusing tool, for it gives the feeling of oneness with "self." It causes one to feel more strength, more direct, more pointed in our belief and thoughts, more totally channeled and challenged in our way of being.

If used right, this stone focuses the mind so that the power of the mind becomes activated, after which we become more aware of our needs and the needs of others. When the power of the mind is activated, sight is given toward the many different points of view, many different areas of life and the many different planes of growth. We begin to relate to our fellow human beings in such a way that we can understand their weaknesses and their strengths as well as learning the weaknesses and strengths within "self."

Let us use the waning energy of Spring to activate the mental powers by performing an inner journey. Hold the tiger-eye in the right hand.

When ready, retreat to a quiet and private place. Ground and center yourself by following the breathing in and out until outside distractions disappear.

Begin by gazing upon the smooth surface of the stone and, as you think on the stone, remember that you must be ever pliable and open, constantly looking to those things around yourself that you might learn the lessons of the Earth; for, as you look upon the stone, you will see that, as you look from side to side, the hues and the tones change. This is necessary for you to be aware of, for even as you look at all relations who walk Mother Earth, you will see that the moods change; that time swings from dawn to dark; attitudes move from right to wrong, good to bad; and energy flows positive to negative. It is well that you learn to seek and watch this and approach others when the timing is right or when the color is there. It is well to be perceptive and aware of other's needs as well as your own needs and change with these as is necessary.[2]

Tiger-eye Journey

When you are ready, close your eyes and breathe the pulsing of the tiger-eye deep into your center. As you feel your body light and free, reflecting the different hues of the stone, travel deep into the center of Mother Earth.

As you rest within the core of the Earth, allow the pulsation of the stone to join with your heartbeat and finally with that of the Earth. Be aware that it is this pulsating energy reaching out and drawing back that is the particular rhythm required to vibrate your soul, connecting it to the universe, which will activate your mental powers and aid you in bringing your focused thoughts on "self" into balance and perspective.

Allow the pulsating energy to begin spinning within your heart. Slowly spinning, throwing its changing hues into your heart, allowing you to feel the different aspects of life. As the swirling energy begins to rise, visualize a path moving up into the light of the universe and rise with it until you come to the point which is your third eye, shaman's eye, and allow the spinning to continue moving faster and faster until it seems as if your mind is clearing and being imbued with clarity and brightness, allowing wisdom to unfold within that clarity and brightness.

Now is the opportunity to see the reflections of all your lives and to realize all that you have carried with you. In this moment of awareness, transformation is made available as you begin to realize the choices that are yours. You can see clearly your path, the lessons of lifetimes, the gifts of your mind unfolding gently before you.

The energy reaches out into this wisdom dance and you glance past, present and future. As the energy draws back, purpose is made known. Your purpose. What it is about "self" that needs to be transmuted into a higher "self."

Mind is clear and your heart is open. The changing hues of life dance with the rhythm of the heartbeat. As you watch this sacred ceremony, the activation of power of mind, you hear the song of your life, for this moment in time, the changes which you will go through as the wheel turns from season to season and you see the meaning of "self" unfold, the way of the heart made clear.

Feel the strength and power of mind. Sense the knowing of necessary transformation. Understand the path which must be walked. Let the pulsating energy quietly diminish, and as it begins to descend, follow it back down into the heart. Embrace the wisdom of life experience there. Continue to follow the receding energy that is now moving back to the stone. Follow it through your center and sense it come back to its place of origin—the tiger-eye stone you hold.

Slowly open your eyes and gaze upon the satiny surface

and reflect a moment upon the journey. When you feel complete, it is important to write down your experience and create the map, just received, for strengthening your "self" identity.

Dates to consider, research and celebrate in the future:

April 1:	Veneralia (Roman)
	Festival of Venus (Aphrodite to Greeks)
April 2:	Battle of Flowers (French)
April 3/4:	Megalisia (Phrygian and Roman)
	The celebration of Cybele as the Great Mother
April 5:	Festival of Kwan Yin (Chinese)
	The Goddess of Mercy (Kwannon,
	Japanese)
April 13:	Ceralia (Roman)
	Festival of Ceres
April 21:	Festival of Hathor (Egyptian)
April 22:	Festival of Ishtar (Babylonian)
April 27:	Floralia (Central and Eastern European)
	Honoring of Flora
April 30:	Beltane (Celtic)

Quando io sar partita da questo mondo,
Qualunque cosa che avrete bisogna,
Una volta al mese quando la luna
È piena... Dovrete venire in
luogo deserto, in una selva tutte insieme, E adorare lo spirito
potente di mia madre Diana. E chi vorrà
imparare la stregoneria, che non la sopra, mia
madre le insegnera, tutte cose... Sarete liberi dalla
schiavitù! E così divennete tutti liberi!...
                                    —Aradia

Aradia

Chapter Three

SUMMER ————————
A Fire Spirit of Life

It is to the south I go
to feel the flaming noonday Sun.
As the White Stallion runs across the dry, desert plains,
*   my passions surge forth:*
"Spirit—my friend,
Engulf this circle I dance within!"

The late Summer Sun smiled down upon us, warming our
faces while purging our illnesses. A cool breeze blew caressingly
over the field of pampas grass in the back bay where we gathered for ceremony. The Mother Earth had been pulling me to
spill healing energy into her, so I had put out the word that
there would be a Ma-Ma Earth Healer's Ceremony and that it
was open to all the Earth Angels who were being called by the
Mother to come together and participate in this ceremony. Five
others plus myself showed up for the ceremony.

Together we set up our ceremony site. The three other women
and two girls arranged grass mats and Mexican blankets to sit
on. Rattles, drums and crystals were laid out. Water bottles were
strategically placed around the circle. I concentrated on the altar,
where I put up a wood A-frame, covered it with my medicine blanket and then hung my east medicine shield on it. In front of the
shield I stuck four large crystals (from the altar in my Temple) in
the ground, point first. We sat on the blankets facing the altar.

The stillness of the noontime embraced us. Even the pack rats, who were normally busy chewing under the foliage of the pampas-grass houses, were quiet.

We closed our eyes and breathed deep, listening to the Earth around us, feeling the breeze and the Sun on our bodies. I brought a smudge stick to life and held it out to Suzanne (18 years old) to begin the purification, preparing us for sacred time. As each female smudged herself, I rattled with a deer medicine rattle over and around each of them, taking them into their centers and a place of groundedness.

After smudging the altar, I brought the smudge stick to the center of the group and had each woman purify a crystal she had chosen or brought to work with during the ceremony. When finished, I walked out to the dirt path and began snuffing out the burning embers of the stick. Upon my request, Sarah (eight), the baby of the group, brought over one of the water bottles. She unscrewed the cap and held it meekly out to me (though she has the energy of the ram running rapid in her). I smiled into her hazel eyes.

"We need to wash the flame away so as not to cause any fires," I explained as I poured the water over the last ember that stubbornly burned and then upon the ground where I had crushed the stick.

"There, it looks out to me, but perhaps you should double-check for me, Sarah." Peering down into the stick and then checking the ground, she confirmed it was out. We went back and joined the others. I began the ceremony.

"Close your eyes and be one with your groundedness, this here and now. Breathe naturally, gently. Begin to feel the warm, golden light of the Sun washing over you, kissing your face and arms and thighs. Open to this warmth, this energy, and allow it to nourish your skin—the cell tissue.

"Bring this golden light to the soles of your feet, and under each foot visualize a golden ball of light forming. Open and allow the light to enter the bottom of your feet. As the golden light expands inside your feet, allow this fire to consume and break up any blockages in your feet and ankles. As it rises into

your calves and into your knees, it continues to burn away the blockages. Up into your thighs it spreads, breaking through, consuming, filling you with pure, golden light.

"As the light reaches the top of your thighs and sits resting at the base of your spine, your pelvic area, allow the golden light from both legs to join together and form a golden ball. Once formed, open your base chakra located at the base of your spine and allow this purging, healing, golden light to enter. The light becomes brighter as it enters your chakra system. From here the light spreads out into your organs. It breaks apart the blockages and moves up into the second/womb chakra, the lower back, the major organs, where it consumes and burns away tension, illnesses. It continues to rise up to the solar plexus, middle back, stomach, burning away the blockages. Up to the heart center, upper back, lungs—the golden, healing light expanding and growing brighter. Up to the shoulders, the chest.

"Here the light divides into two balls where they each travel down your arms, burning through the residues of stress that so often reside in the muscles and at the elbow and wrist joints. Let the light flow into the hands, to the very tips of your fingers, where it pulsates with incredible energy. Let the light rise back up your arms until both balls merge together at the base of your neck.

"The golden light flows into your throat center, breaking apart the blocks which prevent your masculine energy from spilling forth in the form of words. It flows into the back of your neck, consuming the tension. It rises into your face, filling your mouth, cheeks, ears, nose, eyes and back of head with light. Then it moves into your third eye, your Shaman's eye, and here it consumes the doors which have been shut for so long. It blasts them open.

"And finally, the golden light rises to the crown and consumes and breaks apart the last bit of blockages and tension and stress in your body. Feel the light growing stronger and stronger. Your whole being is filled with the golden, healing light.

"Now open your crown and allow this light to shine back up into its place of origin, into Father Sky, the Sun, where all this

light energy was birthed."

In the stillness between my words, the rising of a jet air-plane could be heard. We were being reminded of our everyday world, and that we were indeed urban Medicine Women belong-ing to a Sisterhood of civilization in the modern world. I swal-lowed the sudden apprehension I felt about being so involved with city living; after all, I had always thought of myself as an Earth Mother and despised the thought of having to live my days in the city.

As the loudness of the jet plane subsided, I continued.

"Reach out and pick up your crystal. Bring it to your solar plexus about an inch above your belly button and hold it there with both hands. Make sure the point is shooting down." To both sides of me, hands reached down to pick up different-sized crystals lying on the blanket. As they picked them up, the sun-light caught in the inner prisms of some of the crystals and quick, bright rainbow flashes shot out. All movement ceased.

"As you hold the crystal to your center, tense your solar plexus against the crystal three times and focus on the point of connection between the two points, that of your center and the crystal. A golden light begins to shine at this point and, as you tense your muscles for the third time, send that golden light into the crystal, opening the passageway for your energy to travel down into it.

"Become very aware of this connection—you the generator of healing energy, the crystal the conduit for this healing energy. And when you feel the connection is complete come to the altar and plant your crystal, point down, into the Mother." Very qui-etly we sat; each focused on the work.

The soft rustling of our garments broke the reverie as, one by one, we rose and planted our crystals. The drum began its steady beat and rattles joined in. A chorus of voices began chanting:

Our magic is our give away,
Our magic is our song.
So give away your love today,
And sing the whole day long.

Around and around the altar we moved until we raised the energy, creating the atmosphere in which we needed to work our healing medicine. As we gathered around the crystals and medicine shield, we began to give attention to the ill and dying places of the land. Quietly the instruments continued to set the mood, and one by one we gave voice to those places.

"I feel we should send healing to the beautiful hills of Irvine, which for the last decade have continually been raped and shaved away." Instantly the drums and rattles rose in volume to a tremendous level. After the energy was sent, the volume returned to a low level. Over and over this process went on as we sent healing to the fault lines and the volcanoes and the back bay and faraway places such as the Middle East where all the holy wars have been killing the land and its people. We focused on the tropical rain forests in Brazil and the wasted plains of Africa.

Finally we sang To One Gaia *(page 3), giving voice to our Mother Earth's words.*

We ended the ceremony by coming together and holding hands. Closing our eyes, our bodies began to sway softly, gently. A beautiful, heartfelt song was born. We sang of our oneness, our words taking us deeper and deeper into the reality of the connection to the true life force that dwells within us all. Holy, we were, angels singing to the life that shared this great Mother Body with us. We felt the magnitude of our ceremony being received, even on a subliminal level, by every foot that touched the Earth. We knew we were messengers of healing. We were the new power. The women and the children. We were the new healing. The women and the children. We were the birthers of the new world.

Summer is a combustion of activity. The warmth of the Sun dances across the deserts, caresses the trees of the forests and sparkles off the movement of the waters in the oceans as it rises and splashes against the shoreline or softly gurgles and rushes on downstream. All life is in full celebration of active energy.

This is the season of healing. Dis-ease is the racing of the mind, mind exhaustion. We have now entered the phase of body action and/or awareness. We shed cumbersome clothing and expose our skin to the elements with relish. The Sun becomes our focus as we bathe in its fiery rays, allowing the richness of the Sun's force to soak into our pores, empowering us with new zest and enthusiasm. After a wonderful day at play we are charged with energy and feel as if there is nothing we cannot accomplish. Through our play, we release the stagnate energy held within each cell, and allow the electrical spark within each nerve to jump furiously from synapse to synapse. The action of our internal fire roaring to life engulfs and burns away the blockages of the mind.

Summer is perhaps the only season that we, as a whole people, get immersed in. We join the dance and seem to live in the here and now. If in the Spring we joined with the energy of a positive mindset, the Summer becomes the action or active energy required to manifest our goals into the physical. With a positive attitude already seeded in our cell memory, we can take the necessary steps imperative to set into motion and bring to fruition those areas in our life that must be tended to. With the added energy of the Sun, we can easily overcome the obstacles that once seemed monumental. Because our energy is at its annual all-time high, we can tie up any loose ends without feeling pulled on or overburdened.

Action. Action. Action is the key at this time.

The Correspondences of Summer

The season of the body/action/energy
Progress/fullness/fruition/midday/Full Moon
South/touch/fire/spirit/orange/red
White Stallion/salamanders/large cats
Ancestors of the Native American cultures
Volcanoes/hearth fires/candles/fruit trees/garlic

Summer is housed in the south, the home of energy, spirit, heat, flame, blood, sap, life, will, healing and destroying, purification, bonfires, hearth fires, candle flames, Sun, deserts, volcanoes, eruptions, explosions and volatile emotions. South is the direction we turn to when desiring to understand the child within, the place of innocence. South is the spirit within.

The Element of Summer—Fire

Fire is the element of Summer, south and the body. Fire is the symbol of transmutation. Thus, one of the main tools to be used at this time is the candle, for the substance of a candle becomes transmuted by burning and changes into light.

In Europe at one time there was a mysterious fraternity of the Rosicrucians who were sometimes called *Philosophi per ignem*, the fire philosophers, whose main symbol was the flame of transmutation.[1] By their beliefs and practices, these occult philosophers sought to transmute that which was base into something better in order to attain illumination and enlightenment. They had a mystic saying or motto: *Igne Natura renovatur integra*, "All Nature is renewed by fire."

Fire was considered to be the most spiritual of the elements because the use of fire is one of the things which most markedly distinguishes man from beast. The burning of candles and lamps in temples and churches throughout the world was not done merely for the mundane purpose of having light but as an honoring of the above philosophy.

Wise women have been known to scry (gaze upon) the flame as a form of divination. The technical name for this form of divination is *pyromancy*. Today many of us are not fortunate enough to have a fireplace in which to practice pyromancy; thus, candle burning has become popular (not only as a form of magick, but also during our sacred circles to alter the atmosphere with soft muted light).

Dancing around a campfire or bonfire is an ancient form of temple dancing. Since the movement of fire is fast and upward, the arms and head are the main parts of the body used when dancing the fire dance. The fire symbol (upright pyramid) is made with the hands and held over the head, reaching and flickering for the sky. The movement is shimmery and fiery. The tone "re" (ray) can be sung or chanted with a staccato rhythm, imitating the flickering and unpredictable nature of fire.

When working with fire in its season, the body temperature rises and sparks the ever hidden sensual and wild side of our being. Thus, our sexuality flames awake. We can become very alluring, the enchantress. It is through this very powerful sexual energy that the natural energy of the season—action—is channeled. Because the natural energy of Summer is raw and uncontrollable, it is extremely important for us not to get thrown off balance and become satiated with sexual power and begin manipulating. Rather, we should strive to harness it and use it to the benefit and good will of all. Remember, we of the Goddess community adhere to a very old code of ethics, which is simply: "An it harm none, do what ye will, for the good will of all. Blessed Be."

The Phases of Summer

May

The waxing month of Summer is May. Right off the bat, we begin the season with a Sabbat: Beltane, the wedding day of the feminine and masculine energies of life.

May is the month of Taurus, ruled by the planet Venus. A month of love and sexuality, tenderness and values. It is the month of the Goddess, and if a Friday the 13th should ever fall in the month of May, then hearken all women unto your most holiest day of the year and celebrate in your Goddesshood. And should Friday May 13th ever be graced by the Full Moon, then low and behold, miracles can be manifested through you and the flame!

The power of love,
A force from above,

freeing my soul.[2]

...rang through the room. Pink and red candles were burning; their flames flickered and danced with the energy of the colors and the vibration of the words being sung.

On the wall, the shadowy silhouette of a woman danced. Her long hair whipped ghostly shadows across the paint. Her long, flowing skirt gracefully followed after her body. Her breasts were exposed to the night.

It was the witches' day! Friday the 13th. But more importantly, it was the month of May, and high above, the white, pregnant Moon dripped her moist light upon the Earth. It was the night of love. Exalted love. Goddess Love.

Tears ran silently down the woman's face as she released conscious hold on her body, surrendering to the goddess Ishtar; allowing the Goddess to rise and live through her body.

As the movement and music took her deeper within the erotic emotion of Isthar, the Priestess shed the layers of entrapment crusted around her spirit. The layers of conditioning glued there by the continual preaching of the patriarchy that women were evil sorceresses who tempted man and caused his fall from grace.

Erotically, her hips moved, luring all the men of the world to thrust their penises within the moist folds of her flower. She called forth to the man of her heart. The Priestess of Ishtar touched the place between her legs. Her eyes closed. Slowly, she caressed the yoni of all women. Love. Love. Love swept through her veins and burst forth through the nerve centers of her cells.

For 28 years this Priestess had remained unharnessed by a man, free and virginal in her "one-in-herself" phase, but now she felt ready to open to the man who she knew would one day come to her and heal the feminine wound she had carried into this current life. The wound that was festering. The wound which would be the greatest lesson to learn. Born at the time when Venus was in Gemini, the Priestess knew that ultimately it would be this man who would teach her the diversity of experiencing the wisdom that when she faced her shadow, faced her own death experience, she would be empowered and transmuted and transformed into something else, that to love is to embrace all sides of self, including the shadow self.

She knew she had not yet experienced the love that was possible between a man and a woman, and that the whole experience of love, and love values, was such that she could very much be in touch with the great mystery and the void within, for she had always been aware of the transient nature of relationships and had always been able to love deeply and intensely, if often only in a remote and detached way.

Her greatest love would be the added love for the mind of this man who would take her hand and walk her through the inner fire of transmutation. He would ultimately be the catalyst for her to touch with the true rebel inside, the true artist of the Goddess. This man would be the true supporter of her radicalness, her unusualness and her extreme need for freedom, yet tolerant of her possessive love that seemed to cause her to cling, out of fear, to the soul reflected in his eyes.

And so the Priestess danced and made love to this man of her dreams who lived only within the deepest recesses of her mind.

"Let him come in," she whispered to the Full Moon. "When the time is perfect, let my mate come in. I am ready from this day forward. By all the power of Moon and Sun, as I do will, it shall be done."

Round and round she turned. Losing herself to the twirling, spiraling core of energy her movement created until at last it peaked and she released her wish up to the pregnant Moon to be birthed down into the physical, when the time was perfect.

—Three years later, he came to her as the Summer ended and the season of release fell upon the Earth.

Beltane / May Day (May 1)

There are so many wonderful ways in which to celebrate Beltane that I could easily devote an entire chapter to them.

Beltane is a day of activity that should be shared by women, men and children. It is a day of picnicking and singing and dancing around the Maypole. This celebration must always be celebrated on the green grass barefoot. The focus should be on Love. Love, sweet love.

Lots and lots of flowers are used as the decorations. Flower necklaces and garlands are made and worn. Games such as tug-o-war and tag are played. A feast is enjoyed. And somewhere within the midst of all the activity a traditional Maypole dance is celebrated, for this is the ancient dance of love. The enactment of male penetrating the female, the union of the sexes.

If your celebration only contains women, then the focus would shift to your love of life and the sharing of love between sisters.

And if it be only you, well, your celebration might become the most special of them all.

I climbed further up the rocky crevice. There in front of me stood my place of dedication. The waterfall and the crystal-clear pool. The Sun sat just over the lip of the cliff above (Plate 2).

I took my dress off and waded out to an exposed stretch of sand in the center of the pool. Standing there, I closed my eyes and breathed deep as if taking in all the life, all the elements that surrounded me. Kneeling, I purified my body by washing in the cool stream. I became an open vessel and began filling with the Earth's life force. My words broke the stillness and seemed to become part of the lyrical exchange between the water and the air.

I called forth to Ishtar. I opened my heart and was blessed. I was of the Earth and the Earth was of me. There no longer seemed a distinction between me or anything else. I felt my body connect and merge with this solidness.

Above where the water flowed over the cliff lingered a fuzzy white shine, the life force. It seemed as if I grew ten feet tall, lifting up to meet with the life force resting on the cliff. All the emotions and all the wonders of the world exploded within me. I understood them. Everything became possible in my moment of realization.

*Plate 2—The Place of Dedication. A personal place of power,
where I performed my dedication to Ishtar on a beautiful May day.*

*"I am" was repeated over and over as I entered the realm of
my Queen.*

*I picked up my athame and dipped it in the water and then
held it up to the firelight of the Sun to purify it. I wove it
through the air and charged it with life, dedicating it to Ishtar.
I touched my fingers to the folds between my legs and felt the*

wetness there. I raised my fingers back up and saw the blood glistening on them, sacred blood. Instinctively I wiped the blood across the blade of the athame in an act of consecration. I touched the blood again so I could consecrate myself by wiping it onto my third eye, my heart and then my lips. A third time I felt the wetness on my fingers and ended by bringing them to my lips and sucking the blood off.

With the tip of the blade I marked my skin, cutting a sickle Moon above my left breast. There was no pain, but as the skin broke and the blood beaded out, I felt a release shake through me as if I had just had an orgasm.

Into the sheath of the knife, I carved a new symbol and tanned it with the blood. I sat down and held the athame out in front of me. I centered and listened.

As I sat there I heard the drone of a hummingbird flitting around my head and opened my eyes to see it frozen not more than 12 inches before my eyes. Again I listened and saw butterflies dance in pairs. A sparrow dived down and somersaulted before the waterfall. Lizards crept out to the edge of the rocks, sunning themselves in the warm Spring Sun. Life was everywhere. I was alive.

I looked deeply, fully, richly at all things surrounding me and stepped through the transformation into my new skin. I became the Priestess of the Queen of Heaven, the Opener of the Womb—Ishtar.

As I left the waterfall and climbed back down to the campsite below, I somehow knew this had been my wedding day, but not to a mere mortal man. I had married my soul to the life force and had become its bride.

The Sun set on a Beltane that glowed with sacredness.

It is important to remember that during this waxing month of Summer (May), you should be conscious of your own fire and the flame of the candle, bonfire, hearth fire, lightning, starlight and sunlight, becoming one with all fire and one with the illuminated spirit of Goddess.

Dates to consider, research and celebrate in the future:

May 1:	Beltane (European)
May 2/3:	Fire Festival of Bona Dea (Roman)
May 4:	Festival of Sheila Na Gig (Irish)
	The vulva goddess
May 9:	Lemuria (Roman)
	Peacemaking with the dead
May 14:	Goddess Tithe Day (North African)
	The black-robed Isis is honored
May 15:	Rain Dance (Guatemalan)
May 18:	Feast of Pan (Greek)
May 19:	Bendideta (Greek)
	Dedicated to Bendis, Goddess of warfare and the hunt
May 19-28	Kallyntaria & Plynteria (Greek)
	Spring cleaning of sacred places
May 24:	Birth of Artemis (Greek)
May 24-28:	The Mothers of Arles (French)
	The celebration of the Gypsies "Three Maries of the Sea," the Triple Goddess
May 25:	Celebration of the Tao (Japanese)
	Mother of the world celebration
May 29:	Ambarvalia (Roman)
	Corn Mother festival; Ceres
May 30/31:	Feast of the Queen of Heaven (European)
	The Virgin Mary and Proserpine are honored

June

The exalted month of Summer. Greatly influenced by Gemini and Mercury, the energy is rich with the power of intellectual communication and awareness. We need not fear our words, but rejoicingly and actively seek to speak the truth.

The "I AM" Religious order (The Saint Germain Foundation[3]) makes available through its books many incredible affirmations that one can use. This order has called the art of affirming and/or chanting "Decreeing" and practices it as the single focused form of manifesting change. (Though the organization is based on the teachings of the Ascended Master Saint Germain, and is at times rather patriarchal in its dogmatism, it is an invaluable source for further reading in gaining a better understanding of the power behind the spoken word.)

June is the month that affirmations, or personal chants, become extremely potent, especially if combined with the use of candle burning. Understanding the color vibration is important if you are going to dabble in this art. To begin, acquaint yourself with the spectrum of visible color, which consists of 12 basic colors that offer different sensitive vibrations (red being the most active and powerful, violet the most passive and receptive and black the most stabilizing). The colors of the light spectrum are red, orange, yellow, green, blue, indigo and violet. In addition there are three acromatic (without color) colors to be included: white, black and gray. The balance of the 12 colors are rose or pink, a soft red and brown, an earth tone.[4]

The spectrum colors from red to violet move energy outward and forward as well as inward and backward. Red, orange and yellow are forward-moving colors. Blue, indigo and violet are receiving colors, while green (in the middle) is the color of balance. Rose is the color representing gentle emotion, one usually of love, while the color brown offers grounding and stability. White expedites all color energy; black anchors and absorbs while separating all colors. Gray is not used in color candle burning because it is a void color, neither moving forward or inward.

Each color has a particular adaptation to the energy of light from which the desired result of candle burning is effected. For example, red is a powerfully emotional color. When a red candle is lit, it attracts red to its total light energy, and the power of red relative to the red ray within the light spectrum combines; then the energized red is sent forth, bringing back the desired result.

A green candle releases the green expression of balance relative to the green ray of the visible spectrum of light and a balanced, checked effect is achieved. It is important to keep in mind that it may take three days to see the result of candle burning and, when more than one color is to be burned, all candles are to be lit at the same time.

The following is a basic chart to use for candle burning, but further research is advised.

RED: The longest wavelength. Assist courage, fortitude, physical problems and positive action. Power generation. One of the seven primary rays. It is the lowest center in our chakra system, the base of the spine.

PINK: A combination of white and red. Moves gently but forcefully, with emotional feelings of giving and receiving. Lucky love candles, as they open hearts and bring forth happy experiences.

ORANGE: Second longest wavelength. Moves in a direct line, bringing desired results. Action color, organization and development. Motivation. The primary ray connected to the splenic or womb center.

YELLOW: Expanding wavelength. Combines with light energy to open things up. Yellow candles assist communication, expansion and stimulation. The primary ray connected to the solar plexus center.

GREEN: Middle of spectrum. Has a four-hour to twenty-four-hour cycle to complete its action. Balance, aiding health, clearing confusion and negative energy. Motivate learning. The primary ray connected to the heart center.

BLUE: Passive and shorter wavelength. Faculties of the mind, assists mind expression. Creative expression, decision making. The primary ray connected to the throat center.

INDIGO: Passive wavelength. Stimulates the mind, assists executive capabilities, management awareness and protections. For wisdom. The primary ray connected to the pineal gland or the third-eye center located between the eyebrows on the forehead.

VIOLET: Shortest wavelength. Produces introspection, spiritual development, independence, clarity of thoughts and feelings. The primary ray connected to the pituitary gland or the crown center found at the top of the head.

BROWN: Security and stability.

BLACK: Separates controlling energy. For release of fear from the unknown.

WHITE: Universal color.

When working with your candles, remember that once you light a candle with an intent, it must never be used for anything else. Never leave a candle burning unattended, not even to run to the corner store! When you are finished with a candle and there is a stub left over, either bury or melt it down in a double boiler with other candle stubs and make your own candles.

I spent a weekend going through intensive ceremonies with Black Wolf, a sister from the Sisterhood of the Shields. She had taken me through a series of empowerment exercises and brought me to a place where I was honored by receiving my Power Song. *Though I learned many things from this teacher, I knew this would be the last time we would work together, and when departing I felt a sadness overwhelm me.*

In the days following our weekend together, I walked in the dreamtime for the first time. Black Wolf had taught me that there were two dreamtimes—the dreamtime of the mind and the dreamtime of another dimension, or of the spirit world.

Having been a student of esoterica for years, I had long ago gained access to the dreamtime of the mind. But shortly after ending my work with Black Wolf, I experienced what I believe to have been the dreamtime of another dimension. Though I have not since had the honor of experiencing it so vividly, I believe I have gained access and through dedicated practice will one day be able to traverse it with little effort.

It was during this experience, when I was in the spirit world, the realm of all realities and non-realities, that I found freedom through my own efforts, the belief behind my personal Power Song *and the force behind every word I uttered. The power of word no longer seemed just a concept or an adage we learn to assume when involving ourselves with the New Age movement. I understood; I really got the power.*

During the weeks that followed this experience, I spent many hours sitting before my altar, a single candle burning, shaking my medicine rattle and chanting my personal Power Song. *One particular evening I lit a purple candle, settled myself down on the pendleton blanket I had begun to use for occasions such as this and picked up the medicine rattle.*

I sang my Power Song *three times—once out loud for my own ears, the second time I whispered it for my medicine animal and the third time I sang it within the corridor of my Shaman's eye for the spirit keepers. I sang:*

I am light of woman,
white wolf singing by Full Moon bright.
I am freedom and beauty,
woman spirit of life.

I am ancient and young,
primordial wisdom of time.
I am moonlight and sunlight,
starlight pieces that shine.

I am spirit woman,
walking in dreamtime.

I am white wolf,
disappearing between time.
I am woman of spirit, the Goddess divine.

After a period of time, I stopped rattling and was finally able to open my eyes and fix them upon the flame that sat still at the top of the candle. The Sun had descended and the room was a rich glow.

I stared for a long time at the flame and lost track of time. I remembered the spirit world dreamtime and the understanding of power behind the spoken word. It was then that I gave the fullest power and focused intent behind affirming. Though the affirmation went on for a long time, I was successful in writing it down. The power of those words still rings true in my center and the thought of sharing them with others, who might use them, is extremely exhilarating.

I am that I am
I am that I am
I am that
I am that
I am
I am.

I am all things for the highest of good.
I am shaman
I am positive
I am healing
I am success
I am spirit
I am goddess
I am god
I am peace
I am love
I am balance
I am unity
I am harmony

I blend
I merge
I teach
I give
I receive
I heal
I direct
I learn
I have peace
I have harmony
I have love
I have unity
I have success
I have balance
I have positive light

I have but to speak; my words create;
my thoughts are manifestations
I am an open channel through which flows the spirit of life
I am the flame of spirit
I am connected to the life force;
that which I reach for I achieve
I am the highest of good
for the positive benefit of all
for the good of all
for the healing of Ma-Ma Earth
and all spirits living upon her body

I am that I am.
I am that.
I am.

Summer Solstice (June 21)

There is a very special celebration that can be shared between women at this time. It is an ancient Nez Perce Indian ceremony called "Becoming Relative."

One Summer, while attending the Woman's Alliance Summer Solstice Camp with a dear friend, I was introduced to Norma Cordell, a very powerful teacher from Oregon. She was offering a ceremony to the women who wanted to become spirit sisters, and so Lisa and I felt the calling to participate in the ceremony.

Though I could never recall the experience, because it was so intimate, I would like to give the outline of the ceremony for adaptation. (A request of Norma was that if we shared this ceremony with others we would not share the ancient tongue spoken, and out of respect to a valued teacher, I omit those power words from this outline.)

Before performing the ceremony it is important to share with those attending or participating in the ceremony the story of the Great Water Gourd.

The Great Water Gourd is the Big Dipper constellation. Through the Big Dipper, the peoples of the world are blessed, with the everlasting thirst finally quenched. The Great Water Gourd carries lessons to us, helps us through the lessons, becomes the mirror of honesty and objectivity and helps us move into the starlight.

Within the Drinking Gourd live the seven sisters: She who is survival, She who is love and compassion, She who is will and manifestation, She who is mothering and nurturing, She who is ritual and ceremony, She who is cutting throughs and the Little Sister.

Becoming relative is dropping into the interpersonal arena. It is the relationship of becoming the embodiment of all seven sisters inside.

By becoming the embodiment of all seven sisters inside you:

1. Know when to move/change.

2. Know your limits, when to be not all giving, but honest in your giving, whether it be feedback from observations or feelings, a commitment to be kind in all your honesty.

3. Know how to be supportive on the Earthly plane, helping the creative processing and knowing when to be grounded and

what is realistic.

4. She who rocks and holds commits to soothing pains and letting the pain be experienced by providing a safe space in which to experience the pain.

5. She who makes sacred and remembers the traditions/ carries the stories and lineage is to hold in memory for the other what you go through together.

6. She who holds the sword dispelling illusions/working with emotions/having emotions and cutting through to the anger wrathfully, but loving is taking the risk to reach in and help the other find the dis-ease.

7. The Little Sister is the biggest commitment of all, for we are in her control as of four years ago. The Little Sister stands up in the Great Water Gourd. She is wearing her ceremonial dress and her finest jewelry. We cannot see in the black orbs of her eyes as she reflects everything out.

In her hands she holds an orb, a ball, and she is speaking to the children of Earth. She is saying, "I want to play." She is pleasure, innocence and the restoration of our inner child. As she took control, she tossed the ball to us and it is falling down through the starlight to us. She is in control for 1200 years.

We must catch the ball so we can play with the Little Sister and restore the innocence. This ceremony is for us to restore this lineage of the seven sisters and to drink from the gourd and share what we drink.

As we become relatives, we are surrounded by three magical rings of experience and commitment. The first ring is a commitment to carry the lineage forward. The second commitment is to heal the interpersonal relationship with our relatives, and the third commitment is to the survival of the world.

Women are tribal and feel the loss of not belonging to a tribe today, or having a lineage. Part of why people in general are hurting so much today is that they have no roots, no lineage. The modern family has created disembodiment from the tribe. This ceremony helps align all things. It brings the nuclear family unit back into a tribal unit. This ceremony is an enactment to repair the family. (A healthy family has some type of spiritual belief. A healthy family plays, eats, feels, touches, has faith, genuine affection shared and communication within its structure.)

Becoming spiritual sisters is an important step. It is a commitment that is made for life, all lifetimes. It is a commitment made to assist each other on your spiritual paths forever. Should this bond be broken, a serious karma is created between your two spirits for all times to come. This is a conscious choice being made, for you are creating family.

If you have a blood sister and a time comes when both your blood sister and your spirit sister need you at the same time, you must heed your spirit sister's call. She is chosen family; she comes first.

"Becoming Sisters Ceremony"

Items Needed:
Gift to sister
Ribbons: blue, red, green and yellow
Rose water
Corn meal
Scissors
Feather and sage to purify

This is a sacred ceremony and all participants should dress in their finery.

There should be as many witnesses as there are participants in the ceremony. This ceremony should be performed only at the Summer Solstice when the Great Gourd pours down upon us the light transmissions of the green wind (feminine energy), which is the highest healing potential available to us.

The witnesses make a circle around the participants enacting the sacred hoop and remain quiet and sitting throughout the ceremony until otherwise directed.

The pairs of sisters stand together inside the circle. Cornmeal is sprinkled on their crowns. (It is believed that the first seed released from the Great Gourd to Earth was of the corn. By being sprinkled with the cornmeal you are being reminded of the law of the seven sisters as described above.)

The right wing of an immature bald eagle is used as the smudge feather. It is drawn up the left side of the body and down the right. (This is the only feather used for women in the Nez Perce Indian tradition. It is the female energy medicine. It is drawn over the body as a form of empowerment. However, it is illegal for non-Native Americans to possess eagle feathers. Therefore, the tail feather of a female peacock is a good substitute.)

The sisters face each other. Rose water is poured into their hands. Simultaneously they wash each other's face while reciting:

My Spirit is your spirit.

After both women have completed the above, they remain facing each other and speak:

My path is your path.
My love is your love.
My commitment to you is to embody the seven sisters and to try.

At this time they place their right hand over the other's heart, and hold left wrists. This is the time to be the mother and daughter, and allow the emotions and residue of all life times experienced together to flow between the two. The woman who is leading the ceremony will recite a prayer over them. She will stand in the middle of the circle, before the altar and speak:

I have come through lifetimes from my Elders to you. I have stood before you many times. I am the flame of the fire, the breath of the wind, the sparkle of the water.

After the ceremony leader has finished speaking, she will

move around the circle tying ribbons around the left wrist of each pair of sisters. The time is taken to gaze into each other's eyes and to feel each other; see each other, breathe each other. When the ceremony leader has finished tying the ribbons, she begins the *Sister Chant,* and all women gathered join in. The chant is sung many, many times to allow the emotional and spiritual interchange between sisters.

> *Sister, sister—oh my sister.*
> *How can I tell you how much I love you?*
> *You have given me so much pleasure.*
> *I love you so.*
>
> *Sister, sister—oh my sister.*
> *How can I tell you how I am feeling?*
> *You have given me so much pleasure.*
> *I love you so.*

When the chanting has ended, the ceremony leader asks the witnesses to stand and join hands. She says to them:

> *You represent the great sacred hoop, that which holds all things. As witness to this rite, repeat after me:*
> *We, the great sacred hoop,*
> *now see,*
> *now hear,*
> *now know this sisterhood.*
> *May you stay to your commitments.*
> *May you hold tight to the hoop.*
> *And may you heal the great sacred hoop.*

The ceremony leader travels around the circle cutting the ribbons apart, saying:

> *Forever joined—forever a part.*

Once all pairs have been separated, the ceremony leader

has everyone recite after her:

Ho. Blessed Be. It is done. Ho.

The gifts between spirit sisters are now exchanged. The ceremony has ended.

Dates to consider, research and celebrate in the future:

June 1:   Children's Festival (Chinese)
Festival of Carna (Roman)
    Goddess who opens what is closed and
    closes what is open
Festival of the Oak Nymph (Druidic)

June 2:   Juno Regina's Day (Roman)
    Celebration of women who are in public life

June 3:   Second Festival of Peace (Roman)
    Goddess Pax; peace

June 4:   Rosalia (Roman)
    The celebration of the rose, a symbol of
    Aphrodite and Mary

June 7:   Vestalia (Roman)
    Celebration of Vesta, fire

June 11:   Matralia (Roman)
    Celebration of Mater Matuta, the Goddess of
    Dawn and Death, and the powers of mothering

June 12:   Scirophoria (Thenian)
    Festival dedicated to the Goddess of fruitfulness

June 13:   Feast of Epona (Celtic)
    The horse-headed goddess

June 14:   Birthday of the Muses (Greek)
    The celebration of Mnemosyne (memory) and
    her daughters: Calliope (epic song), Clio (history), Euterpe (lyric song), Thalia (comedy),
    Melpomene (tragedy), Terpsichore (dance),

	Erato (erotic poetry), Polyhymnia (sacred hymns), and Urania (astronomy)
June 17:	Marriage of Orpheus and Eurydice (Greek) The celebration is All Couples' Day
June 21:	Celebration of Yemaya Olokun (Japanese) Summer Solstice Festival of Litha (European and North African) Goddess of fertility, power and order
June 24:	Lady Luck (European) Fors Fortuna, ruler of chance, and the Fates are honored

July

The waning month of Summer. Though the pace of life is in full action, the energy is at a mellow high. July is the time of Cancer, the crab. It is the time of nurturing, touch and security. Ruled by the ever elusive Moon (the female principle), the home, the family and "self" become the center of focus.

This is the time when the Emotional Body is on fire. It is a time of preparing for the release that will be made in the upcoming months of Autumn. Life is at that standstill point, like the sprinter at the moment before the gun goes off and the race begins and is over. This is the time of playfulness and tenderness. Although sexuality has been ignited, the Moon seems to shadow it and subdue the erotica by transforming it into the love of family.

The Goddess Aspect of Summer—Mother

Whenever you have need of anything, and better it be when the Moon is full, you shall assemble in some secret place and adore Me, who is Queen of all the Wise and who is called by many names:

Aah (Egyptian)
Acca (Roman)
Acco (Greek)
Achaaiva (Greek)
Adamah (Hebrew)
Adamu (Assyrian)
Adda (Hindu)
Aegina (Roman)
Aestas (Roman)
Aholibah (Hebrew)
Aima (Hebrew)
Aindre (Hindu)
Aine of Knockaine (Irish)
Akka (Finno-Ugric)
Akna (Yucatan)
Ala (Nigerian)
Alaghom Naum (Mayan)
Alcmena (Greek)
Alphito (Gaelic)
Althaea (Greek)
Ama Gal Dingir (Sumerian)
Amalthea (Assyrian)
Amathaounta (Aegean)
Ambika (Indian)
Amphitrite (Libyan)
Ananke (Neo-Platonic-
   Pythagorean)
Anasuya (Indian)
Anaxithea (Greek)
Anna-Purna (Hindu)
Antum (Assyro-Babylonian)
Anuket (Egyptian)
Apet (Theban)
Aphrodite (Greek)
Aramati (Iranian)
Aredevi Sura Anahita (Iraqi)
Aretia (Chaldaean)

Armathr (Icelandic)
Arma (Hittite)
Arsinoe (Greek)
Artio (Celtic)
Asherah or Asherath
   (Semitic)
Ashima Baetyl (Hebrew)
Ashnan (Sumerian)
Asia (Hebrew)
Asintmah (Canadian)
Assam (Himalayan)
Astarte or Ashtart (Semitic)
Atabei (Haitian)
Ataryatis Derketo
   (Babylonian)
Atea (Polynesian)
Atira (Pawnee)
Athenesic (Zuni)
Auchimalgen (Chilian)
Audhumla (Teutonic)
Aurora (Ethiopian)
Avilayoq (Eskimo)
Awehai (Iroquois)
Axo-mama (Peruvian)
Aya (Assyro-Babylonian)

Badb (Danaan)
Bachue (Colombian)
Baltis (Greek)
Bau (Sumerian)
Baubo (Egyptian)
Belit-Ili (Babylonian)
Beltis (Sumerian)
Bendis (Greek)
Bensozia or Benzozia
   (Basque)
Bera Pennu (Hindu)

Berchta (Teutonic)
Beruth (Phoenician)
Bestla (Teutonic)
Beva Pennu (Bengali)
Bhumi (Hindu)
Bhuvanesvari (Indian)
Bibi Miriam (Hindu)
Birra-Nulu (Aboriginal)
Black Maa Ema (Finland)
Bomu Rambi (Zimbabwean)
Bribsun (Tibetan)
Brimo (Greek)
Britomartis (Cretan)
Buana (Irish)
Buto (Greek)

Cabiria (Phrygian)
Cailleach Beine Bric
    (Scottish)
Calyce (Greek)
Campestres (Celtic)
Candras (Indian)
Caridwen or Cerridwen
    (Celtic)
Carman (Irish)
Carmenta (Italian)
Cassiopia (Greek)
Ceithlenn (Irish)
Ceres (Greek)
Chalchihuitlicue (Aztec)
Chang-O (Chinese)
Charis (Danaan)
Chhaya (Hindu)
Chicomecoatl (Aztec)
Chie (Colombian)
Chih-Nii (Chinese)
Chit (Tibetan)

Citali (Aztec)
Cleito (Greek)
Coca-mama (Peruvian)
Concordia (Roman)
Copacati (Incan)
Corentina (Celtic)
Coronis (Greek)
Cotys (Thracian)
Cyboread (Semitic)
Cypria (Greek)

Dakini (Hindu)
Dakshina (Hindu)
Damkina or Damku
    (Babylonian)
Damona (Celtic)
Danae (Greek)
Dea Dia (Roman)
Deborah (Hebrew)
Dechtire (Irish)
Demeter (Pre-Hellenic Greek)
Derceto (Babylonian)
Derketo (Greek)
Devaki (Hindu)
Devananda (Hindu)
Dharani (Hindu)
Dia (Minoan)
Diana, Diana-Nemorensis or
    Dione (Roman)
Diti (Hindu)
Djet (Egyptian)
Dodah (Hebrew)
Dok (Aboriginal)
Domnu (Irish)
Don (Welsh)
Doris (Dorian)
Dwyvach (Welsh)

Edo or Edjo (Egyptian)
Eilythia, Eleuthera or
    Eleuthia (Cretan)
Eithinoha (Iroquois)
Eithne (Irish)
Elath (Semitic)
Electra (Greek)
Elihino (Cherokee)
Embla (Teutonic)
Enodia (Thessalian)
Epona (Gallic)
Erato (Celtic)
Erce (Basque)
Erditse (Basque)
Ernmas (Irish)
Ernutit (Egyptian)
Erzulie (Haitian Voodoo)
Etain or Edain (Irish)
Europe or Europa (Phoenician)
Euryanassa (Greek)
Eurymedusa (Greek)
Eurynome (Greek)
Evan (Irish)
Eve (Hebrew)
Ezra (Hebrew)

Fand (Irish)
Fatima (Arabia
Fauna (Roman)
Fides (Roman)
Fjorgyn (Teutonic)
Fleachta (Irish)
Flidhais (Celtic)
Fornax (Roman)
Fors Fortuna (Italian)
Frigga (Norse)
Fulla (Teutonic)

Gadda (Chaldaean)
Gamelia (Greek)
Ganga (Hindu)
Garbh Ogh (Irish)
Ga-Tum-Dug (Babylonian)
Gaus (Indian)
Gayatri (Hindu)
Gbadu (W. African)
Godiva, Godan or Gerd
    (British)
Gokarmo (Tibetan)
Goleuddydd (Welsh)
Gouri (Hindu)
Grainne (Irish)
Gula or Gulu (Sumerian)
Gu-Lang (Tibetan)
Gwendydd (Welsh)
Gwenhwyfar, Guinevere
    or Gueneva (Welsh)

Hagar (Hebrew)
Hakini (Hindu)
Haniyama-Hime (Japanese)
Hani-Yasu-No-Kami
    (Japanese)
Haumea (Hawaiian)
Hecuba (Greek)
Heket (Egyptian)
Helen-Dendritus (Cretan)
Helice (Delphic)
Heng-O (Chinese)
Hepzibah (Hebrew)
Hera (Pre-Hellenic Greek)
Hertha (Celtic German)
Hesione (Syrian)
Hestia (Cretan)
Heth (Hebrew)

Hettsui-No-Kami
  (Japanese)
Himavati (Hindu)
Hina-Mitagtor-Of-
  Many-Things (Polynesian)
Hine-Ahu-One (Polynesian)
Hingnoh (Hottentot)
Hinlil (Assyro-Babylonian)
Horsel (Teutonic)
Horta (Etruscan)
Hretha (Teutonic)
Hsi Ho (Chinese)
Huixtocihuatl (Aztec)
Hulda (Teutonic)
Hulla (Anatolian)
Hun-Ahpu-Mtye (Guatemalan)
Hvor (Iranian)
Hyrax (Western Bushman)

Ida (Tantric)
Ikugui-No-Kumi (Hindu)
Ila (Tantric)
Ilithyia (Pheneus)
Inanna (Sumerian)
(Indoea Pad (Javanese)
Indrani (Hindu)
Ineno Pae (Indonesian)
Innin (Sumerian)
Isani (Hindu)
Isis (Eygptian)
Iusas (Eygptian)
Ixalvoh (Mayan)
Ixasaluoh (Yucatan)
Ix Chel (Mayan)
Izanami (Japanese)
Iztat Ix (Mayan)

Jambavati (Hindu)
Jana, Janus or Juno (Roman)
Jarah or Jesah (Semitic)
Jarnsaxa (Teutonic)
Jingo (Japanese)
Jocasta (Roman)
Jord (Teutonic)
Jumala (Siberian)
June Vestalia (Roman)

Kaaba (Meccan)
Kadomas (Tantric)
Kahasuma (Hindu)
Kakini (Hindu)
Kalinde (Hindu)
Kami-Musumi (Japanese)
Kathirat (Syrian)
Kaya-Nu-Hime (Japanese)
Ked (Celtic)
Kenemet (Eygptian)
Kewa (Argentinean)
Khados (Tibetan)
Khon-Ma (Tibetan)
Ki (Sumerian)
Kikimora (Slavic)
Kinkini-Dhari (Tibetan)
Kiririsha (Assyro-Babylonian)
Kishar (Assyro-Babylonian)
Komorkis
  (Blackfoot Indian)
Kono-Hana-Sakuya-Hime
  (Japanese)
Korraral (Hindu)
Krimba (Slavic)
Kubaba (Greece)
K'un (Chinese)
Kuu (Finnish)

Lady of the Beasts (Arcadian)
Lakini (Hindu)
Lamia (Delphic)
Lara (Roman)
Latium (Italy)
Lato (Anatolian)
Latona (Roman)
Lebiyah (Hebrew)
Leshachikha (Slavic)
Leto (Cretan)
Leucippe (Italian)
Libera or Libra (Libyan)
Lilwani (Hittite)
Lissa (Dahomey)
Litha (North African)
Lubchas Guaya (Columbian)
Lucine or Lucina (Italian)
Lugad (Irish)
Lupa (Roman)
Lvan (Irish)
Lysippe (Armenian)

Maan Emoinen (Finnish)
Mader-Akka (Lappanese)
Madri (Buddhism)
Madonna (Hebrew)
Maeve or Medb (Celtic)
Magna Mater (Roman)
Magog (Scythian-Amazonian)
Mah (Arabian)
Maha-Nila-Sarasvati (Hindu)
Mahuea, Mahui I'a or Mahu
  Ika (New Zealand)
Maia (Greek)
Mair (Hebrew)
Maitresse (Haitian Voodoo)
Malkuth (Hebrew)

Mama Alpa (Incan)
Mama Nono (Antilles)
Mama Occlo (Incan)
Mama Pacha (Incan)
Mamat (Arabian)
Manat (Arabian)
Mania (Roman)
Mammita (Assyro-
  Babylonian)
Mannu (Finno-Ugric)
Mari (Sumerian)
Marinette (Haitian Voodoo)
Mary Magdalene (Greek)
Marzanna (Slavic)
Mashongavudi (African)
Mashyoi (Persian)
Mat or Mut (Egyptian)
Mater Cara (French)
Matergabia (Slavic)
Mater Matuta (Greek)
Mati-Syra-Zemlya (Slavic)
Ma-Tsu-P'O (Chinese)
Mbaba Mwana Waresa
  (Nepalese)
Mehurt (Egyptian)
Mene (Pre-Hellenic Greek)
Mensa (Roman)
Mera (Egyptian)
Meridiana (Greek)
Meri-Ra (Egyptian)
Meri-Yamm (Syrian)
Meshkenti (Egyptian)
Meteres (Cretan)
Methyer or Meh Urit
  (Egyptian)
Metis (Greek)
Mezulla (Anatolian)

Mielikki (Finnish)
Mirian (Semitic)
Mnemosyne (Greek)
Mobo (Chinese)
Modir (Norse)
Modron (Welsh)
Mona (Teutonic)
Mother Carey (French)
Mother Clear-Light (Tibetan)
Muldava (Laplander)
Mut (Egyptian)
Muzjem Mumi (Siberian)
Mylitta (Carthaginian)

Nana or Nina
    (Phrygian/Sumerian)
Nanda Devi (Himalayan)
Nandecy (Brazilian)
Nanna (Teutonic)
Nanshebargunu (Sumerian)
Nantosuelta (Gaulic)
Naunet (Egyptian)
Nau Ut Set (Pueblo)
Nebt Het, or Neb-Thet
    (Egyptian)
Neit, Net, Nit or Neith
    (Egyptian)
Nena (Aztec)
Nephthys (Egyptian)
Nerthus (Norse)
Niamh (Irish)
Ninella (Babylonian)
Ningal or Nikkal (Sumerian)
Ninkarrak (Sumerian)
Ninsar (Sumerian)
Nin Sikil (Sumerian)
Ninsun or Ninsunna

(Sumerian)
Niobe (Anatolian)
Nkosuano (Ghanaian)
Nortia (Etruscan)
Notre Dame (France)
Nott (Teutonic)
Nsomeka (African)
Nuah (Babylonian)
Nunbarshegunu (Sumerian)
Nuneit (Egyptian)
Nut (Egyptian)

Odudua (Brazilian Voodoo)
Ogetsu-Hime-No-Kami
    (Japanese)
Opet (Egyptian)
Ops (Roman)
Ora (French)
O'Shion (Romanian)
Otsuchi-No-Kami (Japanese)
Otsukisama (Japanese)

Pachamama (Incan)
Panagia-Arkodiotissa or
    Pangara (Greek)
P'An Chien-Lien (Chinese)
Papa (Polynesian)
Pashadhari (Hindu)
Pasiphae (Cretan)
Pe (Pygmy)
Penelope (Greek)
Philyra (Greek)
Phoebe (Greek)
Pi-Hsia-Yuan-Chun (Chinese)
Pingala (Tantric)
Piria (Peruvian)
Pomona (Roman)

Porrima (Roman)
Postverta (Roman)
Potina (Roman)
Pramlocha (Hindu)
Prisni (Hindu)
Psyche (Greek)
Pukkeenegak (Eskimo)
Purvachihi (Hindu)
Pyrrha (Greek),

Queskapenek (British
   Columbian)
Quinoa-mama (Peruvian)
Qis-Mah (Arabian)

Rahab (Hebrew)
Rait or Rat (Egyptian)
Raka (Hindu)
Rakini (Hindu)
Rangda (Balinese)
Rati (Hindu)
Rat-Taui (Egyptian)
Rauni (Finnish)
Re (Phoenician)
Rhea (Greek)
Rhiannon (Welsh)
Ririt (Egyptian)
Robigo (Roman)
Rohini (Hindu)
Rosmerta (Gaulic)
Rukmini (Hindu)
Rutbe (Costa Rican)

Sadhbh, Sadb or Sadv (Irish)
Sakini (Hindu)
Sambhuti (Hindu)
Sams (Semites)

Sandalphon (Egyptian)
Sangye Khado (Tibetan)
Saning Sari (Javanese)
Sappha (Roman)
Sanjna (Hindu)
Sarah (Hebrew)
Saranyu (Indian)
Satarupa (Hindu)
Sati (Hindu)
Sedna (Eskimo)
Sehu (Cherokee)
Selene (Pre-Hellenic Greek)
Semele (Greek)
Sengen-Sama (Japanese)
Shasti or Shashti (Bengalese)
Shataqat (Syrian)
Shentayet (Egyptian)
Shing Moo or
   Sheng Mu (Chinese)
Shinty (Egytpian)
Shitala or Sitla (Hindu)
Shitateru-Hime (Japanese)
Shushumna (Tantric)
Sien-Tsan (Chinese)
Sif (Teutonic)
Siguna (Teutonic)
Silili (Chaldaean)
Simhamukha (Tibetan)
Singarmati Devi (Indian)
Sinvali (Hindu)
Sirdu (Chaldaean)
Sirtur (Sumerian)
Sita (Indian)
Somagalags (British
   Columbian)
Songi (Zulu)
Sradda (Hindu)

Srahman (African)
Sri (Hindu)
Succoth-Benoth (Babylonian)
Suhiji-Ni-No-Kami (Japanese)
Sukarapreyasi (Hindu)
Sung-Tzu-Niang-Niang
　(Chinese)
Sura (Hindu)
Surabhi (Hindu)
Suseri-Hime (Japanese)
Sutrookaj (Hindu)

Tabiti Vesta (Greek)
Tailltiu (Irish)
Tamra (Hindu)
Tana (Etruscan)
Tanit (Phoenician)
Tara (Indian)
Tar-Anis (Roman)
Tari Pennu (Bengalese)
Tashmit (Chaldaean)
Tatsua-Hime (Japanese)
Taueret (Egyptian)
Tavobe (French)
Taygete (Greek)
Tea (Irish)
Techerauur (Egyptian)
Tefneit (Egyptian)
Telita (Babylonian)
Tellus Mater (Roman)
Tenazuchi-No-Kami
　(Japanese)
Tenth (Chinese)
Tephi (Irish)
Terra Firma (Latin)
Tethys (Greek)
Thalna (Etruscan)
Theia (Greek)
Themis (Pre-Hellenic Greek)

Thetis (Greek)
Thyone (Eleusian)
Tillil (Chaldaean)
Ti-Ya or Ti-Mu (Chinese)
Tlachtga (Irish)
Tonantzin (Aztec)
Toyo-Uke-Bime (Japanese)
Toyo-Uke-No-Kami
　(Japanese)
Trisala (Hindu)
Tsao-Wang Nai-Nai (Chinese)
Tsuki yomi (Japanese)
Tuaret (Egyptian)
Tuwabontums (Hopi)
Tyro (Greek)

Uadt, Uatchet, Udot
　or Ufo (Egyptian)
Ua Zit or Ua Zet (Egyptian)
Ukemochi (Korean)
Uma (Hindu)
Unt (Egyptian)
Urmit (Assyro-Babylonian)
Ursula or Ursel (Saxon)
Urt-Hikeu (Egyptian)
Urvasi (Hindu)
Ut Set (Pueblo)
Uttu (Chaldaean)

Vadaba (Hindu)
Va-Kul (Syrian)
Varahini (Hindu)
Varamit (Chaldaean)
Vennolandua (British)
Vesta (Roman)
Vindemiatrix (Roman)
Voltumna (Etruscan)

Wadjet or Wazit (Egyptian)

Waka-Uke-Nome (Japanese)   Yasodhara (Buddhist)
Wang-Mu Yiang-Yiang   Yatai (Indo-Chinese)
  (Chinese)
Wild Pony (Apache)   Zara-mama (Peruvian)
                            Zarpanit (Babylonian)
Yachimato-Hime (Japanese)   Zhag-Pa-Ma (Hindu)
Ya-Hsek-Khi (Burmese)   Zytniamatka (Prussian)
Yang-Chen (Chinese)

For Mine is the ecstasy of the spirit and Mine also is joy on Earth. For My law is love unto all beings.

The mother remembers us to the sisterhood of all women. And in our remembering, we come face to face with the realization that this sisterhood has been shattered and scattered about the Earth far too long. In this forced segregation, the feminine principle and wisdom of life has also been shattered and lies in fragmented pieces, buried in the soils at the ancient sites where our ancestresses once gathered to revel in this now long-forgotten power. Because of our isolation from each other and the feminine principle, we have lost the center of our management. Through the millennia we have surrendered this authority over to the dominators, the patriarchy.

As the healing energy is native in the season of Summer, women are now in a native season of healing. Vicki Noble (*Shakti Woman*, Snake Power, Oct. 1989) tells us that women "are healing ourselves from the world illness of Patriarchy. We are experiencing a most momentous awakening of this healing power; for we have no choice—we are having a collective near-death experience," and as the fire is the power of the Summer, so the blinding light of our healing can show us how to transform our lives.

Let us use the magick of fire during our empowerment of Mother Goddesshood by remembering that first comes destruction, then creation, and that this is the way of the Goddess, of the Shakti (feminine) energy. As fire burns through the old structures, eliminating them, transmuting their energies to a higher vibration level, then releasing the creative energy to allow the cure—so we too can use the Shakti to transform our spirits and heal our souls.

It is in this season of the Mother that we can become most effective at healing. The Mother Goddess is a powerful force for joy or pain in a woman's personality. She provides us with the capacity to bond, to be loyal and faithful, to endure and go through difficulties with a partner. Through the Mother we can find physical, psychological or spiritual nourishment for ourselves as well as using her energy to draw from to enable us to give to others.

As a woman choosing to heal herself, you must begin by turning the characteristics associated with mother—i.e., nurturing, loving, compassionate, understanding, protective, caretaking, etc.—onto yourself. You must "mother" yourself (so to speak) and place your inner goddess into a new category—that of the Alchemical Goddess, a goddess of magical prowess, containing the elemental power of transformation. You must draw from the Cauldron of Cerridwen, the cauldron of regeneration and healing, to empower your Mother Goddess aspect and become healed as a woman of love and emotion.

The Alchemical Goddess communicates with herself openly and honestly. She acknowledges the dis-ease that rests within and actively seeks to transmute it into a higher vibration. It is this goddess that allows the natural energy of our feminine power to emerge. Through her we experience the multilevels of emotions connected with this power. Through Mother we come to know that, by experiencing the painful, stuffed emotions and by processing them, we can go home. Norma Cordell once shared a very easy rule to follow when dealing with dis-ease, whether it be of a mental, emotional, spiritual or physical level. Her rule is simply: "Change it or die."

The months are zooming by. Summer is here full-fledged and I'm feeling romantic. I'm three days into a fast, which I plan to remain on for ten days. Spirit is calling me to raise my vibration rate, and besides, a good purging never hurt anyone.

After having passed on my Medicine Woman Crystal to Lisa at the time of "Becoming Sisters Ceremony," I began working with Spirit Woman Agate (a gift from Hilary while in Vermont). Spirit Woman is a powerful guide and wasted no time in showing how effective she was by lifting me out of ordinary reality.

Today I sat with her in meditation and once in my inner medicine circle, with my totem quarter powers in place, Medicine Woman appeared. I was happy to see her, for I had feared that she would leave me, as her energy is housed in the Medicine Woman Crystal now in Lisa's possession. Medicine Woman assured me that she was always within and that I was simply sharing her "house" with another sister. I did feel relieved.

Shortly after Medicine Woman appeared, Spirit Woman Agate forced me to look at my hands, which took me completely into the dreamtime. The blue corridor of my Shaman's eye flared around me and exploded into white light. When the light subsided, Spirit Woman and I stood upon the beach, the cool ocean waters splashing gently around our ankles.

She told me, "You are at a transmutative stage. On all levels you are undergoing change." She said, "Don't be worried with releasing at Lammas, because you have been and are releasing much in your life already.

"You have recognized that life is not to be held onto, that this," she motioned to the world with her hand, "is only one picture frame on the movie reel.

"It is your time to disperse the new flow of information. It is your time to cut through, and shine."

Dates to consider, research and celebrate in the future:

July 2:	Feast of Expectant Mothers (European)
July 3:	Festival of Cerridwen (Celtic)
July 4:	Independence Day (American)
	Honor of Lady Liberty
	Kisma's day of birth (America)
July 5:	Sun Dance (Native American)

July 7:   Tanabata (Japanese)
               Celebration of star crossed lovers, Bega and
               Aquila
               Nonae Caprotinae (Roman)
               "Nones of the Wild Figs," festival celebrating
               Nature's growth, dedicated to Juno
July 13:   Celebration of Our Lady of Fatima (Portuguese)
               Festival of Demeter (Greek)
               Obon (Japanese)
               Rememberance of the dead
July 17:   Festival of Amaterasu-O-Mi-Kami (Japanese)
               The Sun Goddess is honored
July 19:   The Marriage of Isis & Osiris (North African)
July 20:   Panathenaea (Greek)
               Athena was honored with agricultural rites
July 19/20:   First Women's Rights Convention in the United
               States, 1848.
               Susan B. Anthony and Elizabeth Cady
               Stanton began the women's liberation move-
               ment in America
July 22:   La Fete De La Madeleine (French)
               The day of Mary Magdalene in the holy cave
               in Provence
July 23:   Festival of the Cat Goddess (Egyptian)
               Sekhmet and Bast
July 27:   Hatshepsut's Day (Egyptian)
               The Queen who ruled Egypt (ca. 1490 B.C.)
               and built great temples to the Goddess

Tiamat

Chapter Four

AUTUMN ————————
From the Water We Rise

It is to the west I go,
to listen to the whispering twilight.
As sister dolphin sings her mysterious song,
My love sprays forth:
"Spirit—my friend,
Enchant this circle I dance within!"

Autumn is the secret time, for it is the twilight of seasons when we are caught between life and death. The turning of the wheel takes us down into the center of woman power. If compared to a woman's Moon cycle, autumn is the waning Moon, the time of bleeding, of the womb, of the blood mysteries.

It is the time of intense color, the turning leaf colors, the shedding and releasing. All life surrenders, leaving behind the fullness of action, and prepares to enter the silence, the season of death.

In this phase of retrospection we come to that place of relationships: family, friends, lovers, coworkers, employers, employees etc. We have become awakened with the Spring and begun actively healing ourselves with the Summer action.

As a woman of power, the journey into darkness becomes an intense time. As power woman walks her path, she must be willing to release the extra baggage from her life and open to the changes that are smoldering just beneath the surface. Being within her power and yet available to others (no matter what that relationship might be) is the balancing of Temperance. It is the wisdom of the Crone that teaches us how to endure and pass through the season of release most effectively and make peace with Death while welcoming Change.

I would like to share with you the tale of a sister who underwent a very powerful releasing ceremony. Faith Barr-Glover had come to a crossroads in her life. Being a woman of spirit, she was very aware that it was time to release, release in the most exalted sense and allow death and change to cycle into her life. She was experiencing a very drawn-out dying process, one which she was refusing to look at. She was experiencing the "death throes of my lazy, naive trust in love of all sorts...of my lifestyle and the attendant beliefs about what I deserve versus what I really want, and of the amusing, rather glittery, make-nice persona, or personality, which had carried me through my late childhood and all my years as a public relations professional and then as a seminar leader."

The series of events which eventually led to the following pivotal ceremony began with her attendance at a Shamanic Intensive Workshop lead by Lynn V. Andrews in Joshua Tree, California, during June 1989. Faith had read all of Lynn's books and found them stimulating and informative, but never felt the pull to experience Lynn as a teacher.

"I hate following 'the crowd' and so have always resisted participating in intensive trainings with mega-popular teachers, but my inner wisdom kept prodding me until I began to listen," she confided in me.

Faith followed her inner voice and found that the Intensive Workshop was timed powerfully with her personal astrology, and so, after deciding to attend, within a 20-minute period was able to make very complex arrangements which included finances and child care for her ten-year-old daughter.

The Intensive led her to many wonderful experiences as well as profound personal insight, the most powerful being the recommendation by Lynn to perform a Native American ceremony that involved the making of "Life and Death Prayer Arrows." Preparation for the ceremony is centered around making two lists: 1) ten things which you will commit yourself to doing within one year; a goal which becomes an *act of power*, alias the Life Prayer Arrow, and 2) a list of things which are keeping you from your sacred purpose and which you are willing to release now; these are usually addictions of some sort, alias your Death Prayer Arrow. [I would like to add that this ceremony requires very pragmatic thought given to the compilation of each list. I, too, have experienced this ceremony (as guided by Black Wolf) and in preparing for my path of power (which became my writing career) found that almost six months of time elapsed from the first day I sat down and titled two pieces of paper Death and Life. It became very apparent that this ceremony was not a toy, but a serious, focused consciousness on changing my life. As will be seen in Faith's story, the depth of the change and the seriousness of it is acute.] I would like to continue the tale, but in Faith's own words:

Although the ceremony which I ended up doing is different from the one Lynn suggested, I want to acknowledge her for planting the seeds and watering them.

At the Intensive, after introducing the concept, Lynn set us to work with a partner to begin our lists, and especially to complete the Life Prayer Arrow list of ten actions which we felt we could promise Great Spirit we would accomplish in one year. My complete inability to do that list was a rather heavy hint about where I needed to focus my efforts.

Of all the tasks given at the Intensive, this one remained uppermost in my mind in the following months. I finally began the process during a slow day at work, nearly two months later; a dark Moon / sunset ceremony I had performed a few days earlier jarred loose the things which needed releasing from my subconscious and so began the process (appropriate for my "9" personal year, numerologically) with death, hoping that it would clear the way for birth.

Before the list was finalized it was five pages long. Knowing the power of words spoken or written in ceremony, I went over the pages again and again, considering the subtle and obvious consequences of each statement, rephrasing each one to be as complete, as purposeful, and as unburdened with preconceptions (especially preconceptions about outcomes) as possible.

Once the list was fairly complete, I began to receive guidance about the ceremony itself. First, I was told that I needed to do ceremony in a nearby national forest which had just been devastated by fire and that I should do the ceremony overnight, sleeping in a bag under the stars, in order to "deeply feel life renewing under the ashes of destruction" and gain hope for my future which my rational mind could not then muster. I was told that I was to commit my Life Prayer Arrow at the following sunrise. The appropriate time for the ceremony would be August 30, 1989, during the dark Moon/New Moon Solar Eclipse (it was also the time of my personal dark Moon, the day before my menses was calendared to begin). I soon discovered that the astrological aspects at this time were harmonious to my natal astrological chart, a welcome relief for someone who had been thoroughly battered by the Saturn-Neptune-Uranus transits in Capricorn! The New Moon also was close to many of my natal planets. In addition, the Solar Eclipse provided outstanding energy support for the shedding of old ways of handling solar issues (fundamental character and outer-world behavior and expectations), with the added benefit of immediate emotional grounding through the New Moon.

Ah, but my Life Prayer Arrow I hesitated over. I hesitated, mainly because what I was doing (which was what my heart was telling me to do) involved leaving my husband, whom I still love, leaving the ashes of a brief career which I had thoroughly enjoyed, and leaving the area (I had lived in for 22 years) to live in Seattle, Washington, where I have felt I was destined to live since I was very young.

I'm still not sure that I would have had the courage to move to Seattle, especially within three months, had it not been for a good friend who, like me, felt it was time to leave Southern California for the Pacific Northwest. My husband absolutely

*refused to go unless he was able to find a job that was a signifi-
cant improvement in pay and in professional prestige (a remote
possibility), even though we had been discussing this move and
talking about "someday" ever since we met more than 12 years
ago. I guess I finally tired of waiting and, at this point in my
life, was uninterested in finding a job which would generate
sufficient income to support the kind of lifestyle he wanted.*

*In any case, my friend said to me, "If I get a job up there,
and if they pay my moving expenses, we'll throw your things in
the back of the truck and you can come with me." I felt the energy shift and, for the first time, felt it might be possible to do it.*

*So, the day before my ceremony, I put my daughter on a
plane to her grandmother's and spent a quiet, noncommittal
evening with my husband. I had, for more than a week, been
moving further and further away from daily life, spiraling
deeper and deeper within. I didn't talk much and was very distracted generally, automatically moving as close as possible to
my center, wanting to draw the preparations and the ceremony
itself from the core of my being.*

*The next morning I packed what I thought were minimal
supplies: sleeping bag, flashlight, matches, candle, water, rice
cakes, my little Pacific Northwest eagle totem, a notebook, the
Medicine Cards, conch shell, hawk-wing fan, high energy
prayer shawl, an extra layer of clothing and a container to burn
my Death Prayer Arrow in.*

*I was very restless and anxious from the moment I woke. Yet
I managed to maintain silence, to block distracting telephone
calls from coming in and to maintain what I call my sacred
focus (a deep, intense, singular concentration which is like a
trance). I gathered the material for my prayer arrows; i.e.,
brightly colored cotton crochet thread, feathers, shells etc. I sat
down and began the final copy of my lists which would be
wrapped around each arrow shaft.*

The Death Prayer Arrow list contained items like:
I give away to Great Spirit:
*Addiction to or reliance on predictable relationships and
life patterns.*

Inappropriate beliefs about what constitutes a secure and worthwhile existence, especially ones based on the material/ monetary or patriarchal belief system.

Addiction to substances (food, alcohol, material goods), behaviors, beliefs, ideas and so on which have a disruptive, weakening or other negative effect on my health, well-being and sacred purpose.

Addictions to authority: having it, obeying it and disobeying it.

Inappropriate beliefs and expectations about my relationships.

Fear of the unknown and desire to control people and outcomes.

And so on. The list was 38 items long. Just as I was finishing the list, my husband called. We discussed something about his work, and just before he hung up, he said, "Just go ahead and do what you need to do." Although he was actually talking about something else, I felt as if his spirit had given me permission to complete the task. And, so, after I hung up I wrote this last item: "I release my husband and our marriage." My intent with this was to release both to become whatever they needed to be. My Death Prayer was then complete.

My Life Prayer Arrow was next. Here is the list in its entirety:

I will live in complete commitment to my sacred purpose: its discovery, its unfoldment and its achievement.

I will move to Seattle by the end of this year.

I will send queries about my book to all publishers located or suggested before moving.

I will send at least 10 networking and/or job-search letters to the Seattle area weekly before moving.

I will remain open, detached and clean in my negotiation with my husband.

I will be open, honest and vulnerable with my daughter throughout this process.

I will diligently pursue money-making to support the move through readings, a class/workshop, a garage sale, indepen-

dent contracts, and any other means which does not deflect me from the major issues and requirements of these changes. *Goal: $3,000 in hand to move with.*

I will be clear headed and responsible regarding financial matters, living and making this move without compromising my responsibilities or my dreams.

I will bend every effort to developing a lifestyle of sacredness and voluntary simplicity which does not deny or avoid the needs of the world around me.

I will finish my manuscript before December 21, 1989.

When the arrows were wrapped with the lists and made beautiful, I packed them and left the house. It was 3 P.M. and a beautiful day.

As I drove out to the national forest I saw many birds. Most prominent was a mockingbird which dive bombed closely to my right. Later, two ravens flew west; then a red-shouldered hawk flew to the east. As I walked up the path out of the camp-grounds, two bluebirds flew in front of me to the west and perched in a scruffy bush and twittered at me. All of these winged ones were close to me and directly in my path.

I found two crow pinion feathers carefully laid across the path, the tips pointing up a hill and off the path. I picked up the two feathers and moved in the direction they pointed. The walk was very hard. The dust and ash was up to my knees in many places. I was seriously encumbered by the amount of "equipment" I had brought, and my hands were full. The float-ing ash and soft ground sucked me under; blackened branches kept grabbing me as I passed by, and I kept worrying about all the people driving by, way down the hill, that might see me. I realized my worry at being seen was a symptom of a deep-down fear of standing in my place of power and being recognized for what I really am, and of being sure that there were a lot of peo-ple who weren't going to like what they saw.

Once at the top of the hill, I dropped the heavy load I car-ried and searched for a good place where I would be able to see the Sun rise. I eventually found the best place right behind *where I had dropped my pack about 45 minutes after arriving.*

I felt increasingly wound up, scared, but very intent. Then I felt sad largely because of my husband's telephone call. Putting my reflections aside, I set up circle. I placed a stone in each of the directions and unrolled my sleeping bag in the sacred space. I unpacked the supples (everything was immediately blackened by the ash) and placed my eagle totem at the east gate and the two crow feathers pointing up from the ash in the north. I noted the hundreds of tiny green shoots at the base of the mesquite and other desert scrub bushes and remembered what my guidance had said about feeling the life stirring. But I was too distracted, nervous and frightened to connect with the meaning in any depth.

I settled in and pulled the crow card from the deck of Medicine Cards and realized that Crow Woman had already come to me in a meditation during Lynn Andrews' intensive retreat as my Sacred Twin. In the meditation she had come from the north and handed me a beaded object which I now realized was wampum, regarding Universal Law. I tried to connect with the magic of that insight but was too anxious to concentrate or release myself into the kind of "high" I usually get when I realize this type of connection.

I called in the directions, preparing sacred space for my journey.

The sunset had begun. It was framed in a V between the mountains soft pink and violet. I tried to center myself and become peaceful, but it was no use. I had entertained a fantasy of having a powerful sunset ceremony, of deeper releasing, but it was all I could do to sit still. I wished I could cry.

When the Sun finally descended, I received the gift of a most incredibly clear and brilliant night sky. The stars were astounding, and as I stared at them in delight I thought that it would take only a few more stars to make a solid blanket of light across the sky. Throughout the night, those stars brought me comfort and wonder to heal my very confused and wounded psyche.

I planned to burn the Death Prayer Arrow during the last

15 minutes of the dark Moon, about 10:30 P.M., but almost two hours earlier, my guidance began to nudge me to do it right away. I resisted, thinking it was just because I was fidgety and needed something to do. But the instinctual wisdom persisted and finally I realized the source of the idea and obeyed. It was time to release and die.

It took me nearly an hour to burn the Death Prayer Arrow! I don't know what physical factors contributed. Maybe there were none, or maybe I'd wrapped the paper too tight; the stick was green or wet; perhaps the night was more damp than I realized? Who knows. I had to work to make it burn, and throughout there was so much smoke that my eyes constantly watered (so what if I had been unwilling to cry and half-hearted or even reluctant about releasing my stuff; it was happening now whether I liked it or not). My reluctance made no difference; the circumstances of the ceremony forced me to grieve and forced me to put tremendous effort and intention on the process of dying. I used an entire box of large kitchen matches and, toward the end, I was having to separately apply matches to each small, unburned piece of paper.

I buried the ashes, as a gift of energy to the Earth, and then became even more nervous and fidgety. I was cold and found my extra layer of clothing didn't help. I was miserable because I had just "killed" many things which I had always considered so vital to my survival. I was scared because it was dark; I was alone and out in the "wild" (a revelation, because I've always prided myself on fearlessness. However, I realized that fear is both a block and a tremendous motivator). I heard gunshots. I heard coyotes yipping. Both were at a distance from me. There was literally no life around me save the little green shoots at the base of scrub bushes. I felt utterly alone.

Finally, sheer exhaustion slowed down my panic enough to again allow suggestions for my guidance. I was told to just crawl in the sleeping bag and lie in it, holding a crystal which had been programmed to connect with Star Woman. I took the suggestion, but found I was still restless, anxious and cold. (Although I must say that it never once occurred to me to pack up and go home.)

I tossed and turned for a while, periodically turning on the flashlight so I could see my watch. Then I received a crystal-clear suggestion to get out of the bag and get my power shawl. I was told that, even though it is of the lightest cotton, it would warm me. I did as I was told, crawled back into the bag, struggling to push the shawl down in the bag and smooth it out to cover me. I lay on my back, wondering at the starry blanket above me, when a voice said clearly, "It is time, dear one, to enter the cocoon. Gently go within and release yourself to the dissolving, trusting your instinctive wisdom, knowing that only death makes room for new life."

I pulled the sleeping bag over my head and closed it at the top. I lay for quite a while in the fetal position, holding my crystal and shivering under the power shawl. And then suddenly I was warm; the soft ashy ground held me like a mother's arms holding her child to her breasts. I was comfortable and at peace. I instinctively knew (although I couldn't resist looking at my watch to confirm it) the dark Moon, Hecate, had passed and had taken with Her my fears and pain and all that I had worked so hard to release and give away. She left at 10:45. The clock face read 10:50!

I slept peacefully and deeply until dawn.

When I rose, I blew the conch shell three times and planted my beautiful Life Prayer Arrow deep in the ash. I shouted my Act of Power Life Prayer list to Great Spirit, to my guides and teachers, to my spirit helpers, to all my relations who would listen. I performed the Cherokee Dance of Life, nine full rounds to integrate and ground my commitment.

I stood waiting for the Sun to rise above the mountains, fidgeting and feeling like I was losing my intent, the sacred power, the newness which I had built up through the night. And yet when the Sun did come, I felt it fill me and felt it feed and empower the eaglet within me. The wind blew and I flew on it. I was a butterfly newly emerged, an eagle newly born.

When the time came, I released the guardians of the directions, Father Sky and Mother Earth. I did so haltingly but with great gratitude. As I came around to the east, two birds flew across the red-gold horizon, moving north to south. As I spoke the words of releasing to the east, I idly thought it was a shame I couldn't see what type of birds these were; I thought their species might have significance on the ceremony. And then, across the brilliant morning air, their reply came: caw, caw, caw! Two crows, blessing the ending as they had blessed the beginning of the ceremony.

I packed, skidded down the hill, and walked to my car without fanfare. As I got to my car, parked across the spaces with its tailgate facing my door was a car with a Washington state license plate ostentatiously displayed. I knew it was an omen.

I drove home with no further messages until I turned the corner on the road home. There was an incredible sight—a huge, tall tree with perhaps 50 vultures sitting in it. The Sun was shining through the tree branches, and it glittered off the morning moisture on the leaves, scattering diamonds of light throughout this tree full of harbingers of death and decay.

Faith left the ceremony site a new woman. Within two weeks her friend found a job in the Seattle area and flew to Seattle to look for a place to live, finding one immediately. Faith held her garage sale and brought in 1/2 of the $3,000. She was booked solid with readings and workshops and brought in the balance of cash required to make the move. Even more surprising to Faith was the amicable manner in which she and her husband came to terms regarding their marriage. Within one month after the ceremony, Faith and her daughter moved to Seattle.

After moving, Faith told me, "I learned I won't die if I take incredible risks (even if I turn out to be completely wrong and misguided), and I won't die if people I have depended on for identity, for love and for support think I'm crazy and withhold what I've sacrificed my 'self' to get from them.

"I have learned that only by letting go, by allowing or even welcoming release and change and death, can I experience rebirth and growth."

The Goddess Aspect of Autumn—Crone / Wise Woman

I give the knowledge of the spirit eternal and beyond death I give peace and freedom and reunion with those that have gone before. Nor do I demand aught of sacrifice, for behold I am:

Aakhabit (Egyptian)
Abere (Melanesian)
Achamoth (Gnostic)
Adraste (British)
Aerfen (British)
Agnayi (Hindu)
Agnes (Danish)
Ahabit or Ahibit (Egyptian)
Akimbimi (Japanese)
Akka (Akkadian)
Alecto (Greek)
Allatu (Babylonian)
Ama (Hebrew)
Amaterasu Omikami
    (Japanese)
Amemait or Am-Mit (Egyptian)
Ament (Egyptian)
Ammarik (Ugric)
Anbotoko Dama (Hindu)
Androphonos (Greek)
Angurboda (Danish)
Ankamma (Indian)
Anna Kuari (Oraons)
Anna Perenna (Roman)
Anrita (Hindu)
Anumati (Hindu)
Aoife (Irish)
Arachne (Greek)
Arani (Hindu)
Ara-Seshap (Egyptian)

Arnaknagsak (Eskimoan)
Argeia (Greek)
Asgaya-Gigagei (Cherokee)
Asherath (Samarian)
Asri (Hindu)
Atargatis (Jerusalem)
Atergatis (Cretan)
Athara (Greek)
Athtor (Egyptian)
Atropos (Spanish)
Attar (Arabian)
Aukert (Egyptian)
Aunt Piety (Chinese)
Az (Persian)

Baalat (Semitic)
Baau (Phoenician)
Baba Yaga (Polish Jedza)
Babelah (Babylonian)
Badhbh (Irish)
Banshee (Irish)
Bau, Bahu or Bohu
    (Chaldaean)
Bean-Nighe (Scottish)
Befana (Italian)
Belili or Baalit (Syrian)
    Canaan)
Belit, Belit-ili or Beltis
    (Semitic)
Bellona (Italian)

Bendis (Thracian)
Bera (Spanish)
Berecyntia (Gaul)
Bhairavi (Hindu)
Bhatta (Hindu)
Binah (Hebrew)
Black Dakini (Tibetan)
Bona Dea (Roman)
Britomart (Greek)
Brunissen (Celtic)
Buannan (Irish)
Buddhi (Tibetan)
Buto (Greek)

Cabar (Turkish)
Caillech (Old Celtic)
Candi (Bengali)
Carlin, Carline or Cailleach
    Bheur (Scottish)
Calypso (Greek)
Cardea (Roman)
Carna (Roman)
Carpet Snake Woman
    (Aborginal)
Cathuboduae (Latin)
Cauth Bodva (Gaulic)
Chamunda (Bengali)
Charybids (Greek)
Chimaera (Greek)
Chitraiya Bhavani (Indian)
Chiu T'ien Hsuan-Nu
    (Chinese)
Cihuatcoatl (Aztec)
Citallnicul (Aztec)
Circe (Greek)
Cloacina (Roman)
Cotytto or Cotys (Sicilian)

Cranae or Cranaea (Roman)
Cunda (Buddhist)
Cyhiraeth (Welsh)

Daeira (Greek)
Dagda (Celtic)
Dainichi (Japanese)
Dam-Kina (Sumerian)
Danae (Nile Deltan)
Daphoine (Roman)
Dark Maid (Chinese)
Dea Syria (Babylonian)
Deo (Delphic)
Derketo (Greek)
Devasuni (Japanese)
Diabolus (Latin)
Dirona (Celtic)
Discordia (Roman)
Dorje-Naljorma (Tantric)
Dornoll (Irish)
Druxan (Persian)
Durga (Indian)

Echidne (Carian, Hittites)
Egeria (Roman)
Ekadzati (Tibetan)
Ekhamoth (Gnostic)
Elli (Teutonic)
Elythia (Crete)
Enodia (Carian)
Ereshkigal (Sumerian)
Erinnys (Greek)
Eris (Greek)
Esharra (Chaldaean)
Eterna (Chinese)
Euryale (Greek)
Eye Goddess (West. European)

Fama (Roman)
Fata Mertsegret (Egyptian)
Fea (Irish)
Febris (Roman)
Feng-P'O-P'O (Chinese)
Feronia (Roman)
Fire Woman (Bornean)
Fraus (Roman)
Fuji or Fuchi (Northern
    Japanese)
Furies (Greek)

Gasmu (Chaldaean)
Gerfjon (Teutonic)
Gestinanna (Sumerian)
Ghul (Arabic)
Gjalp (Teutonic)
Glaisrig (Scottish)
Gorgon (Greek)
Graeae (GreeK)
Grain (Irish)
Grainne (Irish)
Gran Erzulie (Haitian Voodoo)
Guabancex (Haitian)
Gula (Babylonian)
Gullveig (Tuetonic)
Gunnlod (Norse)
Gur (Chaldaean)

Hakea (Polynesian)
Halja (Gothic)
Hariti (Indian)
Harpies (Greek)
Haya (Assyro-Babylonian)
Haya-Akitsu-Hime-No-Kami
    (Japanese)
Heartha (German)

Hecate or Hekat (Pre-Hellenic
    Greek/Anatolian)
Heh (Egyptian)
Hel or Hella (Norse)
Helen (Greek)
Hellotia (Greek)
Heng-ugo (Chinese)
Heqit (Anatolian)
Hetep-Sekhus (Egyptian)
Hina-of-the-Land
    (Polynesian)
Hinenui-te-po (Polynesian)
Hir Nineve
    (Assyro-Babylonian)
Hokmah (Hebrew)
Holla or Holda (German)
Hsi-Wang-Mu (Chinese)
Hunthaca (Columbian)
Huzi (Northern Japanese)
Hvergelmir (Norse)
Hypate (Delphic)

Iacchos (Greek)
Igaehindvo (Cherokee)
Ilematecuhtli (Mexican)
Ilmater (Finno-Ugric)
Inara or Inaras (Hittite)
Indus (Indian)
Istusaya (Hittite)
Itzapapaloti (Aztec)
Izanami (Japanese)

Jael (Semitic)
Jagadamba (Tibetan)
Jezanna (Zimbabwean)
Julunggui (Aboriginal)
Juturna (Roman)
Jyotsna (Hindu)

Kadi (Babylonian)
Kadru (Hindu)
Kagauraha (Melanesian)
Kali or Kali Ma (Indian)
Kalma (Finno-Ugric)
Kamashi (Hindu)
Kami (Japanese)
Karakarook (Aboriginal)
Kari (Malayasian)
Kariteimo (Buddhist)
Keres (Greek)
Keyuri (Hindu)
Khoemno (Egyptian)
Khon-ma (Tibetan)
Kishibujin (Buddhist)
Kipu-Tytto or Kivutar
    (Finno-Ugric)
Knowee (Aborginal)
Korobona (Guaianan)
Korravis (Dravidian)
Kottavei (Indian)
Krake (Anglo-Danish)
Kukuri-Hime (Japanese)
Kulakatya-yani (Indian)
Kunda (Buddhist)
Kurukulla (Dravidian)

Lady Meng (Chinese)
Lamia (Greek)
La Sirene (Haitian Voodoo)
Laufey (Teutonic)
Laverna (Roman)
Laz (Assyro-Babylonian)
Leannan Sidhe (Irish)
Leona (Roman)
Lewa-Levu (Fiji)
Libitina (Roman)

Lilith (Semitic)
Lilitu (Babylonian)
Litae (Greek)
Lola (Indian)
Lorelei (German)
Loviatar (Finno-Ugric)
Lucetia (Roman)

Macha (Danaan)
Mafdet (Egyptian)
Mahacinatara (Indian)
Mala Liath (Scottish)
Ma Ma Cocha (Incan)
Manasa-Devi (Bengali)
Manat (Arabian)
Mara (Indian)
Mari (Hindu)
Maria (Greek)
Marichi (Buddhist)
Marishi-Ten (Japanese)
Mary Gypsy (Greek)
Masaya (Nicaraguan)
Matabrune (Bardic)
Me (Babylonian)
Me-Abzu (Greek)
Medea (Corinthian)
Medhbh (Irish)
Medusa (Aegean)
Meenakshi (Hindu)
Mefitia (Roman)
Megaera (Greek)
Mehen (Egyptian)
Melaina (Greek)
Menkheret (Egyptian)
Menget (Egyptian)
Menrva (Etruscan)
Merrivik (Inuit)

Mertseger (Egyptian
Mesopotamia (Babylonian)
Metsulah (Hebrew)
Meztli (Aztec)
Mictecacivatl (Mexican)
Mihit (Egyptian)
Miru (Polynesian)
Mitsuha-Nome-No-Kami
  (Japanese)
Moingfhion (Irish)
Morgan (Greek)
Morgan le Faye (Celtic)
Muilidheartachi (Scottish)
Murigen (Irish)

Nagis (Hindu)
Nahar (Syrian)
Nahema (Hebrew)
Nahmauit (Egyptian)
Nammu (Sumerian)
Nana (Assyrian)
Nanshe (Babylonian)
Nathair Parrthuis (Old Irish)
Nehellenia (Dutch)
Nekhbet (Egyptian)
Nemea (Greek)
Nemontana (Celtic)
Nemanous (Egyptian)
Nephthys (Egyptian)
Nichta or Nikta (Norse)
Nicneven (Scottish)
Nifl (Semitic)
Ninazu (Chaldaean)
Ninlil (Sumerian)
Ninmug (Babylonian)
Ninsun (Akkadian)
Ninti or Nintu (Sumerian)

Nirriti (Hindu)
Nisacharis (Hindu)
Noctiluca (Gaulic)
Nox (Roman)
Nuliajuk (Inuit)
Nuneit (Egyptian)
Nungal (Sumerian)
Nyx (Greek)

Old Spider (Micronesian)
Omikami Amaterasu
  (Japanese)
Omoroca (Babylonian)
Oraea (Roman)
Oupis (Greek)
Oynyena Maria (Slavic)

Pa (Chinese)
Pakhit (Egyptian)
Pekhet (Egyptian)
Pele (Hawaiian)
Perchta (Slavic)
Persephone (Greek)
Phoenissa (Canaanite)
Phorcis (Greek)
Phuri Dai (Romanian)
Pidrai (Canaanite)
Proserpine (Roman)
Prosymna (Greek)

Quartiana (Roman)
Queen of Elphanme (Scottish)

Ragana (Lithuanian)
Rainbow Snake (Aboriginal)
Rakshasis (Hindu)
Ramnusia (Ethiopian)

Ran (Teutonic)
Ratis (British)
Ratri (Hindu)
Reine Pedauque (French)
Remati (Tibetan)
Renenet (Egyptian)
Rennutet (Egyptian)
Rodashi (Hindu)

Sabitu (Chaldaean)
Sabrina (British)
Saci (Hindu)
Sadwes (Persian)
Saga (Teutonic)
Saitada (British)
Samdhya (Hindu)
Sanzukawa-No-Obaasan or
  Sanzu-No-Baba (Japanese)
Sapas (Phoenician)
Sapientia (Latin)
Sara Kali (Romanian)
Sarama (Japanese)
Saranyu (Hindu)
Sarparajni (Hindu)
Sarpis (Hindu)
Savern (British)
Sati (Egyptian)
Scathach (Celtic)
Schala (Assyro-Babylonian)
Scota (Irish and Spanish)
Scotia (Greek)
Sedna (Inuit)
Sekhmet (Memphis)
Selkhet (Egyptian)
Sequana (Gaulic)

Serkhit (Egyptian)
Shapash (Sumerian)
Shashtradevatas (Hindu)
Sheol (Hebrew)
Shiu-Mu Niang-Nian
  (Chinese)
Sidee (Celtic)
Siduri (Sumerian)
Sindhu (Hindu)
Sionan (Irish)
Sirona (Celtic)
Skadi, Skuld or Scold (Norse)
Smashana-Kali (Indian)
Spider Grandmother (Kiowa),
Srinmo (Tibetan)
Stata Mater (Roman)
Sthenno (Greek)
St. Luan (Irish)
Styx (Greek)
Sul or Sulla (British)
Sun (Chinese)
Surya (Hindu)
Suwa (Arabic)

Tadatagei (Hindu)
Tait (Egyptian)
Tamayori-Bime-No-Mikoto
  (Japanese)
Tamesis (British)
Taranis (Gaulic)
Ta-Urt (Egyptian)
Tauropolos (Cretan)
Tchesert (Elysian)
Tecciztecatl (Aztec)
Tenemit (Egyptian)

Tertiana (Roman)
Tesiphone (Greek)
Thalatth (Babylonian)
Thetis (Thessalian)
Thirst (Hindu)
Tiamat (Babylonian)
Tiawthu (Babylonian)
Tien Mu (Chinese)
Toci (Mexican)
Toma (Tibetan)
Tonagma (Tantric)
Tootega (Eskimo)
Tou-Mu (Buddhist)
Trivia (Roman)
Tuonetar (Finno-Ugric)

Uachet (Egyptian)
Uadjet (Egyptian)
Utahach (Irish)
Uma (Himalayan)
Uni (Etruscan)
Unkatahe (Northern Native
    American)
Ulupi (Hindu)
Ura or Urania (Irish)
Urd (Norse)
Urth (Norse)
Uto (Egyptian)

Vaga (British)
Vajra-Dakini (Tantric)
Valkyries (Teutonic)
Vajra Varahi (South Indian)
Vajra-Yogini (Tantric)
Vammatar (Finno-Ugric)

Varuni (Hindu)
Vechernaya (Slavic)
Vellas (Balkan)
Vellamo (Finno-Ugric)
Verbeia (British)
Victoria (Roman)
Vinata (Hindu)
Vindhyarasini (Hindu)
Viradechthis (Roman)
Virgo Caelestis (Roman)
Viz-Anya (Magyar)
Viz-Leany (Magyar)

Whale (Hebrew)
Wonambi (Aboriginal)
Wnpranili (Australian)
Wurusemu (Hittite)

Yatudhanis (Hindu)
Yemaja (Nigerian)
Yemanja (Brazilian Voodoo)
Yhi (Aboriginal)
Yurulunggui (Aboriginal)
Yngona (Danish)
Yogini (South Indian)

Zaltu (Chaldaean)
Zerpanitu (Babylonian)
Zerynthia (Western Turkish)
Zi-kum (Assyro-Babylonian)
Zillah (Semitic)
Zobiana (Medieval)
Zorya Vechernyaya (Slavic)
Zu-en (Sumerian)

And you who seek to know Me, know that your seeking and yearning will avail you not, unless you know the Mystery, for if that which you seek you find not within yourself, you will never find it without.

I have heard women refer to this current age we're in as being the "time of Kali." Because of this claim, people are calling upon Kali (one of the most extreme aspects of the Crone), to aid them in their ceremonies. Also as a result of this claim, one can pick up various metaphysical and/or women's magazines and find outlines of ceremonies for Kali. In these ceremonies women are instructed to call upon her violence and destruction, beg for her protection against the recumbent male of ignorance, seclusion and oppression. Women are told it is okay to call in the most raw destructive force and use it against life! This is ignorance, for a woman who chooses to evoke Kali into the Earth's plane in such a hostile manner has not learned the lesson of healing herself, finding her balance within, taking back her power and spreading the knowledge and wisdom of Goddess. Rather, the women who choose to evoke Kali in such a hostile way are lost in their own rage. These women are still giving away their power; they are still giving away the management over their lives to the patriarchy.

Goddess women must WAKE UP! Wake up and take the world, take life, take relationships, take themselves and bring the feminine power back into balance with the oversaturated male energy prevalent in our Earth's plane today, but not out of hostility and/or negativity.

We women have been standing up against the oppression that fell over us like a shadow. We have been in the clutches of death, as a power, on this Earth. We have fought against the accepted status of woman. We have raised our voices so that now they are heard. We make a difference.

We cry, "No more war." We cry, "Equality." We cry, "No more pain." We cry, "Feed our children." We cry, "No more."

Why then must we resort to the same means used by the patriarchy and become dominators? Is it not time for us to stand up and show the way? The way of balance? The way of partnershipping? The way of conscious awakening?

If we call upon the mighty Crone for her destructive powers, then we must be willing to accept the mighty consequences of using negativity. The healed woman, the whole woman, the power woman, knows that it is the wisdom of the Crone that must be used. The Temperance of finding the perfect knowledge in which to use the wisdom in order to gain the utopia women have known is possible to have here on Earth. It is this wisdom and knowledge that will bring the darkness and the light back into balance, female and male into balance.

Women have been abused and damaged. This I do not deny. The scars of our oppression run deep as the granite blood veins of Mother Earth. But stop and listen to what it is we have been calling for. Life. Love. Not war. Not pain. Not death. Why then do we want to bring Kali back into the world's consciousness purely in a negative and hostile manner?

Are we not trying to reintroduce Goddess to the world and express her?

I understand that rage and anger is an expression, and one that women have been denied too long to express, but must we use Goddess to such selfish means? By using her to express our rage and anger we are only implicating further harm on life and suppressing our most exalted form of expression.

The world does not want an angry Goddess on their hands. Look how long we have revolted against the angry God of the patriarchy. We're doing the same thing they did. We are striving for dominion through the power of the Crone aspect of Goddess. We are so out of control in our rage, so swept away by our selfishness, that we want to risk losing utopia.

The New Age has begun. The cusp has been embracing us now for years. We are witnessing changes everywhere: the freedom of East Germany, Romania and Panama, the civil uprising and eventual collapse of the social structure of China, the Earth changes that are restructuring the surface of the land and forcing us to take notice. This may be the uprising of Kali but, if it is, she has risen of her own will and is taking the necessary steps to bring about the changes. Who are we to evoke her to do our will? Against the will of others?

In our time of self-empowerment let us not forget the laws. The threefold law: What you send out returns threefold. The rede: An it harm none, do what ye will, for the good will of all. The law of the Goddess: "Love is my law." If we claim to be Priestesses/Daughters of the Goddess, if we claim to be true warrioresses, then why do we want to take the patriarchal stance of force, destruction, domination, negativity, evil?

Find the love, the life, the heart of what all this is about. It is the nuclear family we have been working toward. Women, our power, our wisdom, our insight, our knowledge, our love, our heart is what will shift this New Age into being. Not fighting. Not being better than or more powerful than the male. And definitely not by using Goddess against mankind. She will retreat from us if we continue to manifest her in this way. Can't you hear her crying? Can't you hear her whispering to us, asking us not to be so ignorant, to stop being daughters of men and begin being her?

If, during the season of the Crone, we take the time to journey deep within our psyches, she will bring us face to face with the rage and anger. She will shed her waning light upon it and teach us how to release it and absolve it into the darkness. Crone gives us the wisdom to understand and teaches us to know.

In her harshness we find the true essence of life, of love. It is the Crone who is at the heart of all things, the dancing Wu Li master.

We must approach this master out of extreme respect. We must be willing to look at the aged and see the worth in their eyes, their life, and seek to understand the experiences they have had, for in understanding the experienced we gain a knowledge of what not to repeat, or what can be changed to make it better.

All answers lie within. It is the season of release, of traveling deep into our being that we may find Pandora's box and open it. We will find that amid the waning light, the decay, the changing, there is sustenance, power and enlightenment. It is during the release, the time of introspection when active energy is slowing down, that we have the opportunity to seek the interior recesses of life. Few people take the time. A power woman knows that this is where the key to all lies buried, and so rejoices in the waning and finds release.

The Correspondences of Autumn

> The season of the Emotions/release
> Endings/twilight/waning Moon
> West/taste/water/blue-greens/black
> Sister Dolphin/undines/mermaids/willows
> Ancestors of the African People
> Oceans/seaweed/shells/pearls/moonstones

Autumn is connected to the west, which is the house of emotions, love, the heart. It is the place of nurturing and caring. Through our feelings we find the courage to become daring. This is the place of intuition. If we open, release and surrender to our intuition, it begins to flow into our lives.

When a woman faces the west, she faces the void of her womb, the darkness of the depths of the cauldron, the woman mysteries.

Sand dunes stretched before me. I could hear the lulling roar of the ocean, but could not yet see it. As my legs carried me to the crest of the dune, I stopped to catch my breath and gasped at the paradise of Guadeloupe Dunes. Leslie stood, hand over her eyes, staring out into the ocean. She had reached the top before me.

We continued across the dunes. A cool wind whispered off the water and cooled the brow. The air was tinged with moisture. The sand of the shore was clean and soft and decorated with white and black sand dollars. We ran calf deep into the water and jumped out of its clutch and coldness as soon as the first sharp awareness of its fingers slithered up our thighs.

Laughing, we ran back to the warmer sand and laid out our belongings. Leslie lay face down on a towel. I remained standing. I wanted to perceive the shift before I was completely consumed by the magick.

The magick was all consuming. It turned me into the healer and I kneeled next to Leslie and laid my hands on her shoulder blades. Warmth spread out from the palms of my hands over her back in little sparkling rivets of golden light. I closed my eyes to sense the energy deeper.

"Oh, Leslie," I whispered. At once I saw the yellow ray of her spine spinning through each of the chakra centers. "You are saturated with yellow ray." My hands fell to her lower back above the solar plexus chakra. "In this house is where the yellow should reside. Turning, turning in its mentalness. Birthing forth the thought to be absorbed by the heart and released through the throat." My hands had moved up to the heart/middle of the back, and the throat/back-of-neck areas of her body.

I lowered my hands back to her heart. I felt the grumbling of her green ray, the desire of it to live. "You have very little green ray," I spoke as I strived to brighten the greenness. "Think green," I instructed her. "Think green where you feel my hands." I pressed them against her middle back. "Green," I whispered over and over. Slowly, the yellow ray began to recede and the green flow spread out in its wake. "Ah, that's it," I cooed to the heart beating beneath my hands. I focused on releasing love through my hands and sent my green ray to mingle with the birthing color. I felt overwhelmed by the feeling and pulled my hands gently away. I lay down in the sand next to Leslie with my eyes still closed.

My mind reeled and I began falling into it. I was lost in the sensation of my own body colors pumping in each chakra center and the feeling of the warm sand beneath my body. The song of the ocean and seabirds were the only noises on that deserted beach, and I surrendered to their melody.

Thousands of particles of sand trickled over my skin, tickling me at first. Over and over the sensation of our molecules hitting each other drove me deeper and deeper into sensation. As the sand piled up around me and I was encased like an Egyptian mummy in a tomb of sand, the coolness of the encasing became nourishment.

I opened my eyes and laughed at the memory of being a child and playing at the beach. My brother, sister and I would always bury each other in the sand. I looked up into the laughing face of Leslie. We laughed hysterically. After the laughing, I lay there. Just lay there. I became acutely aware of how the snake feels, the spirit of the snake encased in its skin, and inch by inch I wiggled myself out of a layer of skin.

In my changed state, I stood and walked to the water's edge. I studied the rise and fall of the waves and the way the water receded: trickles of water pulling back, moving around the discs of pentacle and leaving them exposed, naked for all life to see. I stooped over and picked up a sand dollar and touched the surface of it. I turned it front to back, back to front, in my hand, feeling the design with my finger tips, tracing it with my eyes.

I walked south, lazily splashing through the shore-break as it crashed against my ankles, stooping to discover a treasure now and then, watching the rise and fall of waves or flight of seabird. I came to an estuary and stood at the merging point. The sand cut sharp and deep, channeling the flow of the river water into the womb of the ocean. I thought of the Greek word oistros *(estrus in English)—the sexual excitability during which the female of most mammals will accept the male and is capable of conceiving—and wondered if perhaps the place were this water passage, where the tide meets a river current, wasn't another estrus cycle of a different level. Perhaps rivers were the male aspect of water and, when they flowed into the ocean (the womb), the act of fornication was enacted.*

I followed the river leg up into the lush oasis that rested secretly between the sand dunes. I studied the plant and animal life, smelled the water in its different stages of stagnation and freshness. I walked through mossy ponds and squatted to watch the long green hair of seagrass sway and caress fat succulents rising above the water. I watched the tiny blue-eyed, see-through fish dart about in a frantic yet poetic ballet.

The barking of a dog brought my attention back to the shoreline, to the realization that there were now others on the beach. I made my way back and came once more to the place of my speculated estrus cycle and stood on the sand plateau between the river and the ocean. I looked to the north to where the barking was birthed and watched a dog jump in the waves. I watched a mother and daughter collect sand dollars and the child dance like a little angel.

Ah, Priestesses of the sea,
little angel dancing before me,
holy daughters of the sacred land,
take each other by the hand.
Teach the people of this world,
how to be young and free.

The mother joined the dance. And then the dog. They approached me. Stopped to show their beautiful treasures and to smile. I watched them walk away. Watched their dancing forms skip along the ocean, then turned and faced the water crash.

Without warning, my body began to move, and I sang to the water:

Aimlessly walking upon the shore,
I came to see an amazing sight.
Out of the waters,
Venus did rise,
dancing in the breeze.
As I watched her dancing there,
sparkling in the light,
from her lips came these words,
Love will begin this night.

The Sun set. An orange glow rested above the water, the reflection of that big, glowing ball swallowed by the water. We *gathered our belongings together, the sand dollars and beautiful grass reeds of the estuary, and turned away from the west.*

My spirit remained at the shoreline. I watched the two bodies make their way up the dune. For a moment they stood at the top of the world, turned and took in the view. One of the figures blew a kiss to me before she turned her back on me and disappeared down the other face of the dune. I stood there for a long time, looking at that silent place, wondering when my spirit would meet up with those two figures again.

I sighed, took a deep breath, glanced at the ocean, then once more at the dune. I felt disconnected. Sad, but fulfilled. Then I saw the footprints resting in the sand and decided to follow.

The Element of Autumn—Water

Necna and your undines bold,
thank you for your liquid gold.
You cool the fire and quench the Earth.
You start the cycle of rebirth.

Water is the flowing gateway into our inner Emotional Body. Through the water we swim to the bottom or float to the top. It is through this element that we may get in touch with the intuition, the house of secret mysteries.

Our bodies are primarily water. As women, water is our strongest element; we are governed by the Moon and by the heart. The Moon affects the tides (our menses), our menses affects our intuition and emotions (our hearts) and our emotions are processed through the heart.

Water teaches us how to operate from a balanced heart space. If we view life from the calm pools of tranquility, flow with the river of our feelings, pull from the tides of our powers and refill from the deep wells of our inner mind, we won't drown in our emotions. Rather, we will swim through life relatively smoothly, gaining access to cross the breath of experience between extreme emotions and extreme mentalness, never having to tread water to stay afloat or give up and sink.

Back in 1987 the world was said to be changing. The magnificent Harmonic Convergence was forecast. Being of the Goddess/New Age community and not wanting to take any chances and yet not wanting to run away and hide (as many people I know did), another sister and I drove down to Mexico to Campe Lopez (K55), where we planned to spend the 16th and 17th of August and undergo the major planetary vibrational shifting while performing ceremony on a deserted beach.

So Sabella and I packed up a few belongings and headed south at sunset. We arrived at Campe Lopez where her family's beach house was located, just after midnight. After unpacking the car and settling in, we stood on the patio overlooking the ocean below. The sky was filled with shooting stars and the waves shook the stone beneath our feet each time one slammed into the cliff. The ocean scent was ripe and rich with sea life, and the air was warm and soft.

We finally snuggled down for sleep and woke a few hours later. In silence we gathered together the basket of altar tools, tike torches and blankets and left for the beach. The walk through the village was haunting. The climb down the cliff was perilous. We trekked a distance down the beach before choosing a spot to construct our circle.

With tike torches flaming in the quarters and galactic altar set up, we began our ceremony in which we greeted the rising Sun and which finally ended mid-morning.

During the course of our ceremony I spread before me tarot cards using the Thoth deck. I wanted to see if a higher intelligence would speak to me through the cards (Figure 4). It did. The reading came through as follows:

Card 1: Six of Discs. In alignment, balanced, power blossoming. Abilities of communications, from an intellectual energy, will begin to flow. Communications, intellect, energy, love are fully synthesized. Connected with Mother Earth.

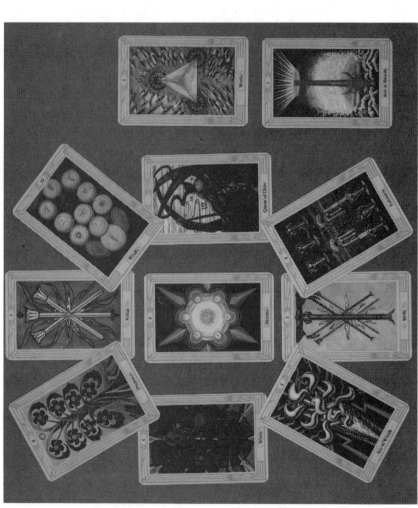

Figure 4—Harmonic Convergence. The tarot card spread I cast for the New Age during a Harmonic Convergence ceremony.
Aleister Crowley Thoth Tarot Deck, U.S. Games Systems, Inc., Stamford, CT

Card 2: Five of Discs. Releasing the plague of confusion and worry, the bound feeling, heaviness. Releasing fully.

Card 3: Queen of Discs. No longer need to look back upon path traveled, for new path patiently waits before me.

Card 4: Five of Wands. The connection with Earth runs deep and the channel of energy is reinforced with the spirit of this connection. Expansion of own spiritual self is evident. Walk new path with confidence.

Card 5: Three of Wands. The divine Trinity flows in from above, and messages mediated through the Sun light my direction. Like the ram, I may now move boldly forward into the blueprint of my life, becoming my fullest potential.

Card 6: Ace of Wands. Creativity sparked is moving in. Energy to begin.

Card 7: Ten of Discs. Wealth gained through communications.

Card 8: Eight of Cups. Allow the dark influences to pass, for the change brings forth renewal and makes way for the new beginning I must take.

Card 9: Eight of Discs. The birthing and growth of me will be nurtured by the strength of the Sun and the messages brought forward. The path will blossom many fruits.

Card 10: Three of Discs. The power of all energies are in motion / the movement is powerful—with practical application I will be able to work wonders in the minds / hearts of Homo sapiens. Spirit will work through me. Spirit will speak to me as a spinning column of white light.

Aside (fell out of deck): Ace of Swords. Strength. You will cut through any and every obstacle.

As I finished the reading, I saw very clearly a golden rod, spiraled by silver, running from my solar plexus (belly button area) up to the sky. In my mind, the words "The new way will be through the light of the heart" danced to life.

We sat there, looking at the cards. Then very quietly Sabella began to sing a song to the melody of an old Hebrew Hymn. Her sparrow voice filled my ears.

By the waters,
the waters of Great Ma-Nu,
We lay down and wept,
and wept for those who knew...thee
remember, we remember,
thee remember,
Great Ma-Nu.

Soon a canon of both our voices blossomed forth, ending our ceremony. The day progressed with breakfast at a neighborhood restaurant that overlooked tide pools, shopping in town—oohing and ahing over ethnic clothing and jewelry—and then a light lunch.

We returned to the shoreline that afternoon. As we sat on the sand watching the playful waves, we dreamed of future days and ceremonies that could be performed as an intensive study on the element water.

In our musing, we became undines and adorned ourselves with the kelp clothing of the sea. Bobbled seaweed became our jewelry, algae and seagrass became ornaments for our hair and shells became our tokens (Plate 3).

We rose out of the water, sister undines dancing the water dance, the haunting call of a conch shell announcing our arrival. We kneeled at the edge of the shore-break, the place where the white foam from Poseidon's horses lay bubbling as the air consumed it.

We lamented for the polluted state the waters were in and the dying relatives that swam therein. We offered our tokens to the rising waves and watched each shell disappear from our

Plate 3—Undine of Ma-Nu, Goddess of the Ocean.

sight. Then quiet at the water's edge, we opened to the ebbing flow of life and witnessed the sparkling energy come to life (the dance between fire and water), and deep inside—in that place of woman power—I felt my own shifting tide and rose as Venus would, out of the clutching foam. Spreading my arms open wide, I turned with laughter, allowing the whole world to feel my otherworldly presence.

"...out of the waters Venus did rise...love will begin..." whispered the breezy voices of the ocean undines as they danced closer and closer to shore, to the place where Goddess stood.

Columns of spinning white light appeared over the ocean gold and silver beams of light shot out from them, piercing my solar plexus, cementing into my belly button—the umbilical cord of life. "The new way will be through the light of the heart," thundered a clear blue sky. My head titled back, laughter exploded from my belly.

I fell to my knees and honored reality. The reality that we take for granted. I wanted to reach out and touch all life, everything and nothing. In that moment of exalted awareness the physical became too much. My body longed to simply be the water, allowing my consciousness to be fully expanded and connected with the inner core of knowingness, flowing with the life current that constantly runs through all things physical, which hides behind all things unknown, to have no limitations or boundaries of mind.

The water of my body seemed to mix with the seawater. Water mingling with water. Current of life. No boundaries. Vibrating out. Ripples of awareness. Rising and falling. Rushing and crashing. Pouring over. Stillness. Reflecting.

We drove home in silence that evening.

Something I learned from that day is this: if we visualize our sense of touch as being as expansive as water, we can feel everything and send out our "feelers" to distances never thought possible. We can check on the status of the Earth, atmosphere, life forms etc., and stay connected and in tune instead of disconnected or isolated, remaining in a selfish mode of reality.

The essence of water is the antenna of awareness to feeling, the teacher of feeling, togetherness, one vibration.

When I work with individuals on the element of water, I have them place their hands in a bowl of water and feel it with their hands, the elusiveness of it, the concrete yet non-physicalness of it. I play a recording of water sounds as I guide them into becoming the water. As my words ebb and flow, I spiral slowly around them, urging them into the very center of the inner pool. I spray water over their bodies, allowing them to rest gently in this inner pool. Then I spiral back out, pulling their awareness out of the pool so that it flows with the current, out and away from them, until they must let go and ripple into the dance of water where they freely swim with all waters of the world.

Just before I end the experience, I pour sacred water on the crowns of their heads and allow the sensation to bring them back into their bodies, the here and now.

The Phases of Autumn

August

The phase of Leo, the male principle, is underway. Ruled by the Sun, we are brought face to face with the identity of ego. Like the proud lion, dignity becomes an underlying element in how we conduct business. The warmth of the Sun sparks our creativity and we roll on our backs playfully.

We are constantly reminded that now is not the time to be selfish or possessive but to join together and form a clan, a working unit.

The energies in August begin to change from active to subdued, and though the shift has not yet completely taken place, it has been initiated. For a moment in the month of August, we rest on the cusp of the wheel at the top. Soon we shall begin the descent, the descent that will take us into the darkness. We must be acutely aware that now we should begin preparing to release our hold on active life and surrender to the regressing energies, following the spiral back within to learn about our own ego and its relationship with life.

The waxing phase of Autumn is the preliminary to introspection. We can use the energy to take a peek at the time of stillness while still actively involved with the element of "action."

I went to Medicine Woman again. I was out of control. I stamped my feet and began crying.

"What have I done?" I kept crying and threw myself on the ground sobbing. Out of obsession I had tracked down a man whom I didn't know. I called him, introduced myself and asked him to meet with me. A time and meeting place was scheduled. When the day arrived, I couldn't think straight. I couldn't think

of anything but meeting him face to face and what I would say to him. Why was I so obsessed with him? Why was it so important I meet him?

On the afternoon of the meeting day, I drove up to Los Angeles and arrived an hour early at a metaphysical bookstore called the Bodhi Tree, our meeting place. I almost choked when he finally walked in. My hands were shaking when I went up to introduce myself to him.

We spent about six hours together. We talked nonstop. Our stories were similar. I was extremely attracted to him and knew I would move to Los Angeles in a minute if he requested it of me. But he didn't. In fact, he had just moved in with a woman who was going to have his baby.

"Ah, so I see," was the only response I could give.

So I left feeling sadness but joy. Our meeting had been the night before, and here I was in desperate need of guidance from Medicine Woman.

Medicine Woman knelt down beside me while cooing softly. The power animals of the directions were anxious and fidgety. She told me it would be all right, that I was crying over an act of power, over Summer Hawk. She cupped my chin in her hand, lifing my face to meet her eyes.

I looked within the universe of her eyes.

"You are ready for your husband, Kisma," she said.

I nodded agreement.

"Your present friend, Kevin, is not him, nor Rick, nor Curt, nor any other man you know at this time."

I nodded in agreement again.

"Summer Hawk is your spirit husband manifested in the physical. But he is not your husband of the flesh. You are, however, in his heart now. He dreams you and smokes you. You are a reality to him now.

"You manifested him just as much as he manifested you. Both of you are equally active in this creation. Both of you knew you had to come together in physical to help the other connect up with the mate of this life." She looked at me through half-closed eyes. "Come," she said, taking hold of my hand.

We began to rise and pass through a rose-colored light. Suddenly we stood on a rock shelf high above the ground. The opening of a huge cave was behind us.

"Look before you," Medicine Woman instructed.

There were mountains and valleys that seemed to stretch on forever.

She continued. "You are at this threshold in your life. You are emerging from your sanctuary. A cave of darkness which taught you the wisdom of hermitage. You are ready to step forward into the light of this physical world.

"Feel your power, how strong it is?" She pressed a crystal into my navel. I could feel the pulsing of my heart beat immediately.

"Jump, Kisma! You are very protected. The Great Spirit honors you and will lift you on the wings of life. Mother Earth will rock you gently into safety. Father Sky cradles over you, protecting you with light.

"Listen." A wolf howled off in the distance. A hawk screeched above. Suddenly, White Wolf (my power totem) was at my side.

"Become," Medicine Woman whispered into my ear.

I felt my body change.

"Run with your power," I heard as I leapt off the shelf and ran with White Wolf down a path.

In prehistoric times, the first day of August was the mark of the beginning of the Harvest season and was referred to as Lammas or the First Harvest, the time of gathering in the foods that grew wild or were cultivated.

Today we can approach this High Holiday with the same feverent dedication but acknowledge it from the ego point of view and use it to "release" our egos, just as Mother Earth releases her hold on the food of her body, providing us with abundance so that our lives may continue.

Lammas / First Harvest (August 1)

Lammas is a cross-quarter day, falling at 15 degrees Leo

(midway between the Summer Solstice and the Autumnal Equinox). It is a day that has traditionally marked the beginning of the Harvest Season. The name of this festival is derived from the Anglo-Saxon word "half-mas," a celebration honoring grain, which at one time was considered the main staple of food. Ancient peoples viewed the grain as a manifestation of the divine force (personified as the "green man," a resilient kind of god-fiqure, growing sturdy and solid through Spring and Summer, cut down by the Harvest scythe, sleeping through the cold Winter in the bosom of the Mother Earth, and returning once again as a reborn infant, clothed in green with the Spring). Our ancestors honored this cycle from birth through growth, consummation, sacrifice, death and inevitable rebirth with rituals, processions, dances and feasts.

The grain also symbolizes ancestry and forms a link to the past, representing as it does the unbroken chain of the consummation of countless generations of life and death. Bread and brew, products of the grain harvest, represent the mystery of transformation, the modification of natural food by fire. This symbolism, the metamorphosis from raw to cooked, can be carried so far as to represent that which we call "civilization." As an extension of this symbolism, the oven becomes a sacral, life-transforming vessel. Thus it plays a role in the female mysteries, for it can be compared to the womb and it comes as no surprise that women once performed their devotions before the oven. In some of the ancient mystery cults the feminine was viewed as the repository of transformation, laying the foundations of human culture, which is transformed nature.[1]

Even though fire plays an active role in the transformation of the grain, I have come to realize that the celebration of Lammas should be the act of releasing, giving away, in order to allow the "fire" of spirit to transform you.

As we prepare for our Lammas celebration, we must give thought to one item we wish to release in order to harvest a desired change into our lives. Therefore, due to the pragmatic nature of releasing, a meditation (whether solo or collectively, if celebrating Lammas with a group) should precede the festivities.

Performing Lammas by the ocean or large body of water has always proved very powerful indeed and is therefore highly recommended. The following outline is a ceremony that has time and time again proven to be successful.

I. Ground and center

II. Purify/smudge

III. Invoke Quarters:

East: *Friends and Spirit of the East,*
Join our Lammas celebration.
Bring forth your power of Air
and fill our circle with inspiration and
*   light!*
Assist us in preparing for release
by adding clarity and insight.
Come, be here now!

South: *Friends and Spirit of the South,*
Join our Harvest rite.
Bring forth your power of Fire
and spark our circle with passion and
*   delight.*
Assist us in surrendering to the energy
of spirit transformation this night.
Come, be here now!

West: *Friends and Spirit of the West,*
join our Sabbat feast.
Bring forth your power of Water
and flood our circle with intuition and
*   love.*
Assist us in flowing with the release
so we may nurture ourselves.
Come, be here now!

North: *Friends and Spirit of the North,*
join our special ceremony.
Bring forth your power of Earth,
and strengthen our circle with wisdom.
Assist us in fully becoming the very
foundation of our harvest wish this night.
Come, be here now!

IV. Invoke Goddess:

Oh Great Mother, hear my call.
This night we assemble to honor you
and the abundance you provide.

Light our circle with your love.
Fill our hearts with your wisdom.
Open our eyes that we may teach your ways.

Inspire us this night,
ground us and guide us
as we fully surrender, becoming one with you.

We love you.
We are love.

V. Invoke God:

Lord of life, hear me this night.
Come join our circle with your protection
and enlighten our lives with your strength.

As we dance the round,
as we sing the song,
let your energies carry us ever higher.

We love you.
We are love.

VI. Raise energy by chanting and dancing:

> *At the harvest we come rejoicing*
> *for the fruit and plentiful grain.*
> *Lady and Lord lead in the dancing;*
> *harvest time is with us again.*[2]

VII. Releasing statement/affirmation

This can be performed by throwing harvested flowers into the water while you speak a releasing affirmation, such as the one Starhawk uses in *The Spiral Dance*. If water is used, have the ceremony leader say to each person before they release:

> *In this water, may it pass from me and mine!*
> *May it pass, may it pass.*
> *May it pass on the outflowing tide,*
> *and burn with the red setting Sun.*
> *As the year dies and fades,*
> *as everything negative fades,*
> *as everything passes, all fades away.*

The participant then responds by saying:

> *I release _____ into the flow of life.*
> *May it pass on the outflowing tide,*
> *burn with the red setting Sun,*
> *transform as the year dies.*

The ceremony leader then asks the participant:

> *What will you harvest?*

And the participant speaks the desired goal.

VIII. Cone of power

IX. Dismiss Goddess:

> *Mother, you who created life on Earth,*
> *Who is the life of Earth,*
> *our thanks go to you this day.*
> *Your presence is seen and felt everywhere.*
> *We know you are always within.*
> *Hail and farewell this Lammas Rite.*
> *Blessed Be.*

X. Dismiss God:

> *Lord of the greenwood,*
> *you who are the protector and provider*
> *of the Lady's children on Earth,*
> *you who are the Lover of the Goddess,*
> *we thank you for your energy this day.*
> *As we end this Lammas Rite*
> *we know that you are ever within.*
> *Hail and farewell, blessed be.*

XI. Dismiss Quarters:

> *Friends and Spirit of the East*
>   *(South, West, North),*
> *thank you for joining our celebration*
> *and bringing your power of Air*
>   *(Fire, Water, Earth).*
> *We bid you hail and farewell*
> *as you depart to your lovely realm.*
> *Blessed be.*

XII. Open Circle:

> *The circle is open, but ever unbroken.*
> *May the love of the Goddess go in our hearts.*
> *Merry meet, and merry part,*
> *and merry meet again.*
> *This rite has ended.*

XIII. Harvest Feast

Lammas began at 4:00 P.M. Sunday afternoon on July 31, 1988. We dressed in soft clothing, long flowing skirts and shawls. We were smudged and led in a grounding and centering by Kisma. She then cast circle, indicating that the circle was to remain intact even though we were to leave and go to the water. Kisma led us in a meditation, taking us into ourselves, that point where we would be releasing from. She asked us to reconfirm that what we had chosen to release was actually what was needed, or to open and allow the real release to become clear.

After the meditation was over, we prepared our offering feast for the first harvest of the season. The feast consisted of raspberries, vanilla yogurt, honey, jam, breads, butter, decaffeinated coffee and wine. We had fasted all day, and the aroma of the food was tantalizing. We sang songs of thanks and received a lesson from Kisma on the importance of the first harvest.

Prior to gathering together, each of us scoured the neighborhood for flowers to be used in the celebration. The flowers were placed in a basket and prepared for the journey. We loaded up and departed for the beach. Upon arriving at the beach, and observing the scene of the masses of people, Kisma took us to a new location.

We arrived at a bluff overlooking the back bay. We ventured over the cliff and worked our way down to a small, muddy beach at the water's edge.

Once there, Kisma asked us to pick a direction and move off into it to prepare for our individual releasing. Alexandra went to the west, I went to the east and Kisma remained in the center. Each of us collected our thoughts and prepared to release. Eventually, Kisma called us, one at a time, to her side.

She motioned for me to sit on a rock next to her and said, "In this water, may it pass from me and mine. May it pass on the outflowing tide and burn with the red setting Sun. As the year dies and fades, as everything negative fades, as everything passes, all fades away."

She looked at me, the eyes of the Goddess looking into mine, and asked, "What do you release?" As she asked me this, she held up the basket of flowers and indicated I should grab a handful of the blooms. She too took a handful. I looked out on the water, noticed the red glow of sunlight kissing the still harbor, and spoke my release. Automatically, I released by throwing the flowers out into the water.

I heard Kisma moving, but could not take my eyes off the flowers that now floated away from me on the current. I felt her arms embrace me. The warm scent of cinnamon and musk filled my senses. She pressed her mouth next to my ear, her breath soft and even. She asked, "What will you harvest?"

I spoke my desired harvest goal, keeping my eyes closed, envisioning it as manifested, and felt her arms tightening around me, drawing me into her breasts. Her kiss brushed against my ear and she set me free.

I stood, slipping in the muddy slush, and made my way back to the harder ground. I joined Alexandra, who had gone first, and together we watched Kisma perform her own releasing. After she was complete, we gathered together, opened the wine, blessed it and poured a libation to the Mother, then drank the rest. We laughed and looked at the beautiful bejeweled harbor, blue water, bright colored flowers and golden, sparkling sunlight. Kisma opened circle and we journeyed back to the place where our feast lay waiting. We then satisfied our hunger with an absolutely wonderful oral sensation.[3]

Dates to consider, research and celebrate in the future:

August 1:	Lammas (Celtic)
	Green Corn Ceremony (Native American)
August 2:	Feast of the Virgin of the Angels (Central America)
August 4:	Feast of the Blessed Virgin Mary (European)
August 8:	Tu Day (Nepalese)
	National Women's Day in Nepal
August 13:	Festival of Diana and Hecate (Roman)

August 15:   Birthday of Isis (North African)
August 20:   Festival of Virgo (Greek)
August 23:   Vulcanalia (Roman)
             Fire Festival in honor of Juturna and Stat Mater
August 24:   Mundus Cereris (European)
             In honor of Ceres
August 25:   Opeconsiva (Roman)
             Holiday of Goddess Ops, Lady Bountiful
August 26:   Ilmatar's Feast Day (Finnish)
             Creatrix of the world, the Water Mother

September

September is the fullness of the Autumn season. We have traveled the wheel from rebirth (Spring) through growth and healing (Summer) and now into the very center of our self-realization (Autumn). The energy is influenced by Virgo, a time when we find we will respond to encouragement and appreciation and have a deep hunger for sharing experiences and self-realization with others. However, we may tend to be emotionally overeager in our desires to share, making us prone to dictate the course of all relationships.

The planet which rules Virgo is Mercury. Mercury represents reasoning ability, the mind and ways of communication. During this month of self-realization and communication, we can use the energies of Virgo and Mercury to go fully into our self-expression. We can usher in the methodical, critical and analytical energy of Mercury and approach introspection from a very practical, cool, logical and almost impersonal manner. We can travel without fear or hesitation into the center of our darkness, our shadow self that we always blame for bringing the negative life situations into our plane of experience.

Now is the time to focus on our shadow, dare to go within and walk that dark corridor. Come face to face with the black mirror and gaze upon it until, within the darkness, we see the stirring of light shine through, illuminating the black edges. So often in the midst of the darkness lies all our hidden power. We are so afraid to claim our power that it has become a villain surrounded by the black cape of shadow. Now is the time to throw back the hood of that black shadow cape, see the face that smiles back—the beautiful raw and wild woman who dwells hidden deep inside the darkness. The woman behind all intense emotions rests in this darkness. The woman who is behind all action. Surprisingly enough, you will find a strong, powerful goddess. (See my book, *An Act of Woman Power*, for The Shadow Queen Visualization.)

Shadow Woman, west.
I danced with my shadow, the tender frightened soul whose fear keeps her in darkness, blackness, peeking out—
Whispering, "See me...see me...I want to be loved, and touched, and held, and told it is going to be okay...it is going to be all right."
She reached out for me, her dark arms moving out from her body. They gathered me in and held me to her breasts.
"I love you," she told me. "I need you," she whispered. "Please hold me."
Her tears slid from my eyes as I reached my arms around her shadow body and gathered her to my breasts.

In order to gain access to your inner darkness, trancing and meditation are helpful. I prefer wearing a black cape and drawing the hood over my head, encasing myself within a manifested cocoon of darkness so that after the journey when I emerge, I actually physically emerge from darkness into the light and continue to wear the black cape around my shoulders as a statement that I gladly embrace my shadow.

For me, Autumn is a time of travel, not only physically but astrally as well. I have found that travel aids me greatly in gaining heightened levels of awareness. During my travels I like to harvest herbs that cannot be found growing around my home. I have been taught that herbs should be approached and used with reverence, for they are filled with the life spirit and many can teach us about the inner side of self.

It was cold. The wind was blowing wet with the beginning of rain. I stood at the edge of the Kern River, its rapids rushing by. I looked down at my feet and saw small puddles of water around my boots, the gravel having allowed water to seep up. "Damn," I swore, and stepped out of the water, shaking my boots. Turning, I spotted a stinkweed bush crawling up the side of the bluff. I walked over to it and kneeled. Touching the leaves, I spoke a greeting in honor of the teaching properties the seeds and roots of the plant contained. Standing, I searched for the male bush I knew would be in the vicinity. He stood about three feet tall off to the right. I walked over and greeted the male energy, then continued walking in hopes of finding more clan bushes. In the short distance I came upon them and, after studying two bushes, chose the one I would harvest.

The bush chosen was a female sapling. I set about speaking to the spirit of the bush, telling my reasons for harvesting it, and after receiving a positive feeling, I gently cut away the thorny seedpods and dug out as much of the roots as I could, using a stick. I was only able to get about two feet of the root, but felt it would be deep enough for what I needed. (I had been taught that the deeper the root, the more intense the properties.)

The day ended up being a teacher-herb harvest day for me. Shortly after harvesting the stinkweed I came upon mugwort, wormwood and a species from which Kinnikiniik (a Native American tobacco mixture) could be made. After safely storing the herbs in their own wrappings, and a good night's sleep, I headed out toward Death Valley.

Cutting off on a beat-up, two-lane blacktop road (Talc City Road to Salene Valley Road), I changed my destination to the Salene Valley. The road eventually curved through high granite cliffs, winding on forever it seemed. Turning a bend, a small stream lay off to the right. Lush green plants grew around the moist dirt. I came to a place where the stream washed over the road. Slowing to drive through the water, the most amazing scent rushed through the open windows of the car. I craned my neck to see what plant it could be and caught site of purple. I pulled over and ran back to the plant. There, in the middle of nowhere, the most beautiful and potent pennyroyal plant I'd ever seen or smelled sat like a flag, waving boldly an acknowledgement that the plant Devas truly existed.

I sat down in the sand next to the plant and stuck my nose into the middle of the bush. I took one deep breath after another and felt the healing antiseptic properties this aromatic, pungent plant gave off. I gingerly harvested the squaw mint.

At last I arrived at the great shelf above the valley and trekked off in the bush. I climbed onto a large, flat rock and sat meditating on the beauty of the landscape. As the noonday Sun climbed in its exalted position in the sky, I prepared to take a journey. I took out the piece of root I brought with me from the car and held it up to the Sun, asking for the light of energy to flood the herb. I found a sharp, pointed rock and began mashing the root, pulverizing it. As I did so, I chanted to the spirit of the herb asking for a safe journey into the core of my darkness, my being, and asked for the light of the Sun to show me the way and reveal those aspects of my shadow I needed to see in order to fully understand the blackness and arrive at the point of embracing the fullness of my blackness into its rightful perspective and balance.

I wanted to know my shadow, the evil one I thought dwelled within and caused me to do hateful things. I had chosen Death Valley (though I wasn't actually in Death Valley, but on the other side of the mountain range just west of it) as the best possible land energy that would assist me to go deepest. I was determined to conquer my shadow.

When the herb was masticated enough, I uncapped a water bottle and poured a cupful. I added the root and set it in the Sun to soak. I pulled off my boots and then my blouse and stood on the sandy Earth facing the valley. I sang my Power Song three times. I called in the directions, acknowledged Father Sky and Mother Earth, and then called in to Shadow. I warned Shadow that I was on my way, that I wanted it to

*Plate 4—As I looked through a shadow hand, I saw
the distant valley, shadowed but there.*

*reveal itself to me, that I was going to conquer it and love it. I
spoke on and on, losing track of everything I said to Shadow.
When I was finished, I bent over and scooped a handful of
Earth. I added enough water to the dirt to make it into a pasty
mud and rubbed it over my face and finished by brushing the
remainder of the mud across my breasts. I was going to go on
this journey as a warrioress!*

*Reverently, I picked up the cup containing the mixture of
water and herb. I held it to my heart and performed a blessing
over it. At last I drank down the mixture.*

*I lay back on the rock, feeling the warm Autumn Sun bake
me, and eventually dozed off. The journey was unclear, not
within my wakeful consciousness. I went deep, into what
seemed like a death-sleep. When I woke, the Sun sat on the
western horizon. I sat up and looked off into the distance. Life*

after life was mused on, or was a residue of my journey. Nevertheless, I sat there, transfixed on the landscape below me, the cool, white adobe, pastel colors of the desert floor (Plate 4). And as I sat there glued to the scene, it dissolved into nothingness. Anxious over the disappearance of the land, I bolted to my feet and stood, hand over my eyes, searching for the valley below. The sky was white; the land was white; everything was simply white. As I dropped my hand from my eyes, the moment the solidness of my hand passed before my eyes I saw that I was looking through a shadow hand. I held it there before me. Dark shadow hand. As I looked through the shadow, I saw the distant valley, shadowed, but there. As I lifted my shadow hand back up to shade my eyes, I saw again only white nothingness.

"Am I the shadow of the land?" I asked out loud. "Does nothing exist without the shadow?" I yelled into the nothingness. Is the shadow the place where the dream is lived? I wondered, as again I brought the dark shadow hand before my eyes and looked through to see the valley below.

I then sat upon the warm rock, placed my shadow head in my shadow hands and rocked back and forth. Nothingness. The world is simply nothingness until it passes through the shadow. It is the shadow that allows creation to be manifested. It is the light that dissolves it into nothingness. I was confused.

I knew that the light was positive, but I'd never thought of it as being nothingness. Then as I looked up and saw the outline of the land take shape, I understood that the physical reality, this physical dream I walked in, requires the shadow in order to give depth to existence. It is the shadow that houses the power of the light. The shadow that is the complement to the light. I knew that if we were to walk the physical dream, we had to be willing to accept the shadow with the light. If we accepted the shadow, we could become balanced and receive the first key of knowledge required to manifest what we needed to fully complete the picture. The light was the canvas upon which we needed but to reflect the shadow and give illusion to those shapes and formations we dreamed were wakeful life.

"In the fullness of understanding, allow your knowledge to be communicated clearly into your life."

Autumnal Equinox (September 21-23)

The Autumnal Equinox, the celebration of Mabon, the time of balance between the dark and the light, the time of balance between life and death, the time of balance between sleep and wakefulness.

This is our true time of thanksgiving, for it is the second harvest, the harvest of all foods grown and reaped. It is the harvest of relations into the family unit. It is the time of rejoicing subconsciously over another abundant season of active life, and the subconscious knowing that the releasing of action must now take place in order to dwell peacefully through the season of darkness. For as the wheel turns, this is the last time (in the current year) to rejoice in its fullness.

The Autumnal Equinox has become, for me personally, the great feast shared with friends and family in honor and tribute to Gaia, Mother Earth.

"We request your presence at a very special thanksgiving dinner in honor of Gaia. Please come join in our Autumnal Equinox Celebration, Friday, September 22, 1989, at 8:00 P.M. promptly," read the invitation. We mailed it out to 15 people. We were having our Thanksgiving dinner and wanted to share it.

At 6:00 P.M. the evening of the dinner, the women of Rose Moon Tribe (my personal coven at the time) gathered in my home. Everyone had fasted that day and were looking forward to the feast we would begin making. After groceries were unloaded in the kitchen, we met in the Temple where we grounded and centered, cast circle (extending it throughout the house), called in Goddess and sang the I Am chant three times.

At 6:45 we returned to the kitchen. After dividing the chores, we set about preparing the food while focusing our energy into the food which would be an offering to Gaia. The affirmation,

Plate 5—The core of Women Spirit Rising gathered at the
thanksgiving table at the celebration of the Autumnal Equinox.
(Left to right: Shelley Bradford, Faith Barr-Glover, Gail Carr,
Kisma Stepanich, Lisa Hill and Linda Sanford.)

"*I prepare this food in honor of the Divine Mother,*" *soon*
became a chant. Once the food was either cooking, or completed,
we set the table, and changed into festive clothing (Plate 5).
At 8:00 promptly, the guests began to arrive. Rick Welt,
Elaine Regan, Patricia Major, Shawn Konecky, Kevin Nelson,
Shelly Bradford, Bette Barr-Glover, Barbara, Suzanne Carr,
and Reitt joined our celebration. Lisa shared the meaning of
the Harvest Time and our celebration and informed the guests
that our meal primarily consisted of items made with grains
and vegetables and that the main drink would be beer. She also

Plate 6—The altar of the harvest, Autumnal Equinox.

informed them that tonight we honored the Grain Mother.

As Lisa spoke, the rest of us quietly prepared the buffet-style table. When the spread (consisting of Russian cabbage pies, a salad with tamari dressing, wild rice stuffing, corn bread, watermelon, oat cookies, herb tea, wine and beer) graced the table, everyone rose and circled the table once, then joined hands. A blessing to Gaia was given and individual thanksgivings and blessings were spoken over the food. Warm smiles were exchanged, and love, and finally we partook of the beautiful harvest feast.

After dinner we shared the story of the Aztec Great Corn Mother, Chicomecoatl. During desert (pumpkin pie), I invited our guests to enter the Temple, approach the altar and give their own personal thanks to the Mother if they so desired.

Conversations and laughter were shared, and a moment of silence was observed before the guests began departing. When only Rose Moon Tribe remained, we bid farewell to the Goddess, dismissed the quarters, opened circle and ended the Autumnal Equinox rite.

Dates to consider, research and celebrate in the future:

September 1:   Thargelia (Mediterranean)
                Festival of the First Fruits
            Radha's Day (Indian)
            In honor of Lakshmi, the Hindu Goddess, who, in her Radha personification, is the lover of Krishna

September 3:   Marathonia (Greek)
            The day of Artemis

September 8:   Nativity of the Blessed Virgin Mary (Roman)

September 10: Eleusinia (Greek)
            Games in preparation for the Greater Eleusinia

September 13: Banquet of Venus (Roman)
            Ceremony of Lighting the Fire (Egyptian)
            Temple fires were kept burning

September 21: Feast of the Divine Trinity (Greek)
            Kore, Demeter and Iacchos

September 23: Autumnal Equinox
            Eleusian Mysteries (Greek)
            Goddess Demeter is honored
            Festival of Libra (Greek)
            The Goddess of balance and justice

September 28: The Holy Night (Greek)
            The Queen of Hell was honored

October

We have moved into the waning month of Autumn, the month of the Crone. It is ironic that the month of the Crone is the month ruled by the planet Venus. Venus, the planet of love on all levels (romantic, familial and spiritual). We also find the astrological sign Libra native in this month. The scales of wisdom, balancing the degrees of love.

It is the star Venus, that blue twinkling light, that teaches us the art of cooperation with our inner wisdom. The Crone appreciates the ignorance of human suffering, applies the temperance needed in order to balance the scales between this existence (the dream reality as seen through the shadow) and the other world (the light of nothingness).

In this month of waning during the waning season, we must look closely at the masks we have worn. We must go within and find new masks, new faces, bring them forth and examine them to see if the eyeholes of the new mask reveals more truth than the old one. We must be willing to come face to face with the monster masks as well as the beauty masks and wear each. It has often been said that "Beauty is in the eye of the beholder" and that sometimes the "Ugliest exterior can house a most beautiful interior."

During the month of October we can use the waning energy and begin making a new mask. Use whatever material you are drawn to; i.e., papier maiché, clay, cloth, wood. Create the foundation of the mask and then decorate the surface of it. End by adorning it with sacred objects. During the entire creation process, *never* put it on. When you are finished with your mask, place it on your altar or under a pyramid to draw the power it needs until Samhain arrives (October 31st) and you celebrate in the Shadow Dance when you will wear your new mask.

Samhain/Hallows Eve (October 31)

Tonight the wheel turns. It is the third and final harvest of the year, that of the livestock. The spirit of the animal kingdom is honored.

With respect, we come to the crossroads between the old year and the new year, between the season of life and the season of death.

The veils are thin this night, and the feast of Hecate, the Crone, is celebrated. At this feast we make offerings to our ancestors, all relations who have gone before us to the Otherside. We commune with our dead, with the spirit realm, asking for assistance in stepping through the death season, asking for their messages to come through our dreams.

It is Hecate who will take us one step beyond the gateway this night so that we might dance in the Otherworld, even if it be but one brief moment, and wear our masks to see if the sight is better through them.

Adorn your altar with the colors of Hecate—black, red, white—and bring forth the cauldron of her magick and fill it with the white trumpet flower. Transform your Temple rooms into caves by hanging black cloth or streamers from the walls. Place your mask(s) around the foot of the altar. She among you who is a worthy vessel for the Goddess Hecate must prepare to become Hecate by drinking Her brew: sage, mugwort, wormwood, stinkweed, raspberry. You must surrender to Hecate fully, never fearing your own death, but willing to come face to face with death and all the attending aspects of death; i.e., fears, expectations, addictions.

When all have gathered together for this festival, a guide of Hecate shall ground and center the participants in a room separate from Hecate's Cave. The participants are purified and black veiled. The quarters are invoked.

East: *Misty breath of spirit light*
seldom seen but by Full Moon at night,
Be with us—slice through the veil
that we may look beyond.

South: *Creatures of the passion flame,*
the journey has now begun.

Be with us—render a gateway
through the veil that we may inhale your spirit
beyond the edge of this world.

West: *From your depths of old,*
          come now creatures of water.
          Be with us—part the mists so we might
          flow beyond the veils of time.

North: *Creatures of the Earth, keepers of time,*
          Guardians of the old age tombs,
          be with us—grant us passage to the land
          where the Fair Folk command.

Take the participants to the Cave of Hecate. Have all sit
with their backs to Hecate. The guide of Hecate steps forward
into the center of the cave and greets Hecate:

O, Hecate, Goddess of Life and Death,
beloved by us all.
Wake from your slumber.
Earth Mother, bless this gathering with your presence.

O, Hecate, Goddess of Darkness,
I beseech thee by the Ancient key—
Achna, Rai, U'ma.
Great Hecate, Guardian Mother of the Gates of Death,
I call thee by the Theban Three—
Hecate, Hecate, Hecate.
Tarry not for the time draws near.
Cast aside the veils, open the gates, for the
two worlds draw near.

O, Hecate, 'tis Hallows Eve.
Set us free.
Ancient Mother, Guardian Crone,
Hear my call. So mote it be.

The guide of Hecate will sit with the others and await acknowledgment from Hecate. She who becomes Hecate remains still until she receives the spirit of Hecate and her energy comes in.

A good sign to use as acknowledgement that Hecate has entered is for the Priestess to stand and ask, "What seek ye?" At this point the participants rise and begin chanting:

Lady, we pray you open the gateway.
Open the gateway for us now.

The chanting shall continue. As it does so, Hecate shall hold each mask up until the owner has stepped up to the altar. Hecate shall then place the mask over the participant's head. When all participants are masked, the Shadow Dance begins and continues until each participant arrives at a place of reconciliation with the new mask and again places it at the foot of the altar.

When all are sitting once again, and the Shadow Dance has ended, time is allowed for Hecate to speak. (I have never once remembered the words Hecate speaks through me. I only know she is there, and oftentimes I am filled with a great sorrow as she looks from face to face and beseeches the wisdom of the women gathered. My eyes still see, and the faces of the women attending the ceremony become very still and awed as the powerful voice that is not my own rolls out. Tears have dropped, mouths have fallen open, hands clasped tight, as the Crone speaks. One day perhaps I shall have the foresight to set up a tape recorder and tape the Crone's wisdom, but that thought always eludes me until after the ceremony when I ask the women what message Hecate spoke. Unfortunately, no one ever remembers the entire message, for they are caught at their own meaningful crossroads.)

When Hecate has finished speaking, she indicates this by turning her back on those gathered. The guide ushers the women back into the other room where the feast of Hecate will begin.

A blessing is said over the food (a spread which should consist of fish/poultry or meat). Each participant will then prepare a very small plate of food in honor of an ancestor (chosen before the ceremony). The plate is carried to the altar in Hecate's Cave and placed on the altar next to a picture of the deceased. A white, red or black votive candle is lit and the following prayer spoken:

To the one who has gone before me,
come now to my aid.
Show the way to travel,
so I might fully honor life.

The candle is placed next to the plate and picture. The participant returns to the feasting area, where they will prepare their own plate.

I usually do a tarot spread after the feasting, as this night of all nights during the year is the most powerful time for divination. Each year the messages given through the cards have proven true.

When all agree it is time, a farewell is given to Hecate. The quarters are dismissed. The circle is opened and the rite ended.

Dates to consider, research and celebrate in the future:

October 1:	Saxon New Year
October 5:	Day of the Holy Spirit (Gnostic)
	In honor of Sophia, the spirit of female wisdom
	Proerosia (Greek)
	Festival in preparation for sowing Autumn crops, Goddess Kore is invoked for fertility
October 11-13:	Thesmophoria (Greek)
	The festival of Demeter and of Women's Rights
October 12:	Holiday of the Goddess of Happy Journeys (Roman)
	In honor of Fortuna Redux

October 19:   Apaturia (Greek)
                The meeting of the Clans, dedicated to family reunions

October 21:   Koureotis (Greek)
                Ceremony of receiving children into the Clan, also a time of dedicating children to their patron deities

October 31:   Samhain (Celtic)
                Feast of Hecate (Wiccan)

Hecate

Chapter Five

WINTER ─────────────
A Child of Earth

─────────────────────────────────

It is to the north I go,
to touch the midnight hour.
As the stag prances on high mountain tops,
My strength bounds forth:
"Spirit—my friend,
Enrich this circle I dance within!"

*I held Medicine Woman Crystal to my solar plexus and
went to my power spot on the sea cliff at the edge of a redwood
forest. I stood at the edge looking down. The mist from the
rushing water below rose in tufts of billowy clouds. The power
of the water lapped at my ears.*

*The forest beckoned me and I turned to face it. Giant red-
woods towered above, shading the ground below with shadow,
pieces of red bark and pine cones. I ran to the edge of the forest
and stopped. It was important to ask permission to enter this
holy ground. Kneeling down, I placed my hands on the Earth
and sent forth "feelers" into her body. I connected with the roots
of the trees and other green growing plants. I connected with
the moist soil around the streams, under stones and fallen
debris. I connected with the flowing lullaby of water. I felt very
welcomed.*

I ran through the trees collecting stones (ten to be exact) and carried them back to the cliff. They tumbled from my arms, hitting the spot which would be the center of my medicine wheel. Beginning in the south I placed a stone in the south and honored the wisdom of "She who bears life." I moved to the southwest, placed another stone down honoring the wisdom of "She who brings dreams." On and on I moved round the circle, placing the stones and honoring each wisdom of the outer hoop: West, "She who heals with forked lighting from her left eye." Northwest, "She who brings balance." North, "She who guards all directions." Northeast, "She who is the energy of movement." East, "She who brings the light" and Southeast, "She who brings peace."

When the outer hoop was complete, I walked around the perimeter of the stone medicine wheel once, honoring the sacred outer hoop, and entered through the south gateway. As I stepped over the south stone I spoke quietly, "For all my relations."

I pulled blue cornmeal from the pocket of my jacket and began creating a second wheel just within the stone one. It was the inner hoop, the representative of the life force. When a circle of blue lay on the ground, I retreated to the center of the circle and unslung the bundle from off my back. I untied the leather thongs holding the bundle together and unrolled it, revealing the red medicine blanket and all my sacred tools contained within. I picked up a tobacco pouch, untied it and held a pinch up to Great Spirit.

"I am thankful I am a part of this life," I told Great Spirit. "I am ready to defend Mother Earth—no compromise! Bring me together with those people who I can help heal the Mother with where together we will accomplish what only one of us could not. My heart is full. I give thanks." I placed the pinch of tobacco in the center of the medicine blanket.

I threw pinches of tobacco to each of the four directions, creating the third and last hoop, the great secret hoop which holds the universe and all its mysteries. I acknowledged Father Sky and Mother Earth and felt the completeness of the medicine wheel. I looked down at the objects lying on the blanket.

There were many objects lying there. I picked up a rattle and sang my Power Song three times. The energy outside of the wheel began to shift. The mist from below flowed over the cliff and engulfed me. Slowly it receded, and once more the beautiful redwood forest lay before me.

Laying the rattle down, I took up my Medicine Shield and walked to the east. I held it up high and yelled, "Come, Grandfather Eagle, Guardian of the powers of the east. Bring your clarity of intelligence. See for me and bring to light the path I must travel!"

A giant eagle flapped its wings above me and perched itself on a pole that now stood in the east gateway. I was amazed at the hugeness of the eagle and felt his power and protection radiate down from under the umbrella of his wings.

I hung the shield on the pole and said to the eagle, "I put in place my shield of power, my medicine tool of the east." As I backed away from the pole, a gust of wind rushed out of the eastern sky and rocked the shield back and forth. The pole stood still, and not one of the feathers on Grandfather Eagle was ruffled.

I moved back to the blanket and picked up the black obsidian blade knife. I walked to the south. As soon as I stood at the gateway, a pure, white stallion came galloping to the edge of the wheel. He reared on his hind legs. I held the medicine tool up to him.

"Power of the south. The innocence of your purity and beauty is overwhelming. Guardian of the south, protect my innocence in this world, so that my connection with Mother Earth is ever strong!"

I stuck the blade down in the Earth. "With my tool of trust now in place, I am ready to journey down my path with all your power and grace." The stallion stood frozen in place on its hind legs rearing, mane flowing in the breeze. The ground shook beneath me. The handle of the knife vibrated.

I went back to the blanket and reached for my sacred drum as I turned to the west, to the ocean before me.

"Come sister dolphin," I called out to the sea. Immediately

she jumped fully out of the water and hung suspended in time.

"The power drum beats your song. In this place of darkness, death and birth, in this place of woman mysteries, I beat the drum, summoning forth the courage to dance the true dance of power."

I threw the drum out to the west and watched as it stopped and hung suspended in the air at the edge of the stone medicine wheel.

"Our connection is complete," I whispered to the dolphin whose skin shone from the light of the Sun as its rays kissed the residue of water clinging to her gray body.

The north was the redwood forest. Granite mountains rose off in the distance. I held my sacred pipe up to the mountains peaks. The largest stag I ever imagined came bounding out through the trees. He stopped at the edge of the medicine wheel, nostrils flaring with white wisps of air. He pawed the ground, shook his giant antlers from side to side and eyed me curiously. I held the pipe toward him.

"Brother stag of the north, Earth power." He stood poised and still, head thrown back, proud and slightly arrogant. I continued, "Bring me your strength and protection, the mighty wisdoms eternal you store within the hollow of your bones. We share the pipe and blend the two worlds."

Placing the pipe at his feet, the curling smoke danced from the stem and reached up for his antlers until it swirled around them like an etheric crown.

"Let the smoke carry our voices to the heavens, to the spirit world." I moved backwards. I stepped on the red medicine blanket and sat down facing the east. I looked down at Medicine Woman Crystal and picked it up. I held it to my solar plexus.

"Come, Medicine Woman," I spoke out loud. "Come stand by my side and teach me."

She stood before me, white braids hanging to her knees, white deerskin dress. She was ancient. Withered from the passage of time and the nature elements, yet somehow eternally young. She stood as a paradox before me, sending my mind into argument over her age and bodily condition.

Without speaking, she stepped over the east stone, crossed the space between us and knelt at the edge of the medicine blanket. Her smile spread across her face transforming it into that of a three-year-old child. Automatically I smiled back and felt her embrace.

I sunk into her arms of endless comfort and disappeared into a space that was all-consuming. A perfect sense of balance and time seemed to exist. My mind ceased to work so hard at analyzing the experience, and I surrendered to her scent, which was that of the damp Earth of the forest and the sea foam spraying high and the delicate essence of Spring blossoms and rich, brown-golden leaves falling. Layer after layer of scent rose from her pores, transporting me into each reality that was brought to life within the realm of my experience. And then the scents took me beyond, into worlds and feelings and understandings I couldn't grasp.

As if sensing my puny limitations, the scent dissipated and I was pulled back to her arms, back to her face, back to her smile.

She stood, taking me with her. As she took hold of my hand, she spoke.

"I will take you forth to learn."

I was aware of her wrinkled hand holding mine, the soft, leathery touch of it. She continued speaking.

"Breathe deep and let us move up. Up. Up," her words soft and elusive echoed through my body. "Up and out of this reality into the next." Mist surrounded us.

"Up. Up. Out of this non-reality into reality." Blue light surrounded us. Then blackness.

"You are blindfolded," she told me. "Where I take you, it must be done in this manner the first time." My hand reached up to the material covering my eyes.

Drumming exploded as our feet hit solid ground. Light flickered around the edges of the material. I could hear the voices of many women. I could almost feel the warmth from their bodies, smell them. Medicine Woman squeezed my hand.

"We are at a gathering of the Grandmothers," she told me.

"There are many here you know or have heard of. Black Wolf is here, Genuve, Zoila, Aranda, Whistling Elk and many others."

I felt the arms of Black Wolf embrace me. I felt my clothing being pulled off and heard several voices say, "She is female," at the same time that I felt many hands touching my breasts and vagina.

Medicine Woman squeezed my hand again and then let go. I stood alone. Wet fingers touched my breasts. "We are painting you," said a woman whose voice I'd never heard before. Slowly my chest, arms and face were covered with heavy wetness. By the time they finished painting me, parts had begun to dry.

"It is time for you to dance," the woman said as I felt her take my hand. She led me closer to the drumming and let go. I started dancing and felt the movement take over. A strange chant was being sung by the women. I joined in, not knowing the words yet somehow knowing them. I felt primordial, and soon I was swirling and stamping my feet with the drum rhythms.

I felt the strong presence of three entities, not knowing who or what they could be, and heard Medicine Woman whisper, "Ah, your power has brought the Grandfathers." I stamped harder, wanting my connection with the Earth. With each movement I thrust my foot harder and harder into the soft soil beneath me. I wanted to plunge deep into the very core of the Mother. With my next stamp, I felt her open and swallow me.

I stood within a cavern, sultry and misty was the air. A deep, orange glow dimly lit the space. I looked down at my body, the blindfold having disappeared, and saw that I was covered from head to toe with a red clay except my hands, which were covered in green. Black obsidian bands circled my wrists and, on each finger, bands inlaid with turquoise. A ruby choker was clasped around my neck with a strand of rubies dangling down my chest, ending at my waist. At my waist the jeweled strand snaked around and ended above my pubic hair, which was covered by a soft skin tied around my hips. Diamonds covered my arms. A crown of topaz and carnelian circled my head. Plumes of blue and orange macaw feathers were fastened to the back of the crown. Around my ankles rested strands of black obsidian, and around each toe silver, gold and copper bands.

"You are of me," a deep rumble in the Earth spoke to me. "You are one with all life."

Suddenly animals and birds from everywhere of the world swarmed around me. White Wolf bounded up and sat on his haunches to my left. Brother Hawk flew up and perched itself on my left shoulder.

"You are friends with all the land." Every type of plant life imaginable sprouted and grew around me; scenes of different terrain flashed before me.

"The waters are your energy." Oceans, rivers, lakes, streams, waterfalls, creeks and ponds flashed by.

"You are a caretaker of all that you have just witnessed. Protect it well."

Blackness swallowed me. The flickering of the light edged the blindfold again and I was still dancing with the Grandmothers. I felt very dizzy and stopped moving. I reached out, searching for something to hold on to. As I faltered in step and tripped over my own feet, I felt strong hands catch me. I was held upright. Roughly the blindfold was removed. The light, though muted, blinded me for a moment. I blinked the scene into vision. All I could see were images of energy.

I was asked if I could identify anyone. I couldn't. I was informed I shouldn't worry about not being able to identify any- one, and that next time I would see. I was also told that my spirit dreamtime eyes were not yet completely developed.

Medicine Woman stepped before me. "It is time to go," she said. "It is time to show you the stars." Taking my hand, the scene changed instantly. We were standing in the middle of the galaxy. I was so amazed at what I had just experienced that I felt exhausted, unable to see the stars. Before I could tell Medicine Woman this, we were standing on Earth again at the edge of a pond. She pointed to the water and was telling me to "see." The images that appeared on the surface would barely come into focus before fading. I glanced up and watched the landscape fade and then reappear.

"I'm tired," I whispered. She understood the full extent of what I meant. In a flash of light we arrived back at the medicine wheel. We stood for a long time in the center. Most of the time my eyes were closed. I could feel that hers were too. I'm not sure when she left me, but she did, and when I finally opened my eyes I was standing alone, I slowly turned to each of my quarter guardians and thanked them for their protection. Each immediately departed. I thanked Mother Earth and Father Sky and ended by thanking the Great Spirit. I still stood in the center of the wheel and looked back to the east. A glowing light stood just within the edge of the forest. I held my hands out to this light.

"Thank you Medicine Woman." I felt her embrace and then the light was gone. I gathered the tools together and placed them with the crystal in the center of the medicine blanket. As I rolled the blanket up, tied it with leather thongs and placed it on my back, I felt the energy begin shifting. The landscape started to dissolve and the medicine wheel disappeared. I stepped over the south stone just as the wheel vanished. I opened my eyes.

I held Medicine Woman Crystal to my lips and kissed it, thanking her for such a wonderful journey. As I wrapped her in red cloth, I felt her arms embrace me.

> Frozen still, the wonderland.
> Silenced to unknowable depths.
> The opaque reflection on the ice,
> sparkles in the stillness of
> the season of Death.

In the Winter all life slows down; breathing is labored silence. Everywhere the stark land stretches, blanketed with folds of white velvet. Birds have long since flown south to where the fire of the land still dances. All is dormant, awaiting the rebirth of the Sun, awaiting the gentle touching fingertips of the solar rays when they reach down and caress the land—planting their essence of warmth to germinate the seeds burrowed deep in the Mother's womb.

Dark and mysterious is the energy at this time, drawing us deep into the center of our own core to dwell quietly with our shadow. During this time we taste the bile of our essence and eventually regurgitate it into the light. Until then, we quietly use our senses to listen and wait patiently for the Spring.

Now that we stand still, all action ceased, except for those actions that are forced on us—such as the Christmas shopping and celebration. We have no choice but to examine our mortality and dream of days filled with sunshine. Death and dreams. Both, if used during this season, will teach us much about our ego and our relationship to others and, most importantly, our understanding of life.

Though it is important to work with death and dreams, it is also important to understand the correspondences associated with this season to become more intimate with it, allowing us to understand this phase of life.

The Correspondences of Winter

The season of spirit/dreaming/death
Repose/regeneration/midnight/dark Moon
North/auditory/Earth/white
Ancestors of the European People
Mountains/rock/structure/soil/gnomes

Winter is the north quarter of the wheel. The north is the power. It is the place which marks midnight, the hour of darkness. In darkness, the mysteries lie. Understanding the mysteries, one can receive the power, the power of understanding that to nurture is to gain. Power of self.

In the north, the element Earth is found.

The Element of Winter—Earth

Earth is the body of the Mother, the life support system we live on. The Earth reflects strength, growth, nature, sustenance, mountains, forests, groves, fields, rocks and standing stones. It is the element of silence, birth and death.

Element Earth is also associated with Pan, the goat-foot god whose lascivious nature is closely linked to the forests and the mountains; for he was the god of the green wood who was worshipped in conjunction with the Goddess. Although he has become closely linked to the Christian devil and thought to be the devil, he was the mythology of the pure, raw nature of Earth. Today, he has almost faded in our memories. Tom Robbins, in his novel *Jitterbug Perfume* (Bantam Books, Inc., 1984), gives an excellent account (though it is fiction) of why this has happened.

> "'Pan is not well,' the nymphs confided.
>
> "I watched him scale the rocks. I watched him set four of you to coming in a row," said Alobar. "He seems fit enough to me."
>
> The nymphs released a chorus of dreamy sighs. "You should have seen him when he was in his prime. He's like a sick dove, nowadays, compared to the goat he used to be."
>
> "Is it Christ who is making him weak?"
>
> "Not Christ but Christians. With every advance of Christianity, his powers recede," said one nymph.
>
> "It started long before Christ," said a second.
>
> "Yes, it did," agreed the first. "It began with the rise of the cities. There simply was no place in the refined temples of Attica and Sparta for a mountain goat like Pan."
>
> A third nymph, who, with a wad of leaves, was scrubbing herself clean of caked secretions, joined in. "It was man's jealousy of woman that started it," she said. "They wanted to drive the goddesses out of Olympus and replace them with male gods."
>
> "Is not Pan a male god?" asked Alobar.
>
> "True, he is, but he is associated with female values. To diminish the worth of women, men had to diminish the worth of the Moon. They had to drive a wedge between human beings and the trees and the beasts and the waters, because trees and beasts and waters are as loyal to the Moon as to the Sun. They had to drive a wedge between thought and feeling, between the lamplight by which they count the day's earnings and the dark to which our Pan is ever connected."

The god of the forest shunned and Goddess driven underground—no wonder our poor Earth has suffered so very much and is today in a state of decay. Current religions have created a hidden boundary, inhibiting the children of Earth from being closely linked to this boundary because of fear of the darkness and the miracles of nature.

Yet, I know it is unfair to blame the separation between people and the Earth strictly on current religions, for it is our advanced technology and the industrial age of man's achievements that have ultimately severed what little thread still keeps us bound to the Earth. Too many of us no longer live on the land, or even have a small garden in which to submerge our hands in the soil. We dwell in high-rises, or surround our homes with low-maintenance concrete lawns because we simply do not have the time to dawdle in the garden and take part in nature and her cycles.

I sit here, looking out onto my small yard with its rose bushes and vegetable and herb plants, with its freshly mowed grass. My fingers have bandages around the blisters I got today while devoting the entire morning to tending my garden, but these blisters are okay because I feel so much closer and connected to the Earth. This garden has become my saving grace, living in my suburban life. I can hear birds chirping, and watch my Echo as she so very slyly sneaks up as close as she can possibly get to them. A saving grace, as I note the zenith of the Sun by the way the shadows fall and which part of the garden is being warmed by its rays. A saving grace, because I am still involved with the Earth, not ignoring her or the spirit of her. I give and she gives back. Time for peace.

Earth Elemental Journey

(A inner journey in which to re-acquaint yourself with the spirit of Earth).

You are in a forest, rich with lush vegetation, trees and wildlife. Everywhere you look you see royal shades of green: the light, lime green of new growth; the olive green of ferns;

the yellow green of tree leaves; green of grass; and the deep hunter green of the foliage that grows where the Sun's rays do not touch. There are so many shades of green.

As you stand in the clearing of the forest, listen to the sounds of life: the dance of the leaves and air, the leaves as they skip off the branches and fall to the ground, the swooshing of ferns as an animal passes, the silent whisper of plants' breathing as they reach out to touch you and drink in your carbon dioxide and refresh you with their essences of oxygen.

As you turn toward the north you see a path and move toward it. It is a dirt path, rich brown. You step onto the path and walk where it leads. The dirt path takes you further into the forest. Further into the rich vegetation. Further into the lush green colors. As you walk, the sounds become still.

There before you is a canopy of vines which blocks the path. You examine the waterfall of vines and realize they are covering the mouth of a cave. You reach out and push the vines aside. The cave is dark and you cannot see in.

You step into the opening of the cave, and as you stand in the entrance you become aware of the rich smells mingling in the air. You can still smell the greenness of vegetation and the freshness of oxygen the plants emit. At the same time you can smell the musky richness of the soil and the dampness of the Earth as it filters out from the cave. You move into the cave, into this damp scent.

As you move further in the cave you become aware that you have stepped inside the womb of the Earth Mother. The firmness and specialness of this world surrounds you. It draws you deeper. The musty odor consumes you and slowly your eyes adjust to the darkness. You catch glimpses of squat-looking faces with funny noses and fuzzy hair. But just as you focus on the little faces, they disappear and you see a fuzziness from the corner of your eye. You have now entered the elemental world of Earth, the kingdom of the gnomes.

You stand still for a moment, wondering if you should continue without their permission. As you stand there you notice the texture of the rock walls around you. They have changed from a rugged texture to a very smooth and slippery one. There are tiny streams of water flowing down the sides of smooth granite. The water collects in small bottomless pools filled with rich minerals. The atmosphere has become humid, sulfuric.

You sense it is okay to continue. With each step the atmosphere becomes heavier and damper, yet you are surprised at how cool you feel and how easy it is to breathe. It is as if you have become the Earth element and your body has transformed itself into the minerals around you.

Onward you travel and suddenly you enter a huge cavern that is filled with molten rock. You have arrived at the Earth's core. The intensity and brightness of the heat is almost overwhelming, but suddenly your body shifts and you once again have become connected to this surrounding. It feels as if your own body is no longer separate from the Earth; there is no beginning nor ending. You simply are connected. You relish the solid feeling which seems to reinforce your being. Strength flows through your veins. You open your consciousness to the Earth and begin to float within the body of the Earth. You have touched your home base. You are the Earth.

As you linger in this connection, you are aware of the gnomes who are coming out of their hiding places to touch you. They are familiars who live in the Earth, and will assist you once you show them your oneness with the solid strength of the Earth. Perhaps you can hear them speaking. Perhaps one will speak to you its wisdom. Listen... For one or several may bring you a mystery... (Allow time for meditation.)

The gnomes are being called back to their hiding places. They want you to know that they are here whenever you need to seek their assistance. They want you to remember they are always found when you journey with Earth. Thank your gnome(s) for the mystery it/they have brought you and exchange your words of farewell. (Pause.)

Once again you are alone. Slowly your body begins to rise above the molten core, above the sulfuric pools, until you are back at the entrance of the cave. Your body is tingling all over. You feel the regeneration of minerals within your body. Your bones have been strengthened and your skin feels smooth and rich. You turn to look back at the tunnel which took you to the Earth's core. It is very dark now. You turn to the mouth where the vines hang and reach out to pull them back. The light of day makes you squint. As you step back into the forest, the freshness of the vegetation renews your lungs. Each breath cleanses and purifies your being. Deeply, calmly you breathe in the life.

As the vines drop back into place, concealing the mouth of the cave, you remember the gnome(s) and the gifts they shared with you. You send a blessing to their kingdom, then turn and travel back down the path surrounded by the lush greens and the sounds of the forests.

You enter the clearing from where you began the journey. When you stop in the clearing you kneel down and place the palms of your hands on the grass. The softness of the blades tickle your palms. You feel the vibration of all you have seen re-awaken inside you. You remember that you are the Earth. You remember that this body of life, this life-support system, is vitally important to you.

Magically your heart center flows open and you share with the Earth Mother, giving thanks for her abundance. You feel as if the energy that stimulates your kundalini, your chakra systems, is moving rapidly between you and the Earth. You have received the blessing of Mother Earth. Your journey has ended.

The Phases of Winter

November

We enter the waxing phase of Winter, ruled by the passionate sting of the Scorpion's tail and the Lord of the underworld, Pluto. We enter the realm of the subconscious, the occult. The deep intensity of our desires is penetrated. We can learn how to be temperate with our emotions and aware of those feelings of vengefulness and sarcasm.

It is Pluto's energy, however, that gives us access to submerging our awareness deep into the core of our being. If we use the energy wisely, we can expose that which has been developed secretly or kept undercover from our own consciousness, and transmute those secrets of self by undergoing an arduous regeneration process which can end in either death (if the secrets be of a negative nature) or birth (if they be positive).

So in essence this energy is prime for us to investigate through deep research, those areas of our psyche that like to hide. It is a time for spiritual and physical regeneration, psychological rebirth and/or degeneration and death.

The above can be experienced through inner journeys and dreams. Through our dreams we can learn how to enter the sacred round and exist at will. The sacred rounds (there are seven) are controlled by the kachina powers. The first round is normal everyday life, the world we live in and the way we normally perceive it. The second round is sleep. The third round is where the dreamers go. It is called, "walking through the gateways between the worlds," and if we were in them we would be spirit, and that would be what we call death.[1]

There are many theories based on the interpretation of dreams. They range from mundane to occult to psychological. However, my experience with dreams have transformed beyond the above aspects of life into an alternative reality where, more often than not, I receive guidance and contact from other dimensions of being. This has come through conscious effort, researching the subject of dreaming and experimenting with different techniques and documenting all my experiences in dream journals. I have witnessed how my dreaming life has transmuted into another world and give credence to the events experienced in that state of consciousness.

We spend two-thirds of our life sleeping. It is ignorant to think that we are simply "checked-out" while lying down with our eyes closed.

Furthermore, the scientific industry has given much research over to dreaming and the dream state. With the invention of the electroencephalograph or brain-wave machine and the examination of brain waves of patients while asleep, a study of the configurations of the brain waves occurring during sleep has led to some interesting conclusions about the nature of dreams and about their relation to sleep. One such discovery is that the brain-wave pattern associated with rapid eye movements (REM) resembles the same patterns found when awake. This suggests that, while we are dreaming, our state of consciousness is more like that of waking life than that of nondreaming periods during sleep.[2]

It is important to understand the dream process before experimenting with it. First, periods of brain activity are short at the beginning of the sleep period but increase in length as sleep progresses. These periods of brain activity coincide with the REMs and indicate the onset of a period of dreaming. This means that our dreams are short ones soon after we have fallen asleep, but those which occur just before we wake up are longer.

Second, during a period of eight hours' sleep, this combined activity takes place at regular intervals of about an hour and a half. The first dream period, which lasts for about nine minutes, occurs about an hour after we have fallen asleep. The second, which lasts for about 19 minutes, occurs an hour and a half later. The third one, which lasts about 24 minutes, occurs an hour and a half after that. After a similar interval the fourth one comes along, and this lasts about 28 minutes. There is another interval of an hour and a half before the fifth period, which lasts until it is interrupted by the sleeping person's return to consciousness. Lastly, the depth of sleep during the later periods of dreaming is less than that during the earlier ones.

Are we entitled to infer that one of the functions of dreaming is to prepare the mind for "waking up"? Waking up our subconscious? At any rate this seems to be what is actually taking place during the mind's excursions into the realm of dreams.

The strengthening of insight and self-knowledge is one of the most important creative functions of the dream. Likewise, to realize that we go into another dimension while we sleep gives us added power. A power that comes from a much deeper level, because it comes from the level of the invisible realm, the realm of spirit.

"Dreams are diving down in the Earth," Agnes Whistling Elk tells us. "They are feminine in character. Male takes the substance and forms it. Dreams are your other-half vision."[3]

Since we are going into the season of hibernation, the most powerful form of magick to use is dreaming. Whether we choose to dream through meditation, trance or sleep, there are many tools that can be made to assist us, but most importantly, the dream journal should be put in use.

Dream Pillows

Dream pillows are wonderful tools, and are easy to make. The stuffings of the pillow can consist of one or more of the following items:

Herbs: Ash, bay laurel, cinquefoil, cloves, costmary, heliotrope, lemon balm, marigold, mint, mugwort, nutmeg, poppy, rose and wormwood.

Oils: Mimosa, nutmeg or sandalwood.

Additive stuffing: Cattails or cotton.

Crystals/Gemstones: Quartz crystal, amethyst, tiger-eye, rose quartz, herkimer diamond.

The material used for the pillow should be a color and/or design that is very subdued and pleasing to the eye. Never use loud, bright colors such as red, orange, yellow or rich shades of bright pink. These color rays are much too active for our mind in the dream state. You will toss and turn rather than find peace and wake up refreshed.

Most dream pillows are small (nine by nine inches is a magical dimension). When constructing the pillow, it is important to do so when the Moon is waning and during the hour of the Moon.

On Sunday, the hour of the Moon is the sixth hour after the Sun sets. Monday is the third and tenth hours. Tuesday is the seventh hour. Wednesday is the fourth and eleventh hours. Thursday is the first and eighth hours. Friday is the fifth and twelfth hours. Saturday is the second and ninth hours.

Remember that Monday is "Moon" day. If you want to work solely with the Moon energy, you would construct your dream pillow on Monday during the third or tenth hour of the night after the Sun has set.

Another tool which can be made is the Dream Catcher or Dream Web. My Spirit Sister, Lisa, attended Sun Bear's annual Medicine Wheel gathering held in Julian, California, in late 1989. During the gathering she was introduced to the Dream-Catcher Ceremony. The ceremony can be performed during New Moon or after the Full Moon. If performed at New Moon (or during the waxing Moon phase), after the Dream Catcher has been made, place it in a south window until the Full Moon. This is done to "charge" the catcher with the energy of remembering your dreams, to add clarity and expansion to your dreaming.

If the ceremony is performed after the Full Moon (or during the waning Moon), the Dream Catcher will also be placed in the south window but kept there until the New Moon. The energy that is being caught in the web is the energy that will assist you in going deeper into yourself so that your dreaming will be on a deep, subconscious level.

The supplies required to make a Dream Catcher are: cornmeal, scissors, paper and pens, embroidery thread, yarn, ribbon, string (any colors you are drawn to), and miscellaneous items such as feathers, crystals, leather, fur, beads etc.

The following ceremony is a modified version of the original one Lisa experienced. Lisa modified it to fit in with her tradition and belief system, rather than the Native American one.

I. Have participants search the neighborhood or an outdoor area for a stick that will be used as the skeleton of the catcher. (It is important to ask permission to cut a branch from a bush or tree if the participant is drawn to a "live" stick rather than one found on the ground. If permission is given by the bush or tree, thanks are spoken and a blessing/gift of cornmeal left at the base of the plant.)

II. When all have found their stick and returned to the ceremony site, smudge, ground and center.

III. Call in the quarters.

IV. Call in the Goddess aspect Minerva, who is Queen of the Moerae (or the Fates), weaver of time known as past, present and future, who is the spinner of the thread of life.

V. *Dreaming* Chant is sung:

> *I am opening up in sweet surrender*
> *to the luminous love light of the one above.*
> *I am opening up in sweet surrender*
> *to the luminous love light of the one above.*
> *I am opening, I am opening.*
> *I am opening, I am opening.*

VI. Colors of thread, yarn and/or string are chosen and cut into pieces. Miscellaneous items are chosen. All items, along with the stick, are smudged.

VII. A guided journey to the Special Star is then taken. (Stick is held in the left hand to receive the feeling into the skeletal section of the Dream Catcher. Close eyes and focus on the Special Star in the night sky. When Special Star is located, hold the stick up to it so the Star can see it and then place the stick in front of you. Raise your left hand up to the Star and ask Spider Woman, who resides on the Star, for her energy to come down through your arm and hand to help you weave your Dream Web. When the energy is felt, open your eyes.)

VIII. Weaving. Hold the stick in the right hand and weave the web with your left hand. When weaving is complete, the catcher can be adorned with the miscellaneous items. Hold the catcher up to Star and Spider Woman. Thank both entities and ask if there is anything else you need to do to the catcher.

IX. Personal Chant/Affirmation. Time can be allowed to create and write down a personal chant/affirmation that will be said out loud each night to empower the catcher.

X. Pass the Dream Catcher through sage smoke once more.

XI. Thank Minerva for her assistance.

XII. Dismiss quarters.

XIII. Open Circle

The Dream Catcher is placed immediately in the south window. The south window is chosen because it receives both Sunlight and Moonlight. (Note that you can continue to add miscellaneous items to the web during its incubation period.)

When the incubation period has ended, the Dream Catcher is placed over the headboard of your bed. The life of the Dream Catcher is six months. During that time, if anything falls off the catcher—i.e., branch, leaf, thread, miscellaneous items—do not throw it away. Place it back in the web.

At the end of the six month period, it is important to "give away" your Dream Catcher by giving it back to the Earth. It can be burned, buried, placed in the ocean or a river, or dismantled and left for nature to use i.e., the yarn, string and/or thread to be gathered by birds for nest building.

The ability to control your dreams eventually moves them into the state of astral projection. Crystals can be used to assist you in developing this ability.

The sleeping state not only replenishes the strength of your Physical Body but also rests your Astral Body. On its own plane, your Astral Body is almost incapable of tiring. However, on the physical plane, it soon tires of its exertion brought about by the interaction with the Physical Body. When you sleep, the two bodies separate and ultimately find rest.

When you are using your Astral Body consciously, it usually hovers above your Physical Body. In essence, you are not really asleep; only your Physical Body is. However, most people are not consciously aware that they are using their Astral Body in the dream state.

The best crystals to use for dream work and the astral plane are herkimer diamond crystals. A double terminated crystal can also be used. This crystal should be stored in a special place and not be shown to others or handled by them. You want to make sure that the crystal vibrates purely in harmony with you.

Dreaming With Crystals

There are four steps to follow for this method.[4]

Step I: Each night before sleep, program the crystal so that you will remember your dreams in the morning. Place it under your pillow so that it lies beneath your head. As you drift off to sleep, try to maintain your focus. Realize that this conscious focus may take months to develop. So don't give up; be patient. Remember that you are in the season of hibernation and you are not going anywhere. In the morning, write down any dream(s) remembered. Do not clear your crystal between nights. This way the vibrations of your programming will continue to build.

Step II: When you begin to consistently remember your dreams, select a dream that has continually reappeared or that has had a consistent pattern. Before you sleep, program your crystal (as in Step I) that you will dream this dream again. Place the crystal under your pillow. Maintain your state of concentration as when you programmed the crystal and slowly lie down in bed. Visualize yourself as becoming more and more filled with golden light. See yourself becoming so filled with this light that it spills outward from your skin and extends outward

from your body. In your mind's eye see the light extended outward about six inches from and roughly in the shape of your
body. Concentrate on this form of light. See it as being separate
from your body. Do not drop your concentration from this form
as you drift to sleep. This is the beginning of learning to control
your dreams. Continue this step until you can consistently
dream this particular dream. This is helping to build the
Etheric (Astral) Body. (Anytime you do not dream this dream,
clear your crystal).

Step III: When you can continually repeat Step II, clear
your crystal and program it for your travel to a place that you
have not necessarily been to in your dreams but have been to
in your waking state. Again put your crystal under your pillow
and concentrate on your luminous form. As you gaze at your
luminous form, maintain your focus on the place that you
would like to visit in your dreams. Make this your last thought
as you drop off to sleep. Again, record your dreams the first
thing upon waking. Clear your crystal if you dream any other
dream. Always reprogram it whether you have cleared it or
not. When you can consistently visit the intended location,
move on to the last step. You will begin to develop the power to
travel astrally.

Step IV: Now program your crystal for your visit to a location in your dreams that you have not been to on the physical
plane. Use the same process to program the crystal and drop
off to sleep as you did in Step II. When you wake, record your
dreams. Continue this process until you can visit this location
with ease.

When you have mastered this last step you now have the
ability to be anywhere or visit anyone on the astral planes. The
etheric bridge will have been built for you to be able to move
freely between the astral and physical planes with no loss of
conscious memory. Let me mention here that being conscious
during the dreamtime takes continual practice. It is not a state
of mind that is ever perfected, but a life-long process of retain-
ing balance between both worlds.

The goal for learning to be in the dreamtime should be for

the wisdom gained, the act of learning from it, expanding your sense of reality and likewise the sense of who you are until limitations seem to drop away. When limitations begin dropping away, you can gain a better view of death. By gaining conscious awareness of being in the dreamtime, or on the astral, fear of death will cease to exist because you have experienced that you exist beyond your Physical Body, mind and emotions. Dreaming gives you a state of quiet inner contentment and fulfillment.

If you are not quite ready to experiment with the dream state, a good place to begin in preparing your mind is with trancing. Trancing is a state which takes you out of this realm into a place that is between wakefulness and dreaming—a suspension of time, if you will. The most intense spiritual experiences all seem to involve the suspension of time. It is the feeling of being outside of time, of being timeless, that is the source of ecstasy in meditation, chanting, hypnosis, psychedelic drug experiences and trancing. Although it is briefer and less lucid, a timeless, egoless state (the ego exists in time, not space) is achieved through orgasm, which is precisely why orgasm feels so good. Though we have mastered the art of space in a hundred different ways, and know a great deal about space, we know pitifully little about time. It seems that only in the mystic state do we master it. The most profound mystical states are ones in which normal mental activity seems suspended in light. In mystic illumination, as at the speed of light, time ceases to exist.[5] Through the art of trancing, we can begin to understand the full meaning of space and the dreamtime.

Trancing can be done through the use of herbs, chanting and clapping. Performing Guedra (an ancient Moroccan Shamanic ritual) with a circle of women is most powerful and brings on an intense altered state for everyone in attendance.

It was 40 degrees outside. I was lucky, I had been told. I had come to Vermont during a warming trend! Lucky or not, warming trend or not, I was still cold and bundled in my Californian Winter clothing.

A group of women had collaborated on flying me back to their part of the country to teach Guedra, an ancient shamanic ritual that was practiced by the women societies in Morocco.

Guedra became part of the many traditions I teach. I attended a Middle Eastern Folk Dance and Music Camp one Summer up in beautiful Mendocino Forest in Northern California. One of the classes being offered was Guedra, taught by Katrina Burma. I went to Katrina's class every afternoon to learn the movements, chanting and clapping of this ancient ceremony. It was, to my surprise, a tradition that taught the art of trancing.

Katrina succeeded in ten days in taking us through the experience of meeting the quietness of movement, so very delicate and precise. She guided us through the energy as it shifted because of our chanting. We experienced our faces becoming transformed with smiles of serenity, and the sacredness that followed each trancing.

One sunny afternoon we gathered inside a large, wood building. The walls were lined with windows that allowed the Sun's rays to skip in and frame the beauty of the pine trees and mountains, allowing nature to still be a part of our circle. It was on this afternoon that Goddess spoke very strongly to me.

She said, "You must take this tradition and teach it to the sisters. You must form a core group. When the need arises to heal or bless or transform, this core group must come together in ceremony. Begin again. Send forth the sacred vibration through your clapping, your chanting, your movements.

"Women hold Power. Together you can direct that power to become caretakers once again of the Earth, and all forms of life. The time has come for this tradition to live again."

Katrina interrupted our chanting on this day. She smiled shyly and in her quiet voice said, "You are going too far out. This is only practice, not for real. You see how much power there is and how easy it is to go into trance?" We all mumbled an agreement.

"I can hear in your voices that you are getting out there." We laughed. "You know they say that the Western people are espe-

cially trance prone, or they get tranced easily because they are so trance deprived.

"*It's not that you are totally trance deprived,*" *Katrina continued.* "*Because, I guess when you are out driving in your car on the freeway you just sort of go. Or when you watch TV you get like this. But we don't have a focus for trance in our society, or a use for it.*

"*So, they say (in the Middle Eastern culture or in other cultures where they have more use for trance or more old traditions associated with trance), they say that when Westerners participate in them they get out there,*" *she snapped her fingers,* "*right away.*"

When we were finally ready for ceremony, we gathered in a lush green meadow. The sky above was unusually blue and cloudless. The small group chose a spot among the rush grass and pennyroyal stalks and sat in a circle. Soon the meadow filled with the sound of a kettledrum and clapping hands. We added our melodic voice to the music with an ancient Moroccan chant. Together we felt our bodies pulsing with the heartbeat of the kettledrum.

One woman with a black veil over her head moved into the center of the circle. The chanting drew around her, holding her within the very core of the chant's vibration. From under the black veil, the woman's hands appeared. Her fingers delicately danced, beckoning the spiritual realm to move closer. She reached out to feel the vibration of the beings that were joining the circle.

With hand movements from her heart, the woman began blessing the circle of sisters surrounding her. Raising her arms in praise to the Universe, she opened her crown chakra and filled with spirit light. Lowering her arms, she placed the palms of her hands on Mother Earth, grounding, completing the connection. (Plate 7)

Her body and mind gave over to the trance of spirit and she danced into the dreamtime.

The beauty of that day is still etched upon my memory. The tradition of Guedra now lives within my heart. The above scene

Plate 7—Guedra Circle.
An ancient Moroccan shamanic rite.
It is part of the women's traditions that I teach.

was one of the many Guedra circles I had the honor of attending during the camp.

I left camp with a new tradition that was ancient, and a new direction from the Goddess. Yes, the time had come for this most sacred ceremony to become integrated into our traditions and ceremonies of today. I vowed to keep the tradition of Guedra alive.

And so here I was, in Vermont teaching Guedra. This was the second time I had been flown out. During the last day of the workshop two women volunteered to trance. I would end the circle and the workshop as the last trancer.

When we first got together that morning, we shared our feelings about what we would like each of the circles to be. We agreed that the first circle would be for healing the broken spirit of women. The second trancing would be for the empower-

ment of women, and the final circle, in which I would be the trancer, would be for bringing the Goddess in and allowing each woman to experience the Goddess energy within. After taking a break before the ceremony began, three other woman decided they too would like to experience trancing during ceremony, and so, it was agreed that there would be two trancers per circle, which meant I would also double up.

Quietly, we reassembled in our circle. Some women constructed tiny altars before them; each wore a beautiful colored veil over her head. After grounding and centering, I called in the directions.

"The first circle," I reminded them, "is going to be for healing. Sisters, keep your focus on bringing the healing energy into the trancers." I continued giving instructions, while the two trancers chose which part of the floor in the center they would move to when the appropriate time came. We placed two pillows for them to kneel on, and I gave each a black veil to wear.

"Remember, do not move into the center until you are ready," I said.

When everyone settled in place, I began a steady beat on the drum. After allowing the beat to calm and center us, I nodded to the right side of the circle. They began clapping in time with the drum beat. After several beats, I nodded to the left side to join the rhythm with an off-beat. The drum and clapping continued for a few minutes at a steady pace.

Closing my eyes, I sent "feelers" around the circle, driving my energy through each of the women present, connecting up, until it made its way round and back into me.

I opened my eyes to see all eyes glued to my face. Smiling, I began the chant. All joined in with their specified part.

"Esh Hassan Tanih,
Esh ana amalih."

Simultaneously, the two trancers moved into the center; black veils pulled over their heads. Onto the pillows they crawled. Tiny, delicate hand movements reached out to touch the energy and find the pockets of coldness or blockages which needed to be released. Fluttering fingers moved in the air. Thumbs *flicked the negative energy away. Palms pulsed with the heart-beat and held the index finger up for all to see we were one. Open hands grounded the energy. Fingers touched the womb, heart, third eye and crown and reached up to the Universe, signaling openness to become a conduit for the healing energy to enter and travel through.*

The beating inched faster; the clapping hands matched the beat. The movements grew larger, arms swinging up and out, heads rolling from side to side, body arching and contracting. Total abandonment. Trancing. The energy escalated. The chant evolved.

"Wa howajah,
Ha heyajat."

The energy swirled in a cone. The trancers reached their optimum level of channeling the energy and released, bodies falling to the floor. The drumming went wild. The clapping went wild. The chant reached its peak.

"Jaoui,
Haoui."

The cone released. Silence but for the sound of the trancers breathing.

All hands rested palm down on the floor. All heads were bowed. All eyes were closed. Together we drew in the healing energy, channeled it through us and around the circle. Then we sent the residue into the Earth for healing.

Slowly the trancers moved out from the center, back to their spots within the circle. Patiently we waited for them to look up, eyes still wild, faces white and drawn. Then light, knowing smiles spread across their faces.

I nodded to each, smiled back, and opened the space for discussion. Messages were shared, as were the visions. A bit of speculation and the answers to questions.

The mention of anger was brought up, and with it a musing poured out of me. A musing that has become a pet peeve of mine regarding the so-called acceptance and continual usage of rage during women's circles. I acknowledged that rage was an important aspect of processing during healing, but that many women

—and it seemed more prevalent in lesbians—couldn't seem to process and work through the rage. Instead they held onto it as if it had suddenly become their life line, an anchor to being a feminist.

It was this surmising that brought a defensive remark from one of the sisters. She felt it important to tell me I had better watch what I said. I immediately knew she was a lesbian and expounded on my point by saying that first of all I clarify often enough that when I speak I do so from personal opinion and that I do not expect all my opinions to be readily accepted. I went on to inform her that my experience with lesbians was not limited and that more often than not "rage" was the fuel used during their ceremonies as well in their attitudes toward men. In conclusion, I elaborated on the opinion that when a woman gets stuck in the rage, she is not able to complete the healing process and move forward, and that until women are successful at moving through the counter-femi-patriarchy,* they would not be able to come to a balanced state in which they could then successfully find wholeness.

Our circle was dampened by this less-than-positive exchange, and though I felt rather attacked and put on the spot, I recognized that this was a recurring message I seemed to be put in a position of conveying.

I thanked the woman for her willingness to discuss this issue with me. A quick break was needed.

Circle number two—woman empowerment—was an interesting session. One of the two trancers was the woman who had been offended by my remarks. I'm sure she had been affected by our discussion. I know I was, and I attribute part of the chaos experienced with the session to her state, because the second circle took a bit longer for the trancers to reach their zenith, and one in particular just couldn't seem to find her releasing point. As a result, the energy became defused and drawn out. When the release finally came, the sisters in the circle were more than

---

* The term "femi-patriarchy" I use to describe women who are feminist and Goddess worshippers, but who take the same stance against men as the patriarchal stance taken against women.

ready to release as well. As a result the circle ended quite abruptly.

Silence embraced the room for a long time. The two trancers lay in the center for a long time. When both crawled to the outer circle, my debate partner broke down and cried. Sobs shook her body and wails rose up from deep within her. I motioned to a sister to my right to play her flute, and then initiated the circle into holding hands. We sat this way, allowing the wailing and the flute to dance.

In that moment it became so apparent that she was truly crying for all of us.

When her sobbing quieted and only her sniffling intermittently broke through, I began singing the Sister Chant (see page 103). The energy quieted down. The chant slowly ended. I asked if she was ready to continue. She nodded her head. Latter she told us that she had been unable or unwilling to share the reasons for her tears then but that they had come because after her trancing, when she lay in the center of the circle and knew the time for leaving the center had come, she felt so sorrowful, for she felt as if she was in the center of woman power and the womb-secure effect it had had on her was great.

"Trancing," I simply replied to her testimony.

The third circle was for the Goddess, and I was to be the trancer, joined by Deborah, a beautiful sister whose tender spirit I am dearly in love with. Separately, we pulled the black veils around our heads and, without words, settled which pillow we would occupy. We sat quietly waiting for Emily (who would be the circle leader) to begin the drumbeat.

As soon as the beat sounded out, I pulled the veil over my head. I clapped with my side and sang a few rounds of the chant, then closed my eyes and linked back up with the sisters in the circle by sending my energy through each until it returned to me. When I felt the returning energy enter my left hand and hit my heart, I gathered my veil in hand and crawled out to the pillow.

I focused first on myself, releasing blockages in my solar plexus, opening my heart and third eye, grounding my energy, all movements of which were done under my veil. Then slowly my fingers fluttered out to feel the energy being raised; no need to dispel any.

The urge to remind the circle of our oneness sprang to heart, and I held the sign up to each woman, making contact with tmy debate partner. Opening my self up to the spirit of the Goddess, I held my arms up to her. I included the sisters in my journey with a broad sweep. The ancestors were acknowledged, as were the present-day relations and the generations of tomorrow. I was ready and invoked the Goddess into our circle.

She was stubborn. Her form rested behind me just outside an east window. I beseeched her, and whispered words of praise to her, and showed her with my broad, surrendering movements that I was willing to receive her.

In a gust of wind she flew in to us, entering the room through the large window. She danced above our circle, blue gown flowing, hair wild and free. She was strong and powerful and I rose up to greet her.

"Tell them," she spoke to me, "that they may have my spirit. Tell them that I bless them." The room flared with light—sparkling, golden light. I reached up to touch her feet.

The drumming and clapping went wild and released. I lay on the ground panting, trying to catch my breath, unaware of the fact that I had tranced out and lost track of when I released. The quietness consumed and intensified the sound of my labored breathing. My heartbeat resounded in my ears. I opened my eyes and stared up at the gallery ceiling. Deborah moved to my left, bringing my attention back to her. I had forgotten she journeyed with me. I looked over at her. A white face with wild eyes greeted me.

Slowly she moved out of the center. I too crawled out. We sat there in silence. No one dared look at me and I suppose I dared not look at them. I wasn't quite in my body and I felt sick.

I heard Deborah mutter, "I don't understand what happened." I looked at her. "I lost all track of time," she added. I nodded and then looked away, pulling my veil over my head. Her words broke the ice and other women shared their visions. The Goddess had indeed graced us with her presence, and most everyone had felt her within.

In a few minutes my heart beat normally and my breathing regained its composure. I pulled the veil off and, after discussing the session, graciously thanked the women for honoring Guedra enough to bring me out. I closed the ceremony by having everyone, in her own way, move from quarter to quarter, dismissing the elements. The Guedra workshop had come to a close.

Guedra is a ceremony that was performed by the wise women. This ancient shamanistic ceremony has almost died in its homeland. Its survival has happened quietly. Grandmothers shared this sacred tradition with Mothers, and Mothers pass it on to their daughters.

Though the ancient ceremony of Guedra has faded, the current generation of female dancers in Morocco (more recently in the United States, as perpetuated by belly dancers) has managed to keep a rendition of it alive by converting it into a dance performance. Unfortunately, any time we take a ceremony and convert it into a performance, much of the magical sacredness is lost. The energy of the dancers lacks the focused vibration created by a chanting circle of sisters (which is nonexistent in a dance performance), and the movements become empty remnants of the past.

Guedra is a tradition that lives only through women who come together as a group, as a sisterhood; otherwise it will fade away and die. We as a sisterhood now have the opportunity to give new life to ancient traditions such as this one by coming together, by learning, by ceremony and by making ancient traditions part of our lives today.

However, if you are not learned in the art of Guedra, trance can be achieved by making a clairvoyant brew and allowing the herbal properties to take you off into a dream state. Shredded bay laurel leaves, mugwort and cinquefoil can be thrown into a boiling pot of pure spring water. A lid is placed over the pot to allow the herbs to steep. Carry the pot to your altar area, which has already been prepared for the journey. When you feel ready, lift the lid and inhale the vapors deeply several times. Do this for a few minutes, alternating between steam and air. (In magick, better results will be obtained by using the diaphragm while breathing. To find your diaphragm, touch yourself just above the navel, below and between the rib cage. As you breathe in, push this area out with your breath. This is natural breathing, very useful in magickal operations.[6]) When you begin to feel calm, relaxed, peaceful and slightly drowsy, stop inhaling the vapors and sit very quietly.

Allow the properties of the brew to take you into trance. When you return always record your experience in your dream journal.

Animal totems can also be worked with at this time, especially all creatures that hibernate, such as the Bear and Snake.[7] They are the dreamers and can give aid in bringing power to your vision eye.

In Native American tradition, the Bear represents introspection. In the Winter, it is the Bear that enters the womb-cave to hibernate, to digest the year's experience. To become like the Bear and enter the safety of the womb-cave, we must attune ourselves to the energies of the Eternal Mother and receive nourishment from the placenta of the Great Void. The Great Void is the place where all solutions and answers live in harmony with the questions that fill our realities. All answers to every question we believe in resides within us. Each and every being has the capacity to quiet the mind, enter the silence and know. Native Americans call this space of inner knowing the Dream Lodge, where the death of the illusion of physical reality overlays the expansiveness of eternity. It is in the Dream Lodge that their ancestors sit in Council and advise us regarding alternative pathways that lead to our goals.

This is the power of the Bear, the female receptive energy that for centuries has allowed visionaries, mystics and shamans to prophesy. Wearing the mask of Bear will help you walk the path of silence, calming the internal chatter. From the cave of Bear, you can find the pathway to the Dream Lodge and the other levels of imagination or consciousness.

The power of the Snake is that of transmutation, the life-death-rebirth cycle as exemplified by the shedding of Snake's skin. It is the energy of wholeness, cosmic consciousness and the ability to experience anything willingly and without resistance. Through accepting all aspects of your life you can bring about the transmutation through the emotional plane of dreams into the spiritual plane of wisdom, understanding, wholeness and connection to the Great Spirit. Through Snake, you can alter your consciousness enough to gain access to your dreams.

Dates to consider, research and celebrate in the future:

November 1:   Reign of the Goddess as the Old Woman
    (Celtic)
    Feast of the Dead (Mexican)

November 2:   All Soul's Day (English)

November 3:   Festival for the New Year (Gaelic)
    Hilarai (Egyptian)
        Harvest festivities dedicated to Isis
        and Osiris

November 8:   Festival of the Goddess of the kitchen range
    (Japanese)
    In honor of the Goddess Kami,
    Goddess of the hearth

November 10:   Celebration of the Goddess of Reason
    (French)

November 13:   Isis resurrects Osiris (North African)

November 16:   Night of Hecate (Greek)

November 22:   Festival of Artemis (Greek)
    The day of the Amazons

November 25:   Feast of Gaia (Greek)
    Thanksgiving Day (American)

December

The full phase of Winter is December. We are in the realm of the archer Sagittarius, and the expansive energy of Jupiter. This energy takes us actively into the higher mind, the super-conscious. Aspirations in life move into perspective and through the natural energies of this phase we can see into the lessons we learn through living.

This is also the time of visualization, preparing to give birth to new plans for future manifestation. In the darkest time of the year, we can begin laying the foundation of optimism and enthusiasm toward our future. We can begin creating a new philosophy, aspiring to reach new levels of higher education—the education of internal wisdoms.

During the waxing phase of Winter we began implementing dream work, and now in the fullness we can add the tool of visualization to our repertoire. Creative visualization, as Shakti Gawain, in her book *Creative Visualization* (Bantam Books, Inc., 1987), tells us, "is the technique of using your imagination to create what you want in your life. Imagination is the ability to create an idea or mental picture in your mind."

Since this is the season of hibernation rather than action, the energy is perfect for such inner, mental work. The technique for visualization is really quite basic. To understand how it works it is important to first understandably conceive a few basic principles: 1) the physical universe as an energy, 2) energy as a magnet, 3) form follows ideas, 4) the law of radiation and attraction, and, 5) using creative visualization.[8]

The physical universe is energy. Our physical universe is not really composed of any "matter." Its basic component is a force or essence which we call energy. Things appear to be solid and separate from one another on the level at which our physical sense normally perceives them. On finer levels, however, atomic and subatomic levels, seemingly solid matter is seen to be smaller and smaller particles within particles, which eventually turn out to be pure energy. Physically, we are all energy and everything within and around us is made up of energy. We are all part of one great energy field. Furthermore, this energy is vibrating at different rates and speeds, and this is the reason for separate qualities of solidness. Thus, all forms of energy are interrelated and can affect one another.

Energy is magnetic. One law of energy is that energy of a certain quality or vibration tends to attract energy of a similar quality vibration (like attracts like). Thought and feelings have their own magnetic energy which attracts energy of a similar nature. We can see this principle at work when, for instance, we receive a phone call from someone we were just thinking of.

Form follows idea. Thought is a quick, light, mobile form of energy. It manifests instantaneously, unlike denser forms such as matter. When we create something, we always create it first as a thought form. A thought or idea always precedes manifestation. The idea is like a blueprint; it creates an image of the form, which then magnetizes and guides the physical energy to flow into that form and eventually manifests it on the physical plane.

The law of radiation and attraction. This is the threefold law; the principle that what goes around comes around. What this means from a practical standpoint is that we always attract into our lives whatever we think about the most, believe in most strongly, expect on the deepest levels and/or imagine most vividly. So the more positive energy we put into imaging what we want, the more it begins to manifest in our lives.

Using creative visualization. The process of change does not occur on superficial levels through mere "positive thinking." It involves exploring, discovering and changing our deepest, most basic attitudes toward life as we have been doing for the last three seasons. That is why learning to use visualization during the Winter season can become a process of deep and meaningful growth. In the process we often discover ways in which we have been holding ourselves back, blocking ourselves from achieving satisfaction and fulfillment in life through our fears and negative concepts. Once seen clearly, these limiting attitudes can be dissolved through the creative visualization process, leaving space for us to find and live our natural state of happiness, fulfillment and love. When the seasonal wheel turns us into Spring we can approach the next cycle with a honed awareness and plant our action seeds from the already-laid foundation of creative visualization.

Creative visualization is magick in the truest and highest meaning of the word. It involves understanding and aligning yourself with the natural principles that govern the workings of the Universe and learning to use these principles in the most conscious and creative way.

With the peaceful effects reached during trancing and the use of affirmations, there are only four basic steps for effective creative visualization.

1. *Set your goal.* Decide on something you would like to have, work toward, realize or create (i.e., job, house, relationship, change in self, increased prosperity, happier state of mind, improved health, beauty etc.).

2. *Create a clear idea or picture.* Create an idea or mental picture of the object or situation exactly as you want it. Think of it in the present tense as already existing the way you want it to be. Picture yourself with the situation as you desire it now. Include as many details as you can. (You can make an actual physical picture of it as well if this will help you visualize it better.)

3. *Focus on it often.* Bring your idea or mental picture to mind often, both in quiet mediation periods, and also casually throughout the day when you happen to think of it. In doing so, it will become integrated as part of your life, becoming more of a reality. You will begin to project it successfully.

4. *Give it positive energy.* As you focus on your goal, think about it in a positive, encouraging way. Make strong, positive, present-tense affirmations. See yourself receiving or achieving it.

If we think of life as containing three levels of existence: *beingness*, *doingness* and *havingness*, we can achieve our desired goals much easier.

Beingness is the basic experience of being alive and conscious. It is the experience we have in deep meditation, the experience of being totally complete and at rest within oneself.

Doingness is movement and activity. It stems from the natural creative energy that flows through every living thing and is the source of our vital energy.

Havingness is the state of being in relationship with others and the Universe. It is the ability to allow and accept things and people into our lives, to comfortably occupy the same space with them.

These three levels of existence are like a triangle where each side supports the others. They are not in conflict with one another. They simply coexist. From this triangle of existence, this wheel of learning, we can easily see that first we must be who we really are, then do what we need to do in order to have what we want.

This is the basic concept of visualization: to connect with our *beingness*. To focus on our *doingness*. To increase and expand our *havingness*.

December is the point of mid-Winter. The Sun travels to its zenith away from the Earth, marking the Winter Solstice. On a cosmic level (refer to Chapter I), the Great Goddess is giving birth to her new born "Sun," and on an elemental level, the Earth Mother after being impregnated by the Sun Father gives birth to her children, the plant kingdom. In celebration of these two esoteric happenings, we can use the energy to prepare for our own rebirth and, through ritual, release into the darkest phase of the year those attitudes and addictions that have been holding us back, making room for the planting and manifestation of our creative visualizations.

Winter Solstice / Yule (December 21-23)

Winter Solstice can be celebrated in two ways: 1) honoring the Great Goddess giving birth to all creation and 2) giving our negativity away to the darkness so that we can rebirth into our visualized persona with the new solar Sun of Spring. In both of the above ceremonies, the following guided meditation can be used.

A Winter Meditation

The quiet darkness consumes our world, the longest night of the year, the deepest and darkest of all on the wheel.

This night hangs over us like death. Icy coldness sweeps over the land. Greens have turned to orange, and orange has turned to yellow, and yellow has faded with the waning season to brown. It is the time of sleep and stillness.

From the north, icy fingers blow, piercing the spirit, separating the warmth from the fire. Frozen and still, the waters become opaque, reflecting not even the barren image of the sleepy land. All is still, all is as death in this season of repose.

Now is the time to journey deep and come face to face with that part of you that is opaque and icy. The part of you that pierces, not only your heart, but the hearts of those you care about. Look long and fully at this coldness and see how in its murky state it reflects no warmth, no spirit. It emits only coldness. Coldness and darkness.

Take this part of you, which hurts yourself and others, and direct it into the land of sleep. As it slips into a deep sleep, its breath becomes labored and weak. The coldness, in its deep sleep, becomes death.

Detached, without emotion, allow the funeral of this cold, piercing, hurtful part of you to take place. Shed no tears. (Allow time for deep meditation.)

Hear the moaning of the Mother as she labors in birth, pushing and sweating with each heartbeat toward giving forth new life. As she releases the child from the darkness of her womb, it is received into the light, illuminating the night with its pureness.

The Sun of the Mother is born this night. Out of darkness comes the light. After death comes birth. Darkness and light. Death and birth. One does not exist without the other, for they parallel each other; intertwining and overruling each other, constantly in change.

In this time of darkness, when you have buried your negativity, allow the vision of who you want to be form in your mind, your heart. When the image is strong and every detail is in place, sense the waxing light birthing within you, reaching and growing outward from the deathbed of the darkness.

See and feel how the light illuminates your center, your heart, your mind, your body. See how the light illuminates and animates the new image of self.

Feel this light growing so intensely within. Know that you are the light, and shine brightly. And in your rejoicing receive from the Great Goddess and her divine child a gift to birth and nurture in the season of the waxing light. (Allow time for a second meditation.)

Filled with the light of the animated new you, holding the divine gift in your heart and mind, allow yourself to gently regain contact with the physical here and now. As you become aware of your body and the bodies of those around you, allow the light within you to continue to shine.

Tonight, the longest night of the year passes, and with it your old self. Tomorrow, the solar Sun will be rebirthed, and with it your new self vision.

When you are ready, gently open your eyes.

It was going to be a very quiet Yule ceremony for Rose Moon Tribe. Only three of us were in town and would be meeting. Because of this and the fact that I had just moved to a new house, I told the others that we would only be meeting for about an hour and to bring a white, red or green votive candle and candle holder.

When all three of us were gathered, I sat us down in my livingroom before the brightly lit-up Yule tree. I passed sandalwood for smudging and then grounded and centered us.

I planned to use the Winter Meditation and, as a prelude to taking them on their journey, I shared my views on how important I felt this Winter Solstice was. I told them,

"One decade is ending; a new one beginning. I believe that now is the New Age. I know many people believe the New Age won't officially begin until the year 2000, but I can't help but feel that it is now. Too many intense happenings are going on

all over the world at this time—not only on an elemental level but on a social-political level as well.

"The shifting and breaking down is going on at the end of this decade.

"What I really want to focus on tonight is the birthing of the 'woman' who is to be our foundation for the next decade.

"As we journey into the darkest part of ourselves, during this darkest night of the year, I want you to release all that you have learned and been for the last ten years. Leave it behind. Let it go." They nodded their heads with determination. Their enthusiasm renewed my fire. I continued.

"Once you have released, allow the darkness to consume you, and from the depths of existence allow the foundation to rise. Let it come in one of the following two structures: I am the woman of___, or I am She who___. Do you understand?" They did. I shifted position onto my knees.

"Okay, know this: as we come out of the meditation, you will have left behind, in the darkness, the residue of the last ten years. You will come out in a resting mode, prepared to become the woman foundation that comes to you during the meditation, but not until tomorrow morning. So, tomorrow morning, the first thing you do, before anything else, is face the Sun. The newborn Sun, and birth into your new woman foundation."

I led us through the meditation. When it was over, I let the silence surround us, the resting mode. I picked up the green candle before me and held it in my hands. I began chanting: "I am the woman of laughter." Soon, both Alexandria and Elaine picked up their respective candles, white and red, and began reciting their affirmations of "I am the woman of light," and "I am the woman of power."

When the energy felt right, I lowered the wick of my candle into the altar candle and lit my candle of rebirth.

"I am the woman of laughter," I said, holding my burning candle up to the ceiling. Alexandria followed suit. Elaine as well. We sat our candles down in their holders and looked at one another. No one spoke.

The candlelight danced off our faces, creating shadows on

the walls. I looked at the Yule tree, at the boxes beautifully wrapped underneath and then at the pentacle platter holding the bread. Reaching out, I picked up the platter.

"I bless this bread with new foundations of womanness," I said over it, and cut a piece off and placed it on a plate. I turned to Alexandria. "I pass this bread to you as the woman of laughter."

Automatically she responded, "I receive this bread as the woman of light." Alexandria in turn took a piece and passed it to Elaine saying, "I share this bread as the woman of light."

Elaine took the platter and said, "I take this bread as the woman of power."

The chalice of wine was passed in much the same way. We got silly as we ate and drank.

"I eat as the woman of laughter."

"I am satisfied as the woman of light."

"I am nourished as the woman of power."

"I am happy as the woman of laughter."

"I am blessed as the woman of light."

"I am strong as the woman of power."

We acknowledged each other in ten different ways. And finally, I broke out in hysterical laughter and could not stop, to which the other two responded, "You are the woman of laugher," and, "I hear you laughing as the woman of laughter." It was wonderful and special and powerful and just pure delight. Instead of trading gifts, we simply became the gifts.

When we quieted down and got serious again, I had us hold hands and reminded us that as the wheel turned, we were leaving behind in the darkness our hold on the last ten years, and that tomorrow when we faced the newborn Sun we would birth into our new woman foundation.

"It is up to us," I added. "We, the women, to bring about the change, the new attitude. It must begin with us. And so, if we choose to enter the new decade from a place of power, an act of power, than we will be the stabilizing factor of the New Age."

Dates to consider, research and celebrate in the future:

December 3:	Feast of Bonna Dea (Roman)
	Goddess of Justice
December 4:	Pallas Athena (Roman)
	Goddess of wisdom, experience and study
December 5:	Sinterklaas Day (Dutch)
December 8:	Immaculate Conception of the Virgin Mary
	(European)
	Festival of Ixchel (Mexican)
	Mother Goddess
December 9:	Feast of Tonantzin (Mexican)
	An apparition of the Virgin Mary in 1531
	to Juan Diego
December 13:	St. Lucy's Day (Swedish)
	In honor of Lucina, the Sun Goddess
December 17:	Celebration of Ops, Saturnalia (Roman)
	Goddess of plenty and fertility
December 21:	Winter Solstice
	Yule (Celtic)
December 23:	Fool's Day (European)
	Larentalia (Roman)
	Festival of Goddess Acca Larentia
December 24:	Mother Night (Anglo-Saxon)
December 25:	Juvenalia (Roman)
	Day of the children
	Celebration of Astarte (Semitic)
December 26:	Haloa (Greek)
	Festival dedicated to Demeter by holy
	rites at Eleusis and public feasting
December 31:	Hogmanay Day (Scottish)
	Fire Festival
	Festival of Vesta/Hestia (Roman)
	Goddess of fire, hearth fires relit

January

We have traveled the wheel of seasons into the most ardent waning phase, the waning phase of the season of death. Truly within the house of death, with all life at a perfect standstill, we can come to terms with truth.

Influenced by the scrupulous yet practical qualities of the seagoat, Capricorn, and governed by the taskmaster of the zodiac, Saturn, January is the most abstruse energy to be used in making contact with the Earth element. This can be done through the very bones of our skeletal system, which seems to depict the reality of death to our very immaterial minds.

One Winter during the waning of it, I took Rose Moon Tribe through a three-week intensive study on embracing Death. The first week, I asked the women to bring a bone (such as a turkey thigh bone) that was approximately six inches long. I led them into a deep journey, taking them to a safe place deep inside while holding the bone. The purpose of the journey was to connect up with the bone and allow the significance of the skeletal structure to be experienced, but most importantly to allow one to three symbols and one to three colors to intuitively present themselves to each woman. I ended the first week by focusing on the element of Earth and our bodies as an extension of this material.

The second week I again led the women into a deep journey while holding their bone, but this time I took them into the bone structure of the Earth and their own bone structure. I invoked the Crone aspect of the Triple Goddess, and informed them that we would be turning the bones into Death Goddesses or Owl Goddess figurines. After an extended journey, I allowed time for the symbols and colors received the previous week to be painted on the bones. (Between sessions, I had painted owl eyes on each bone.)

I spoke to them about death. I told them, "I believe that if we can come to that place where we willingly embrace death, we can transcend it. We know that our body returns to the Earth and we like to believe that our spirit moves on to other dimensions. Well, I believe that if we can truly understand death and conquer it, understand the connection, then we can choose *when* to leave this physical body and in doing so give this body as a sacred 'give-away.' " I said ideas that I'd never spoken out loud before and quite frankly don't remember all that I did say, but I knew I gave them brain food to digest because of the amazed expressions some of them wore.

Before ending the second session on death, I asked them to invite the Death Goddess into their dreams that night so she could bring them her wisdom.

The window looked in upon my bedroom. I stood at the sill and looked in past the lace curtains, through the brass poles of the headboard of the bed, down at two sleeping figures, the top of the heads the most prominent part of their bodies.

I pressed my face against the window pane and peered further into the room. I followed the lines of their bodies, molded under layers of blankets, to the footboard of the bed. I squinted at the movement I detected there. In the darkness, a black shape loomed. The shape flowed over the footboard and encroached upon the sleeping figure of the woman. Inch by inch the blackness covered her form. I became agitated standing there watching.

At the moment the blackness reached her head, I began screaming uncontrollably. For some reason, I was smothering. As my screams ripped through the night, the woman's body began struggling. Moans slipped through her dreamy, waking throat. They grew louder. The man who lay sleeping to her right lifted up on his elbow.

"Echo," he spoke. "I mean, Kisma. Are you all right?" He rolled over and reached out to shake her awake. "It's okay; you're having a bad dream." His arm came across her chest.

I screamed and opened my eyes. Jack's body leaned over me. I cried out and pulled the covers over my head.

"You called me Echo," I mumbled. He cooed comfortingly to me. "I was being swallowed by a black shadow, Jack." I told him. I rolled on my back and looked out the window.

"I was standing outside the window looking in on us, and I watched this black shadow come over the bed and swallow me." I was scared. Jack groaned and lay back down. He was getting used to my crazy night awakenings, but this time I had startled him.

It was difficult to go back to sleep. In fact I never really did. It was important for me to understand what had happened. I was sure I had been out to the Temple (I often woke up on my stomach looking out the window), but the shadow was frightening and I had reacted so strongly against it.

I opened my mind and called out to Goddess. She stood in the darkness, a shadow. Her voice streamed through the air.

She said, *"You called me into your dreams tonight."*

The Death Goddess!

"It is important that you never make another Death Goddess figurine. The one you have made is the only one you will ever need." My mind leapt out to the Temple altar where all the Death Goddess figurines now lay; the paint drying on the white, sun-bleached bones. Images of how the figurines could be used flashed in mind. I knew I had the power to call death in on myself or, worse, on others, if I ever chose to.

"Never invite me into your dreams again until you are ready to leave your Physical Body behind." A shudder passed through this physical body.

"You come too easily with me. You always have."

It was easy for me to leave my body. On several occasions, after leaving, I desired to keep going. It was always the black shadow, in the act of taking my body, that brought me back. I didn't fear death. I never really had.

Pain exploded in my heart. I thought of the other women who I had instructed to invite the Death Goddess into their dreams. Had I instructed them wrong? Would they be okay? Or would they all die in their sleep? I shut my eyes tightly and mentally reached out for the images of their sleeping forms. I surrounded each body with protection, wrapping it in a cocoon of white energy. In the next instant, the wind chimes hanging around the Temple danced lightly. I knew they would be okay. As in every-

thing else, each of us was at a different level of awareness sur-
rounding death. Each of us would receive our own wisdom and
instructions from this Goddess and the figurines we had created.

The final session on death was the sharing of the above
experience and the consecration of the Death Goddess figurine
as a tool to be used only during the waning Moon and especially
during the waning season. Each woman ended the intensive
study with a greater appreciation of death, a deeper understanding of the connection between her bones and the Earth, a
Goddess figurine, and new thoughts regarding the preparation
of relinquishing the physical when the chosen time arrived.

Dates to consider, research and celebrate in the future:

January 1:   Gamelia Festival (Greek)
               Hera and marriages celebrated
January 3:   Inanna's Day (Sumerian)
               Nativity of the Lady; Celebration of
               Inanna's birth as the evening star
January 5:   Kore's Day (Greek)
               Corn maiden, Lady of the fresh fields of
               wheat and barley; celebration of her nur-
               turing and protective power
January 6:   Feast of Kore (Greek)
January 8:   Justicia's Day (Roman)
               Goddess of justice. Themis can also be
               acknowledged.
January 8/9:   Carnival; Fasching (European)
               A yearly time of celebration just for fun
January 11-15: Carmentalia (Roman)
               Celebration of the birth Goddess
               Pregnant women offer prayers to her for
               easy deliveries.
January 30:   Festival of Peace (Roman)
               Pax is the Goddess of peace.

Though I choose to associate the Winter with the Great Goddess, the Crone can also be worked with in conjunction with the death aspect of Winter, as we have seen above. However, the time has come in the celebration of our Goddesshood to now embrace the Great Goddess within, that aspect of the feminine that wholly depicts the three faces/phases of a woman's life. She is the root or foundation of woman power.

We began working with the triple aspects: Virgin, Mother, Crone. By doing so we ease into the full body of Goddesshood. We come to understand that the changing of our attitudes throughout the year, let alone monthly, are a reflection of the seasonal energy shifts. We experience different degrees of woman power through these changes which prepare us to come fully into our own power.

The Great Goddess is the exalted form of woman on the most high level of feminine existence.

The Goddess Aspect of Winter—Great Goddess

Listen to the words of the Great Mother, whose cup of wine of life is the Cauldron of Cerridwen that is the holy grail of immortality, who is the Mother of all things, whose love is poured out upon the Earth, and who of old was called:

Achyls (Greek)
Adishakti (Hindu)
Aditi (Aryan)
Aeon (Gnostic)
Ahura Mazda (Iranian)
Ahurani (Persian)
Albina (Danaidic)
Ama or Amu (Sumerian)
Ama Tu An Ki (Sumerian)
Amari De (Romanian)
Amayicoyondi (Amerindian)
Amba Bai (Hindu)
Amenta, Amn, Amen or Amun
    (Egyptian)

Amirini (West African)
Amunet (Sudan)
Amma Attar (Arabian)
Anagke (Danaan)
Anann (Irish)
Anastasia (Roman)
Anatha Baetyl (Hebrew)
Ancasta (British)
Angerona (Roman)
Anna-Nin (Hebrew)
Anu (Sumerian)
Apsa (Babylonian)
Ardharishwar (Indian)
Ardvi Sura Anahita (Persian)

Ariana (Iranian)
Arinna (Anatolian)
Arnhemland (Australian)
Aru or Aruru (Sumerian)
Ashtart (Arabic)
Ashtoreth (Semitic)
Ashtaroth (Babylonian)
Asmun Nikal (Anatolian)
Ataertsic (Iroquois)
Atl (Aztec)
Audhumla (Norse)
Au Set or Au Sept (Egyptian)
Ayizan (Haitian Voodoo)

Ba' Alat (Arabic)
Bahu (Hindu)
Baju (Semitic)
Belit Aba Sha or Belit Mati
    (Semitic)
Birrahgnooloo (Aboriginal)
Boann (Celtic)
Brede (Manx)
Brigit, Brigantia, Briginda,
    Bridget or Brigidu (Celtic)
Briid (Hebridan)
Brizo (Aegean)
Buddha Krotishaurima
    (Tibetan)

Cabira or Cabiro (Phoenician)
Cardea (Latin)
Carnea (Roman)
Cesara or Cessair (Irish)
Chantico (Mexican)
Chimalman (Aztec)
Chomo-Lung-Ma (Chinese)
Clothru (Greek)

Coatllcue, Coatlicue or
    Coatlique (Aztec)
Cunt or Cunti (Oriental)
Cybele (Phrygian)

Dana, Danu, Donau or Danube
    (Tuatha de Danaan)
De Develeski (Romanian)
Deshtri (Hindu)
Devi (Indian)
Diakosmos (Pythagorian)
Diamond (Tibetan)
Dianoia (Gnostic)
Dol Jyang (Tibetan)
Dolma (Mongolian)
Druantia (Gallic)
Dudu Hepa (Anatolian)
Dynamis (Gnostic)

Ea (Celtic)
Edda (Norse)
Eide (Greek)
Elat (Canaanite)
Ennoia or Ennoe (Gnostic)
Enthumesis (Gnostic)
Epinoia (Gnostic)
Erua (Babylonian)
Esaye (Celtic)
Eshtar (Syrian)
Estsan Atlehi (Navajo)
Eurynome (Pelasgian)

Freya or Frigg (Scandinavian)

Gaia or Gaea (Pre-Hellenic
    Greek)
Garmangabis (Roman)

Ge (Celtic)
Gefjon, Gefion or Gefn
    (Scandinavian)
Ghe (Phoenician)
Gingira (Semitic)

Habondia (Roman)
Hagia Sophia (Gnostic)
Hanenca (Polynesian)
Hanna Hanna or Hannah
    (Anatolian)
Har (Babylonian)
Hathor (Egyptian)
Hebat or Hebatu (Anatolian)
Heimarmene (Pythagorian)
Held (Scandinavian)
Hepa or Hepat (Anatolian)
Henti (Anatolian)
Herit (Egyptian)
Heth (Hebrew)
Hilde (Scandinavian)
Hokhma (Hebrew)
Holda (Scandinavian)
Horn (Scandinavian)
Hsi Wang Mu (Chinese)
Hubur (Assyro-Babylonian)
Hudigamma (Hindu)
Huruing Wuhti (Hopi)

Idea (Gnostic)
Ilmatar (Finnish)
Imberombera (Aboriginal)
Inanna (Babylonian)
Ino (Centaurian)
Io (Phoenician)
Iris (Greek)
Ishtar, Ishtar Bel Daini,

Ishtar Latashiat, or Istar
    (Babylonian)
Isi (Celtic)
Istadevata (Tantric)
Ivi (Polynesian)
Ixcuina (Aztec)
Iyatiku (Navajo)
Izanami-No-Kami (Japanese)

Jagad Amba (Indian)
Jagad Yoni (Hindu)
Jnanashakti (Indian)
Jumala (Siberian)

Ka-Ata-Killa (Pre-Incan)
Kala-Nath (Semitic)
Kana-Yama-Hime (Japanese)
Kangra (Hindu)
Kefa (Egyptian)
Khamadhenu (Hindu)
Kobine (Polynesian)
Kriyashakti (Tantric)
Kubebe or Kupapa (Anatolian)
Kunapipi (Australian)
Kundalini (Hindu)
Kybele (Anatolian)

Lalita (Hindu)
Leucothea (Greek)
Levanah (Chaldaean)
Libyao-Pelasgian (Greek)
Lilwani (Anatolian)
Lukelong (Micronesian)
Luonnotar (Finno-Ugric)

Ma (Pontian)
Maat (Egyptian)

Magna Dea (Roman)
Maha Devi (Indian)
Mahuea (New Zealand)
Maiso (Guianan)
Maja (Vedic-Hindu)
Malinalxochitl (Aztec)
Malkatu (Semitic)
Malkatu Ashar Amaim
    (Arabian)
Mama, Mamaki, Mami or
    Mammitu (Mesopo-
    tamian)
Mamokuriyona (Yanomamo)
Mamaquilla (Peruvian)
Mami Aruru (Semitic)
Mantrikashakti (Tantric)
Marah (Hebrew)
Mardoll (Finnish)
Mari (Basque)
Marihan (Persian)
Marratu (Chaldaean)
Matrikadevis (Buddhist)
Matrikamantra (Hindu)
Matrona (Latin)
Matur Matuta (Roman)
Mawu (West African)
Mayuel or Maya (Aztec)
Mboze (Zaire)
Mebeli (Congolese)
Meh Urit (Egyptian)
Mem-Aleph (Hebrew)
Messak Kummik Okwi (Cree)
Methyer (Egyptian)
Metis (Greek)
Michal (Hebron)
Miti (Chukchi)
the Morrigan (Celtic)

Mommy Waters (Togo, African)
Mulaprakriti (Hindu)
Mu Olokukurtilisop
    (Panamanian)

Nammu (Sumerian)
Nana (Phrygian)
Nannar (Sumerian)
Nari (Hindu)
Netzach (Hebrew)
Ngame (Ghanaian)
Ninmah, Ningal, Ninhursag
    or Ninshuber Amamu
    (Sumerian)
Nintu (Sumerian)
Nefertim (Egyptian)
Negran (Arabian)
Nikalmati (Anatolian)
Nimue (Celtic)
Nin (Sumerian)
Ninti (Sumerian)
Nokomis (Algonquin)
Nu Kwa (Chinese)
Nungeena (Aboriginal)

Omeciuatl (Aztec)
Omicle (Phoenician)
Omphale (Lydian)
Orore (Chaldaean)

Parashakti (Tantric)
Philosophia (Medieval)
Phronesia (Gnostic)
Plastene (Centaurian)
Prajna (Tibetan)
Prakriti (Hindu)
Prithvi (Hindu)

Qadesh (Egyptian)
Qodshu (Canaanite)
Queen of Heaven (Hebrew)

Ragno (Pomo)
Ra Nambasanga (Fijian)
Rashith (Hebrew)
Renenti (Egyptian)

Salmaona or Sal-Ma (Eastern
    Mediterranean)
Sarvayoni (Hindu)
Savitri (Hindu)
Sept or Set (Egyptian)
Setlocenia (British)
Shaddai el Chai (Celtic)
Shakti (Indian)
Shala (Sumerian)
Shapash (Levantine)
Sharrat Shame (Babylonian)
Shayba (Arabic-Aramaean)
Shekina (Jewish cabalistic)
Siduri Sabitu (Babylonian)
Sige (Gnostic)
Sinkisha Amur (Semitic)
Sirius or Sothis (Egyptian)
Sitch-tche-na-ko (Pueblo)
Slatababa (Siberian)
Sophia (Gnostic)
Spider Woman (Pueblo)
St. Bride (Scottish)
St. Bridget (Swedish)
Sushumna (Hindu)
Sussistanako (Pueblo)
Syr (Scandinavian)

Tabor (Hebrew)

Tait (Egyptian)
Tamar (Hebrew)
Tanit (African)
Tao (Chinese)
Ta Urt or Taurit (Egyptian)
Tawawannas (Anatolian)
Tebunah (Hebrew)
Teeree (Hindu)
Teteu Innan or Teteoinian
    (Mexico)
Titania (Greek)
Triformis (Greek)
Thinking or Thought Woman
    (Pueblo)
Tho-Og (Tibetan)
Til-bu-Ma (Tibetan)
Tlazolteotl or Tlalteutli
    (Mexican)
Tohu (Hebrew)
Tonacacihuatl (Guatamalan)
Turquoise Woman (Navajo)
Tyche (Roman)

Unen-Em-Hetep (Elysian)
Urkittu Sharrat (Semitic)

Vari-Ma-Te-Takere
    (Indonesian)
Vidyadevis (Buddhist)
Virgin Mary (Hebrew)
Vivien (Celtic)

Walanni (Anatolian)
Waramurungundju
    (Aboriginal)
White Goddess, The (Britain)
White Woman (Honura)

Xmucane (Mayan)   Yolkai Estan (Navajo)

Yeshe-Khadoma (Tibetan)   Zipaltonal (Nicaraguan)
Yesod (Hebrew)   Zoe (Gnostic)

*I call upon your soul to arise and come unto me. For behold,
I have been with you from the beginning, and I am that which
is attained at the end of desire.*

Great Goddess moves with us through life, supporting the
many roles we play, laying the foundation for making possible
the manifestations we create, providing the structure needed
to release and allow death and change to cycle in and through
our minds, bodies and souls.

When we claim our power, or take back our power, it is the
Great Goddess who we are portraying. When we stand up for
our beliefs and the welfare of others, it is Great Goddess. She
is the motivating factor behind the most magnificent strength
portrayed through women of substance who initiate change on
a social/political/economical and ecological level. (The Triple
Goddess aspects are the energies used when evolving and/or
creating change on a personal level.)

Women such as Elizabeth Cady-Stanton, Vivienne Verdon-
Roe, Shirley Chisholm, Joanne Woodward, Patricia Shroeder,
Joanna Rogers Macy, Helen Caldicott, Susan B. Anthony, Mary
Harris Jones, Fannie Farmer, Jane Addams, Beatrix Potter,
Maria Montessori, Eleanor Roosevelt, Dorothy Day, Margaret
Rudkin, Margaret Mead, Rachel Carson, Katherine Graham,
Jessica Mitford, Elly Jansen, Gloria Steinem, and Winnie
Mandela (to name only a few) channel Great Goddess, though
some may not be aware or in control of her energy. They are
strong "movers" in society because they *believe* in the rights of
women and are striving to make this world and the conscious-
ness of man a more positive place to live in.

In addition to supporting women's rights, these women go a
giant step beyond and strive for the survival of our world, the
care of our children, and the balance point of partnershipping

and promoting peace throughout all nations. Much of their effort has been on nuclear warfare.

The threat of nuclear war became a reality to our consciousness when the Hiroshima bomb was dropped in World War II. After the dropping of this bomb, the minds of men went crazy (literally) with becoming world controllers. As a result the combined destructive power of the U.S. & U.S.S.R. alone equals 1-1/2 million Hiroshima bombs.[9] A devastating figure for our minds to swallow.

Because of the out-of-control military spending that resulted from the mind-dominator-craze of our government, our nation has experienced levels of poverty that should never have existed in a country so rich and abundant.

In the early 1980s, companies that provided the military with weaponry, such as Boeing and Lockheed, made profits of over $1 billion each.[10] Yet they paid no taxes, while the middle-class and low-income families of "our country 'tis of thee," went into debt making up for this injustice.

Due to the channeling of government funds into military spending, our children have also paid.* Ten thousand American children die each year from poverty.[12] Every child nutrition program in the U.S. had been cut or eliminated since 1981. A study in 1986 showed that if 5% of the U.S. military budget was directed toward feeding these American children, not one would remain in a hungered state of poverty. It is estimated that four days of worldwide military spending each year would end all starvation.[13]

"From the standpoint of conserving and preserving the most

---

*In 1991, 71 heads of state met at the United Nations for an unprecedented world summit for children—the largest gathering of national leaders in history. The summit brought forth the following startling statistics: Fifteen million children under the age of five die every year around the world—40,000 a day. The summit participants agreed on a specific plan to try to save as many as 50 million children this decade.

In the U.S., children are in desperate need of real presidential and congressional leadership to reach these goals. With nearly 13 million poor children, we have a Third World within our nation. One out of every four U.S. infants and toddlers lives in poverty. [11]

important resource that any society ever has—and that is its children—women have to become involved. So I really deeply feel that women can no longer be shrinking violets in a world which is threatened more and more and more by annihilation.[14]

These words were spoken by Shirley Chisholm (former member, U.S. House of Representatives) during an interview for the video "Women for America for the World." The survival of our children, the survival of our planet, has come into the hands of the women. We can no longer allow the men to solely "rule." We must take an active role in the political system and change what needs to be changed in order to guarantee the safety of life.

Addie Wyatt (also interviewed in the above video), Vice President, United Food and Commercial Workers Union, summed it up best when she said, "We [women] conceive the nation in our bodies, we carry the nation in our bodies, in pain and suffering we grunt the nation into being. We nurse it and we nurture it to help the nation to grow up. It certainly is our responsibility to help decide which way the nation goes."

It is never too late to sit up and take notice of what is happening in the government. I have never been a political person. My attitude was one of "leave it to the politicians" until I came face to face with some of the realities facing the welfare of my life and my future children's lives. It became quite clear one day that there might not be a future, so why bother ever having children? At 32, I still have not had the courage to give birth, but I have become more politically awake regarding military spending, world hunger and my country's homeless problem.

Has it ever occurred to you that the human is teetering between two worlds of reflections? Touch the Earth, for the Mother is awake. The Earth is alive and dreaming.
—Agnes Whistling Elk[15]

Ishtar

Chapter Six

REBIRTH ————
Of a Living Goddess

Throughout and about, transformation begins.
Within and without, the wheel doth spin.
Clear, white or black,
the center of Spirit
comes dancing and flowing to my circle
of life once again!

I woke Medicine Woman from her deep slumber. She yawned and opened her eyes. She sat up and sat there looking at me.

"It has been so long since you came to me," she said as her old figure rose stiffly, long white braids falling to her knees. "Where have you been?" she asked, not looking at me. "I have gone to sleep and in my slumber almost forgot you."

It had been a long time since I sought her out. I did not have an excuse to give, so stood there meekly in front of her. The head of White Wolf appeared through a hole in the air, then quickly disappeared. Medicine Woman stuck her hand in the hole and pulled him through by the scruff of his neck. White Wolf thanked the old woman lavishly with wet licks all over her face. Youth colored her high cheeks as a childish smile broke across her lips. Her smiles always made me smile.

"It has been too long." Her sudden scolding made me jump. "I have grown old."

White Wolf rolled on the ground between us, then sat down by her. He was happy to be with Medicine Woman.

"I am not ready to take you on a journey," she grumbled as she turned away. "It is not the time to journey anyway." She motioned to the sunlight dancing across the landscape outside a window. "It is Spring. So, I will sit down next to White Wolf and teach you a song." She sat down on a blanket next to the wolf, who automatically lay next to her and placed his white head in her lap. The whiteness of his fur and her braids blended together.

"You must learn it now," she mumbled as she stroked his head. "Then you can take it back with you. Sit down, child." She waved an impatient hand at me. I sat.

"Is it just for me," I asked. "Or can I teach it to others?"

Her hand stopped stroking the wolf. Black eyes studied my face. Finally, a smile curved her lips. For the first time since arriving in her domain, I relaxed.

"Do what you want with it," she spoke before beginning the chant in a language I did not know.

I finally memorized the chant after being scolded a dozen times, and then we sat in silence. As we sat there I wondered what the words were when translated into English. Before I could ask, she spoke.

"This chant," she began, "is for you to use when you cannot get to me but need my assistance. In singing this chant I will hear you and will be there."

I reflected on her words a moment.

"Maybe this time," she continued, "you will not stay away so long." Our eyes met. As we sat locked in the embrace, I heard her voice as it circled around my head like smoke rising from the sacred pipe.

Medicine Woman, where art thou?
Medicine Woman, come now.
I am right here.
I am right here, right here.
I am with you.

I am with you.
Deep, deep within you.

"Thank you, Medicine Woman."

And so once more the great wheel of life turns and we are brought back to the season of rebirth, the season of Spring. We have traveled through the phases of annual life, working hard and deep to gain access to the hidden Spirit of our inner Goddess through the doorways of the mental, emotional, physical and spiritual corridors of the subconscious.

We have become politically awakened in the sense of realizing the important part of life we have a role in playing, the woman power of life perpetuation, the safeguarding of Gaia, our Mother Earth, and the survival of our children and future generations.

The birth of the New Age is through the women. The revival of the feminine energy of life is through the Goddess of each woman. The love and the natural laws are taught through the power of the sisterhood. The societal consciousness change will be through the coaching and nurturing of the feminine balance.

Initiation

As you continue the celebration of goddesshood in the time of rebirthing, the second celebration you will participate in during the second season of Spring is one of initiation.

Women traditionally honor the initiation of a sister goddess at the time of Candlemas (February 2), which is the celebration of the waxing light, the waxing light of the soul, the waxing light of the Living Goddess on Earth.

The time of initiation comes after traveling a conscious path of evolution when you first desire to expand your consciousness. In celebrating goddesshood, you choose to enter into the spiritual arena of life. The word initiation comes from two Latin words: *in*, into, and *ire*, to go; therefore, the making of a beginning, or the entrance into something. In its widest sense, initiation takes you into the first level of being a Living Goddess and furthermore places you on the Path of Holiness in being a representative of the feminine nature or energy of life.

In choosing to be initiated, you are accepting the burden (if you call conscious evolution a burden) of actually changing the focus of your mental vision, developing it to a point where you have "tuned up" your whole being in order to be able to take on a higher vibrating rhythm. This rhythm is imposed upon your body by the Ceremony of Initiation itself, which in turn produces a greater awareness, a wider viewpoint, a deeper certainty. You become divinely stimulated. From the time of initiation forward, things which you could not accept or understand before become clearer; things which you could not do before become possible for you; things which you could not believe before become facts for you. By passing through initiation you become anchored to the depths within you and are no longer at the mercy of the currents and tides of human life. Vistas open up before your inner vision and you begin to sense the Path ahead.[1]

In preparing for initiation, whether you were consciously aware of this preparation or not, you entered into the university, or Hall of Learning, the courses in learning of which are based on *Knowledge, Understanding* and *Wisdom.* When you have passed through this school and graduate, you do so with a degree as that of a Wu Li Master of Compassion. You become a "spiritual" woman in the most technical sense of the word.

The courses on *Knowledge, Understanding* and *Wisdom* are reflected upon before undergoing the Initiation Ceremony itself. It is important to understand the difference or the connection between the three.

Knowledge can easily be termed the sum total of human discovery and experiences, that which can be recognized by the five senses and be correlated, diagnosed and defined by the use of human intellect. It is that about which we feel mental conviction, or that which can be ascertained by the use of experiments. It is the textbook, so to speak, of the arts and sciences. It is the components required for the development and building of physical things. Therefore, knowledge is the concerns of the material world, or material side of evolution, the matter in the solar systems, in the planets, in the evolution of humans and of our bodies.

Wisdom is the development of life within the form, the progress of the Spirit through the ever-changing vehicles of physical form, as well as the expansion of consciousness. It deals with the life side of evolution. Since it deals with the essence of the physical rather than with the physical itself, it is the intuitive discernment of truth apart from the reasoning faculty. It is the innate perception that can distinguish between the false and the true, between the real and the unreal. It is also the vision, the harmony, realizing the true inwardness of the great pageant of the Universe. It is the realization of the inner Goddess. Perhaps it might be expressed as the gradual blending of the paths of the mystic and the occultist—the rearing of the temple of wisdom upon the foundation of knowledge.

Wisdom is the science of the Spirit. Knowledge is the science of matter. Knowledge is separative and objective, while wisdom is synthetic and subjective. Knowledge divides, wisdom unites. Knowledge differentiates while wisdom blends.

Understanding is the faculty which enables us to adapt the things of the physical form to the life of the spirit and to take the flashes of inspiration that come from wisdom and link them back to the facts of knowledge, in essence, bringing to light the luminescence in which knowledge and wisdom eternally dwell and are linked within. One cannot exist without the other. One might say that wisdom concerns the "self," knowledge deals with the "not-self", and the understanding is the point of view of the ego or its relationship between the two points of wisdom and knowledge.

It is the initiation that places the ego in its rightful perspective, for it is this act that leads us to the mount of existence where vision can be received, a vision of the eternal Now, wherein past, present and future exist as one, a vision that encompasses all levels of evolution of our systems—mineral, animal, plant, deva and elemental—holding in unison and pulsating with life as can clearly be seen in the regular rhythm or cycle of life.[2]

And so initiation is a ceremony that not only takes place in the physical but on the higher subplanes of mental consciousness.

Making the conscious decision to undergo an Initiation Ceremony places you into a new category of living. It is one that disallows you to claim "ignorance" to life's twists and turns. You take a giant step into the supernatural or that of immortality because you are agreeing to go beyond the self-imposed limitations of society into the outer reaches of possibilities. When moving forward on this path, you begin to truly understand the dynamics of life and come to a level of awareness where life and death become one and the same thing, an event that can be controlled or surrendered to.

Though you choose to become a "spiritual" woman, let's face it you are going to have those days when you just want to put everything on the shelf and be dumb. Thank Goddess those days are far and few between, and when they do arise are short-lived. It is just simply too hard to play at being a mundane human after undergoing a spiritual initiation. When days such as these happen for me, I find that I withdraw and bury myself in the daily chores around my home. If I'm scheduled to teach or perform ceremony, I always cancel. I never force myself to be spiritual when my mind needs to refuel. This is just part of the cycle, a phase that will come and go.

Nevertheless, undergoing initiation is very personal and a very momentous occasion in your goddesshood. After making the decision, it is important to give serious thought to *why* you want to be initiated. Is it just to belong to a higher order? Or is it a very deep, spiritual calling? Understanding the motive behind this decision will help you prepare honestly for your ceremony.

Preparation for Initiation

Focusing on the vibration rate of the body becomes important. To help facilitate the change that the rate will undergo, minimizing your diet is extremely important. All forms of sugar, alcohol, caffeine and junk foods must be eliminated. Eating pure and whole foods begins the shifting on a physiological level.

Taking sweats or steam baths to open and flush out the toxins in your system is very good to do. Dry scrubs are also helpful. Drinking herbal teas is another gentle manner in which to flush out the system.

Daily meditation and affirmation are ways to begin transforming your consciousness. Realize that just because you decide to undergo initiation does not mean you are really "ready" to do so. By beginning a preparation regimen one to two weeks prior to the ceremony, you can confirm that this is what Spirit is guiding you to do. I have known people who, on the eve of their "Big Day," received a message during their meditation that the time for initiation was not yet here and that they must not undergo the ceremony. When this happens, it is best not to go through with the initiation. If you receive the "green light," get ready to celebrate.

I always advise my apprentices that it is best if they fast from 24-72 hours before the ceremony. During their apprenticeship they have had to undergo the mastership of controlling the body, and fasting for 72 hours (though always a major commitment) is easy to achieve. I request my apprentices to fast for two reasons. The first, simply because I had to undergo fasting in order to be initiated. But secondly, and most importantly, fasting is the spiritual acknowledgement that your body is indeed a temple, and that you are releasing all hold on your current life to be "born" into your Priestesshood.

When we fast our bodies can vibrate at a higher rate, allowing an easier transcendental state to be achieved. The senses become sensitive to the energies and your inner Goddess can rise to the surface.

For me, initiation is a very serious act of power. It is not an act to be taken lightly. This ceremony is a threshold, and once crossed you can never go back. When I hear of initiations that are made available in the course of one weekend, I always feel a bit disheartened at the "master" who is offering the initiation.

I often wonder, how one can become initiated in any tradition in such a short period of time? Ah, but the New Age is upon us, and many of the New Age teachers feel their guidance has made initiation possible in that time period. Perhaps they are right; who am I to judge their path?

The Initiation Ceremony

There are many ways in which to conduct an Initiation Ceremony; each tradition has its own. Therefore, realize that you can create ceremonies that are appropriate for each individual. There is no sense performing a standard ceremony just because it was performed by countless numbers of people in the past. These ceremonies become empty and a burden. We learn from them, however, and incorporate those components that carry meaning for us into our ceremonies while letting go of the useless aspects.

The following is a list of certain factors that make the ceremony intriguing (many of them having come from older and more traditional Initiation Ceremonies), which add a flavor of the past, or archaic, to the event.

1. Novice is blindfolded; this exhibits the trust the novice is portraying toward the circle of sisters gathered and the ceremony they are all about to undergo. It is a surrendering of being in control, of allowing oneself to be led, of flowing with the energies, of moving from darkness into the light.

2. Novice has wrists bound together, a reminder that all are bound when living in this world of the physical, and that we are bound when we willingly enter the kingdom of death.

3. Novice has one ankle bound, a symbol that the feet are neither bound nor free and that novice stands in balance, that all decisions to go forward must come from spirit.

4. Novice is halted at the gateway before entering the circle

and given a warning; the time has come for the novice to stop and reflect on her heartbeat, to confirm verbally for all gathered that her assent is, "yes," she does want to undergo initiation of her own free will.

5. Novice undergoes first challenge: the reciting of pre-agreed-upon passwords. The traditional passwords are "perfect love and perfect trust."

6. Novice is taken around the circle. At each quarter watchtower, she undergoes a challenge. This is done as a reminder that there are four directions, four elements, four powers, and four energies to be accepted and acknowledged.

7. Novice is read the coven/group *Charge*. (This is the code of ethics by which the group operates and/or adheres to.) The reading and acceptance of the *Charge* binds the novice to the core of the group. When novice accepts the *Charge*, she is then unbound and the blindfold removed.

8. Dedication to the Goddess. For those trained in witchcraft, the traditional Fivefold Kiss would be enacted on the novice.

9. If the coven/group has a sacred cord, the novice's measurements are now taken and added to the cord. If no cord is used, the novice is recognized as a sister/initiate/witch/wiccan/goddess/medicine woman etc.

10. Gifts are now given to the new initiate. Hugs and kisses are shared.

11. The new initiate is taken to each of the quarters and presented using her sacred/power/coven name.

The above are some of the traditional items that can be incorporated into an Initiation Ceremony. The ceremony can be, of course, as elaborate or as simple as each group deems necessary. Most importantly, remember to listen to the heart and allow the ceremony to birth from this power center. The ceremony is only as powerful as the person leading it. So keep it at the group's level. Do not try to stage a production. Leave these type of ceremonies to the ceremonial magicians.

I was cold. My teeth were chattering. The ground under my feet was damp and my toes were beginning to go numb. I stood off in the distance behind a patch of trees, alone.

My stomach growled and hunger pains shot through me. I had been fasting for three days. My body was more sensitive to the elements because of this, and I kept trying to open and become one with the chilly night.

Earlier in the evening I lay in a warm bath. I had been given a muslin bag stuffed full of lavender, salt, rosemary and dragon's blood to use for purification. The water had turned slightly reddish from the dragon's blood, and the slight fragrance of the rosemary and lavender rose with the steam. I tried to visualize the warmth of the water around me now.

The sky above was clouded, and the Full Moon was trying to break through. A light wind ruffled the otherwise silent trees. In the distance I could hear the muffled words of invocation being called out to each quarter in the circle where the other members of the coven stood. I peered through the trees trying to catch a glimpse of the circle but saw only an occasional red glow from the fire as it danced in the center of the stone circle.

A shiver scorched through me. I wrapped my arms tightly around my body, feeling the white cotton gown that covered my nakedness. I looked up to where the Moon sat hidden behind gray. I wanted more than anything to be blessed by her light. My arms rose up to her. Into the darkness I called forth to her, reconfirming that this night was the night of my initiation, the night that would confirm my chosen path which I would walk as a Priestess of Ishtar. Consumed by a feeling of ecstasy, I sang out the Charge of the Star Goddess.

"I who am the beauty of the green Earth and the white

Moon among the stars and the mysteries of the waters, I call upon your soul to arise and come unto me, for I am the soul of nature that gives life to the universe.

"From me all things proceed and unto me all things return.

"Let my worship be in the heart that rejoices, for behold, all acts of love and pleasure are my rituals. Let there be beauty and strength, power and compassion, honor and humility, mirth and reverence within you. And you who seek to know me, know that your seeking and yearning will avail you not, lest you know the mystery.

"For if that which you seek you find not within your heart, you will never find it without. For behold, I have been with you from the beginning, and I am that which is attained at the end of desire."

I opened my eyes. Before me shone, in full glory, the face of the Triple Goddess, Que bella Luna. I felt blessed and empowered. I took her shining as an omen that she would indeed light my path, both in full light and in times of darkness. I was truly becoming a Priestess of the Goddess, and I knew—deep, deep down inside I knew—that this night would change my life, altering the path I had been walking up to that very moment.

The crunching noise of footsteps forced me to turn and face my visitor. It was Morgana, the sister I had chosen to be my sponsor. It was clear she had witnessed my interchange with the Lady. She stopped before me and looked from my face up to the Lady's face.

"A blessing," she whispered. I nodded. "Well, they are ready for you." She presented a blindfold and tied it gently around my head.

"Hold out your wrists," she instructed me. As I did so, she proceeded to tie them together saying, "And she was bound as all living must be who would enter the kingdom of death."

She tested the tightness of the twine around my wrists and then stooped. I could feel her tying one end of the twine around my left ankle. As she did so, she said, "Feet neither bound, nor free."

She then asked me to whisper my new sacred name to her. I did so. After that she led me through the night to the stone circle. I was aware of being close to the circle. Garments rustled, and the edges around the blindfold glowed a soft orangish-white. I stumbled on a rock. A sharp pain interrupted my concentration, reminding me I was vulnerable.

Suddenly a hand pushed against my chest, bringing me to an immediate halt. Morgana's hand rested on my arm. From the darkness a voice spoke.

"Novice, I shall initiate you into the ways of the Wicca. Yet first I give you warning. If your heart holds doubt, please turn and return back to the life of the mundane. If you are of the same mind, answer with these words, 'perfect love, and perfect trust.' "

My voice cracked when I first tried to speak. I cleared my throat and then very loudly answered, "Perfect love and perfect trust."

Very aggressively, the sharp point of a knife blade was placed against my neck. Morgana's hand squeezed my arm. I believe I stopped breathing.

"Novice," I heard very clearly, "you who stand on the threshold between the lands of mortals and the realm of Spirit, hast thou the courage to make the journey? For I tell thee now, it is better to rush upon my athame and perish than to make this journey with fear in your heart."

"I have two passwords," I offered. "Perfect love and perfect trust."

"All who bring such passwords are welcome." The blade was removed from my throat. I breathed. The voice continued. "I shall anoint thee with the oils of consecration that thou be pure to enter the Temple of the Goddess."

A warm and oily finger touched my third eye. The voice spoke, "Let the mind be free." The hand moved down to my heart. "Let the heart be free." The hand moved again and touched my vagina. "Let the body be free. You are now anointed and consecrated. The journey may now begin. Do you still seek to join the Wicca?"

"Yes," I replied very assertively. Morgana once more led me forward by the rope which bound my wrists together. I was helped by unseen hands over the stones outlining the north gateway. In darkness I followed where I was led. We walked for a while. I lost sense of the directions, except the center which was clearly illuminated by the fire. After a period of being led around and hearing snickers and giggles coming from every direction and little pinches and caresses surprising me, someone stepped in front of me and I was forced once again to stop.

"Halt! I am the guardian of the East. Who goes there?"

"It is I, Kisma," I answered.

"What do you seek?"

"I seek to join the Wicca."

"From where do you come?"

"I come from the darkness, seeking the light."

"What passwords do you bring?"

"Perfect love and perfect trust."

"All who bring such passwords are welcome. You may continue your journey. Blessed be."

The guardian stepped aside. I was tugged gently forward. At the three remaining watchtowers I was challenged in much the same way. At last I was brought to the center. By this time my feet were no longer numb and I had long forgotten the chill in the air, in fact, I was sweating.

The warmth of the fire embraced me as I was guided to my knees before the altar resurrected next to the fire pit. I heard Morgana move behind me and then felt her hands rest on my shoulders. I felt protected by this stance she took. She suddenly became my support in this most sacred ceremony of my goddesshood. I secretly sent a prayer up to the Fates, wishing bushels and bushels of blessed love to flow into her life.

The "voice" interrupted my blessings.

"This is the Charge," it said. "That you will keep secret what you are asked to keep secret, and never divulge the names or dwelling places of our people unless by their consent.

"That you will learn and try to master the Art Magickal but ever remember the rune: 'What good be tools without the inner *light? What good be magick without wisdom-sight?'*

"That in due course you will strive to find a worthy pupil in magick, to whom in future years you can hand down the knowledge you acquire.

"That you will never use the Art Magickal merely to impress foolish persons, nor for any wrongful end.

"That you will try to help the Craft of the Wise, and hold its honor as you would your own.

"That you consider these vows taken before the Old Ones, before your sisters, before your Goddess, and that if you betray this Charge you accept as your just reward that retribution of Destiny which overtakes those who basely betray the trust and confidence that others have placed in them. Know that none can escape the Fate, be it curse or blessing, which they make for themselves, either in this life or in another life.

"Will you answer truly this Charge *and keep it in your heart?"*

"I will," I answered.

The blindfold was instantly removed by Morgana, who then unbound my wrists and ankle. Before me stood the Priestess Goddess. She held a pentacle platter out to me.

"Place your hands on this pentacle and repeat after me." I did as I was instructed.

"I have heard this Charge *and understand it."*

I repeated the words.

"I swear to abide by it. May the Old Ones, my sisters, my Goddess, witness my words."

After I repeated her words, the Priestess Goddess set the pentacle down on the altar and lowered a paper containing the written out Charge into the fire flame. She looked at me.

"As the smoke of this burning arises, so these words can never be revoked. By the Earth and the Moon and the Sun, in the name of magick be it done."

All eyes watched as the paper curled black, disappearing in the fire. The Priestess Goddess moved around the fire and kneeled next to me. She placed one hand at the top of my head and the other on the soles of my feet. Her words boomed into my ear.

"Do you vow all that is between these hands to belong to the Goddess?"

"I do," I answered.

"So mote it be."

A choir of "so mote it be's" rippled through the circle.

As the Priestess Goddess rose, she brought me up with her. For the first time she smiled. Without speaking, she lowered to her knees before me. She bent over and kissed my feet.

"Blessed are your feet that have brought you in these ways," she said and then kissed my knees.

"Blessed are your knees that kneel at the sacred altar." She rose onto her own knees, leaned forward and kissed my vagina.

"Blessed is your sex, without which we would not be here." She stood and kissed each breast.

"Blessed are your breasts formed in strength and beauty." Lastly, she kissed my lips.

"Blessed are your lips which shall speak the sacred names."

My head was spinning from the force of my kundalini. I was drunk and ecstatic and wanted to dance and laugh, but knew the ceremony was not yet over. Two women stepped forward and began taking my measure. One held the end of the cord at my crown while the other squatted and cut it away from the spool at my feet. One end of the severed cord was drawn around my head and a knot tied in the cord. Again the cord was drawn around my chest and knotted. When this was complete, the cord was handed to the Priestess Goddess, who then came to me.

She held the cord out to me, and as I took it spoke.

"In burning times when each member of the coven held the lives of the others in their hands, this would have been kept and used against you should you endanger others. But in these more fortunate times, love and trust prevail. So take this. Keep it or burn it, and be free to go or stay as your mind and heart lead you."

I took the cord from her and tied it around my waist. The Priestess Goddess placed her hands on my shoulders and looked me straight in the eyes.

"I recognize you as a Wiccan, as a Priestess of the Goddess. Be henceforward as a stone of the ancient circle, standing firmly based and balanced upon Mother Earth, yet open to the winds of heaven and enduring through time. Coven's Oath, keep troth!"

With that, a cheer went out and all gathered around me. Arms hugged me, lips smacked at me, smiles pressed in on me, and gifts were placed in my hands or hung on my body. A coven robe was wrapped warmly around me and a special medallion slipped over my head. When this welcoming ended, the coveners held hands and circled round me singing: "Look, look, look who's here; the Goddess is alive; the Goddess is alive." They sang it over and over, circling round, making me high from their energy.

Without warning the Priestess Goddess broke from the circling faeries and took both my hands in hers. She raised them to her lips and kissed them, then raised them to the air. Dropping one, she stepped aside and faced the Full Moon.

"Great Lady of the night," she yelled, "behold Mari-Ishtar, who has now been made Priestess and Witch in honor of Goddess this night." Cheers erupted.

I was taken to the east quarter. My hand was raised up to the watchtower.

"Great ones of East, and mighty ones of the craft, behold Mari-Ishtar, who has now been made Priestess and Witch in honor of Goddess this night."

I was taken to the south, west and north. When I was brought back to the center, I was told to give thanks to the Goddess, dismiss the quarters and open the circle, ending the rite. I did so with reverence and emotion. I felt powerful and blessed. One year and a day of apprenticeship had just been celebrated and a new path begun. I was officially an Initiate, an Initiate of the Sisterhood, of the Goddess.

When we circle round to the time of Candlemas, when there will be no Initiation Ceremony, we come together to

Plate 8—The Fertility Bed, in honor of Mother Earth and Father Sky, on Rose Moon Tribe's Candlemas altar.

honor the rebirthing of light, life and the inner Goddess Spirit. Candlemas can also be an act of dedicating a service to the caretaking and welfare of Mother Earth.

Candlemas / Imbolg (February 2)

A passage of power takes place at this time. The regeneration/impregnating power of the Sun's rays are passed into Mother Earth, at which time she receives them, beginning the incubation/germination process of nature within her dark, rich loam womb. That is why at Candlemas we make the Fertility Bed and place, side by side, an image of the Corn Goddess and a phallic image representing the God (Plate 8). We focus on the

*Plate 9—Rose Moon Tribe's Candlemas Altar in the
Temple of the Garden of the Goddess.*

Fertility Bed with the understanding that this is the night
when Mother Earth welcomes her lover into her vagina, and so
we encourage their communion. By performing such an act, we
are creating a sympathetic link with the Earth. Our magick,
therefore, works on a more subliminal level, not really altering
anything physical, simply joining with a natural course for
added impact and power.

Candlemas is a magickal ceremony, for the element of
fire is acknowledged and actually honored. Our altars are
floodlit with candles and/or (if you're lucky like my coven
Rose Moon) your altar will contain a fireplace wherein a
dance of salamanders will enhance the power of your ceremony (Plate 9).

The Triple Goddess is also acknowledged on this night as a

representative of the life phases, a reminder that we are but a spoke on the wheel and that, though we rest in between the point of life and death (Candlemas is the true point where the breath is both an intake and outlet), that movement is indeed only a breath away. This is the night where we breathe, gather our thoughts, prepare for action and move forward all at the same time.

The following outline can be used as a guide in creating your own ceremony. It is a basic ceremony that allows the aspects mentioned above to be worked with. (Remember, like any ceremony, it can be created to focus on one aspect or many. Above all, it would be best to always acknowledge the Triple Goddess or the Fertility Bed in order to connect with the energies turning the course of events on the physical at this time.)

I. Ground and center: focus on releasing hold of the Winter and the previous year's lesson. Be here, willing and ready to embrace the new cycle, opening to the stimulating energy and reactivation of the Mental Body. Be aware that this is the season wherein we prepare for the time of action by stimulating the energy of creativity, developing a strong, powerful and positive attitude toward the goal(s) we want to attain in the next year and setting up the new foundation from where we will journey forward.

II. Cast Circle
   A. Purification/smudge of each participant
   B. Scribing/outlining the circle
   C. Consecration with Sabbat Oil of each participant

III. Invoke Quarters

IV. Invoke God/dess. We invoke both Goddess and God, because on this night we acknowledge the male energy required to perpetuate life. (We are dealing with esoteric cosmology and, to keep balance, both powers are vitally important.)

V.   Raise Energy

   A. *Fire Chant*[3]

Chorus: *As we dance in the firelight,*
      round and round our spirits bright.
      As we dance in the candle glow,
      round and round our power grows.

      Oh Power of fire, we call to thee,
      May this night blessed be,
      Hail, Brigid, join our dance,
      Your bright strength our lives enhance.

Chorus:

      At the sacred forge we shape our lives.
      Up through the flames our spirits take flight.
      Hail, Brigid, join our dance,
      Your bright strength our lives enhance.

Chorus:

   B. When energy is raised, the lighting of the cauldron candle is enacted.

      Behold the burning flame of life.
      Behold the distant stars of fire this night.
      As transference of life and power begins,
      the time of Winter comes to an end.

VI. Triple Goddess is acknowledged. If you are celebrating with your group, three women can either volunteer or be chosen to represent each of the aspects.

   A. Virgin/Maiden dresses in white and wears flowers in her hair. She carries a broom, and when she is asked to come in she walks around the sacred space deosil (clockwise), sweeping out Winter, making way for Spring. As she walks she will recite a passage (below). When she has completed her round and stands before the altar, she lays her broom on it, removes the flowers from her hair and offers them as a blessing, setting them in the east quarter of the altar. When finished, she returns to the center of the circle.

B. Mother dresses in red and wears a candle-crown on her head. She walks the circle deosil, holding her hands in the "receiving" position. She is bringing forth the rebirth of light and life of nature. She too will recite a passage (below), and when she stands before the altar, she removes the crown as an offering, sets it down next to the flowers and joins the Maiden in the center of the circle.

C. Crone is dressed in black and wears a black veil over her head. She carries the cauldron in her left hand and moves her right hand over the top of it as if scrying the Fate of the next wheel. She walks very stately, deosil, round the circle, a reminder that though we are leaving her season and entering Spring, death always follows rebirth. She will recite a passage (below), and when she completes her round, she offers the cauldron and places it next to the other objects, joining the other two in the circle's center.

Before the Triple Goddess comes in, the circle leader prepares the space by acknowledging their arrival.

> *Behold the Triple Goddess: Enchantment, Ripeness, Wisdom. She who has three faces, yet is ever One. Without one aspect the others cannot exist.*
>
> *Like the Seasons, without Spring there can be no Summer. Without Summer, no Winter. Without Winter, no new Spring.*

Virgin *I am young, virginal, free.*
I carry the flame of life within me.
Sweeping out the Winter night,
I am the Spring's new seed of life.

Mother: *I have the secrets of the green Earth,*
I am the womb that forever gives birth.
I am the moon and the crystal blue sea,
and I call to your soul, arise and follow me.

Crone: *I am the wisdom of the Universe.*
I am the death after birth.
I am the darkness of mysteries rich and deep,
that none living dare to speak.

VII.   Visualization. All gather in the center and hold hands. Connect the group breath, have all close eyes.

You are going within to a safe and magickal place of renewal and insight. Begin to feel your body bathed with waves of warmth as the new Sun touches you. Slowly let your breath take on the natural rhythm of those waves of warmth as they wash down over you. Feel your body grow lighter, as your etheric self begins to glow with this warmth.

As you glow with light, you find you are in a place of safety and privacy where you can speak freely with your higher self. Know that Wisdom awaits you. Take time now to set a new goal with the Goddess—a goal that is a dedication and commitment to helping Mother Earth. This goal can be studying the things of the Earth i.e., herbs, plants, flowers, animal husbandry, gardening, ecology etc. This goal should be something that will unfold throughout the Spring.

(Silence for inner guidance.)

As the clear new sunlight nourishes the seed within the Earth, so this spirit nourishes your newfound awareness of how you can connect more intimately with Mother Earth this Spring.
Become aware of an inner force within you now.

This force is pushing and pushing, beginning its out breath after a long sleep. Sacred darkness slowly yields to your newborn light.

From this stillpoint of outer death, you have touched the wisdom of the Earth in Winter. Regeneration now streams from the Holy Earth to you and you are full.

Gather to you now the lessons you have learned during the Winter season so that they may empower you. Add this wisdom to the new light birthing in you and channel this life-giving force for the good of all.

(Pause.)

As you fill with your light and new dedication, gently open your eyes and come forward to the altar. Receive the passage of power by lighting your candle from the cauldron candle. As you do so say:

"I receive the power of light that the Mother be fertilized and the Wheel of Life be renewed."

Then speak out your dedication.

When the passage of power has taken place and individuals have lit their personal candles and spoken their dedication, everyone gathers around the Fertility Bed.

VIII. Bridget's Bed. We honor Bridget on Candlemas (however, use the Goddess personification that you feel most comfortable working with). I use Bridget because she is acknowledged as the "flame" of life and it was her Vestal Virgins that kept the Temple hearth fires burning. At Candlemas, we are the Vestal Virgins because we are tending the hearth fire and overseeing the creation act of nature.

A traditional call is "Brid is welcome, Brid is come!" This is said in honor of the male deity who is acknowledged as Brid. In ancient times, ashes were strewn around the bed. The ashes were checked in the morning for the footprints of the male deity. I leave two candles (on either side of the bed) burning all night to help light the way and show the willingness of Mother Earth welcoming "in" her lover.

Today, we sing a chant three to nine times over the bed to help raise the energy around this sacred place:

Thus we banish Winter,
thus we welcome Spring.
Say farewell to all that's dead,
and greet each newborn thing.

IX.   Cakes and Wine

X.   Give thanks to God/dess

XI.   Dismiss quarters

XII. Open Circle/ending rite

As you walk forward on your goddesshood path, there are many variables to deal with, such as different aspects of Goddess groups, whether one should hex or not, traditional versus New Age, as well as the personal accusations you will undergo from friends and family who do not understand what all this Goddess business is about and who are still suffering from the mindset forced upon all society through the conditioning of current religions. It is important to prepare yourself to experience them all, for on this path the above encounters are inevitable.

Different Aspects of Goddess Groups

Goddess is ancient. Her tradition and worship existed long before current civilization was even dreamed of. This has become a proven fact thanks to women such as Merlin Stone and Marija Gumbutus, who have devoted their life work to uncovering her existence and presenting it to the world through a very socially accepted manner: academia.

The worship of Goddess did survive all these thousands of years through an underground tradition that has been called a "cult," more commonly known as "witchcraft." To those of us active in the Goddess community, this is old knowledge, and we no longer cringe at being associated with the word *witchcraft* or being called a *witch*, because we have expanded our consciousness and gathered the true meaning of the word *witch* to our hearts. To us being a witch is simply being a wise one, learned in the Arts Magickal, which is the *Knowledge, Wisdom* and *Understanding* of the seasonal energies and cycles of life.

However, today Goddess groups are popping up all over, and as a result there are different aspects of this tradition with labels such as Gardnerian, Saxon, Celtic, Wiccan, Ceremonial Magician, Elfin, Dianic, Welsh etc. Because of this, we have become similar to the current-day religion of Christianity with all its various subgroups that fight among themselves, each claiming that they are following the teachings of Christ properly and condemning the other. Ugh! I shudder to think that we of the Goddess tradition can allow this to happen among us, to allow our love of life to become just another manifested, dogmatic religion.

Those of us actively involved in Goddess tradition should never claim to be the birther of this consciousness, nor claim that we have to have a certain sexual preference to rightfully claim to be a Priestess. We should not have to take certain political stances to qualify, either. We must live and let live, and join together, creating strength and support for all of us who honor this consciousness.

I believe that it is okay to fall under a certain traditional label, if that is the label under which you traveled the path of initiation, but let us not be so close-minded as to claim that our label is the rightful one or that all the others are less. We have the ability to truly exhibit the meaning of the concept behind the word "one."

Most importantly this understanding needs to take place between the lesbian Goddess worshippers and the heterosexual Goddess worshippers. We're all in this together. We can love one another as sisters and support each other in our individual paths. After all, we are all women, which makes us sisters, living goddesses on Earth. Let us acknowledge our connection and accept and understand and support and empower one another. I am not lesbian. I love and enjoy men, but this does not make me less of a Priestess. I am not politically active for gay/lesbian rights, but this not disqualify me as a supporter, either. My background is Celtic/Faery, but mine is not the rightful one, nor the only one. In fact, today I simply say I am of the Gaia Tradition, the Earth Tradition—no label, no origin other than that of Mother Earth.

In this moment of acceptance, I pay honor to all women who have brought forth Goddess awareness, whether she be of a grassroots level or of a public level. To those whose names appear, and to those whose names go unwritten:

May Goddess bless each and every one. May she bring us together, a sisterhood in life, showing the many aspects of her existence. Let the oneness, the sweet umbilical cord of our feminine energy connect us, bind us and empower us within our support of one another, giving us the power to birth forth real unity. Let our strength in numbers create the matrix, the foundation, the structure upon which the social/economic/political framework of life is changed and formed anew. Our breath, our voices sing in harmony, in unison, each song valid, each word an encouragement to all women. We are the new community. Let us not forget that now is the time to birth balance, not revenge toward the history of social evolution. May Goddess instill in us the wisdom and knowledge required to bring about a true partnership in life, where both sexes live harmoniously. A life that guarantees the safety of our planet and a playground for our children, seven generations unto seven generations unto seven generations. May Goddess adorn us with the tools that are necessary to change all oppression. Let us not fall prey to the ignorant dominator stance already taken, the stance which has proven to be destructive and negative. Let women not become femi-patriarchs. But most of all, may Goddess begin the changes needed by bringing together women as sisters, as friends. To all my sisters, I love you and I honor you.

I offer this blessing to:

Margot Adler
Debbie Aimes
Vera Stanley Alder
Paula Gunn Allen
Lynn Andrews
Maggy Anthony
Susan B. Anthony
Margaret Atwood
Jean M. Auel
Alice B. Bailey
Faith Barr-Glover
Ruth Barrett
Noel Phyllis Birkby
Jean Shinoda Bolen
Alicia Bonnet,
Alla Renee Bozarth
Marion Zimmer Bradley
Zsuzsanna Emese Budapest
Christina Budeweit
Anne Cameron
Che Queesh Auh-Ho-O
Carol P. Christ
Joanne Colbert
Norma Cordell
Meinrad Craighead
Imogen Cunningham
Mary Daly
Rosalie David
Helen Diner
Christine Downing
Brooke Medicine Eagle
Riane Eisler
Elsbeth

Janet Farrar
Lenonor Fini
Felicity Artemis Flowers
Dion Fortune
Selena Fox
Yvonne Frost
Phyllis Galde
Kay Gardner
Joy Gardner
Ina May Gaskin
Shakti Gawain
Marija Gimbutas
Alicia Goldman
Starr Goode
Marilyn Gotschall
Mary K. Greer
Susan Griffin
Rita M. Gross
Sue Handley
M. Esther Harding
Beverly Harrison
Lisa Hill
Hele Hoke
Josephine M. Harper
Jean Houston
Hallie Iglehart
Carol Isis
Charlotte Kelley
Colleen Kelley
Faye Kicknosway
Ochazania Klarich
Ladyhawk
Susan Lark

Ursula K. Le Guin
Sandra Lewis
Noel Lightbourne
Audre Lorde
Gay Luce
Johanna Rogers Macy
Diane Mariechild
Deena Metzger
Joni Mitchell
Barbara Mor
Nelle Morton
Nancy J. M. Mostad
Jean Mountaingrove
Ruth Mountaingrove
Shekhinah Mountainwater
Maureen Murdock
Barbara MyOwn
Vicki Noble
Mayumi Oda
Vonda Osmon
Kiyomi Ota
Jeannine Parvati
Kristin Peterson
Ellen Cannon Reed
Melvina Reynolds
Rhiannon
Anne Rice
Margaret Ronan
Sandra Roos
Gabrielle Roth
Anne Kent Rush
Mello Rye
Jody Sager

Ntozake Shange
Marsha Smith-Shaw
Monica Sjoo
Tamara Slayton
Charlene Spretnak
Elizabeth Cady Stanton
Starhawk
Diane Stein
Gloria Steinem
Betty Stepanich
Veronica Stevens
Merlin Stone
Patricia Sun
Luisah Teish
Lisa Thiel
Thora
Judy Tolley
Doreen Valiente
Vivienne Verdon-Roe
Karen Vogel
Wabun
Linda Waite
Alice B. Walker
Barbara G. Walker
Iona Wasbourn
Susun Weed
Marion Weinstein
Leslie Kanes Weisman
Anne Williams
Nina Winter
Monique Wittig
Diane Wolkstein
Patrice Wynne

and to so many others whose names have eluded me in this
moment of blessing.
    Blessed Be.

To Hex or Not to Hex

To use Zsuzsanna E. Budapest's words (*The Grandmother of Time,* Harper & Row, 1990), the subject of hexing is "thorny and scary," but one that must be understood and on occasion used. Z. also has written one of the best (if not only) pieces of advice on this subject that I have read. She says, "The craft advises us to 'do as thou wilt and harm none.' But what happens when we need to use magic for self-defense? We can call down the Dark Mother and ask her to help us. Killers exist only on the physical plane, their souls are saddened by the evil they are doing. We can call on their own souls to stop the evil, and their own souls will make them make 'fatal' (the Fates are our helpers) mistakes so they can be apprehended and taken out of circulation. Why is that more difficult to accept than taking self-defense lessons and learning how to gouge a man's eyes out or pull off his testicles? I prefer to do my spells without touching men at all. Isn't that the safest way for a woman to defend herself?"

I quite agree with Z. However, I do believe that a novice should never perform an act of hexing without the assistance and/or guidance of a qualified teacher. Even the initiate should give serious consideration before performing such an act. In any situation where a woman feels that a hexing is the rightful action to take, it is wise to discuss this with her group and/or contact women who are active in the Goddess community and discuss the issue with them.

I've used a hexing spell twice. Surprisingly, neither time was against the man who raped me when I was 18. At the time I was raped, I didn't understand the art of hexing. I only understood the *Threefold Law* and was confused about why such an act came my way. Also, I felt only pity and sorrow for that man. (His wild eyes still haunt me to this day, but I called for just retribution in whatever manner needed to happen.) Needless to say, that event did alter the course of my immediate life and took me further into my feminist stance. Today, if that were to happen (which it won't, nor will it in the future. So be it!), I must confess I would fill with rage and hex the holy shit out of him. But I would do so after contemplation, and discussion with my sisters. I would not perform such an act out of raw revengefulness nor from a state of wild emotion. I would ask for assistance and temperance and the wisdom of the Goddess community to guide me through the hexing.

In doing so I would enforce the safeguard of not calling further harm on my life by going crazy with my hexing and expanding the direction of my focused energy to encompass all men who oppress women, for, you see, I have no right to interfere with unknown aspects of life even though I know (through the media) that such oppressive acts go on every minute of the day. I will, however, come to the assistance of each and every woman who asks me to help protect her against the evil doings of another person (be that a man or a woman) and/or perform a hexing on her attacker to stop the attacker from inflicting further harm on sisters.

The hexings I have performed have been against gossipers who have sent harmful energies my way through their words. My hexings have consisted of making a poppet (a doll) of the gossiper and stuffing it full of certain herbs and a piece of paper with their name written on it. Before the hexing I work at understanding, whether or not I have substantiated the reasons for the gossip. I meditate, and if I clearly receive that the gossip is a negative trait of the individual, I continue with the hexing. Over the doll I chant that the gossiper learn the power of their negative energy. In the hexing I put up a "mirror" of protection around me which causes their negative word vibration to bounce off my energy field, reflect back to them and be absorbed into their own bodies. I take the poppet and bury it in the ground as far away as possible from my domain. As I am doing so, I chant over the grave, giving power to the lesson the gossiper needs to learn, with the affirmation that, as the doll deteriorates, the negative trait will be subconsciously understood and learned.

Whether I have a right to perform such a hexing or not, in both cases it has eased my involvement with the person considerably—though on one occasion the person complained to me over the development of severe stomach pains.

Let's face it; sometimes we are brought into a working environment with people we would normally not associate with. It is these types of situations that can be most unbearable on a long-term basis, and action on our part must be taken.

Furthermore, I also agree with Z. that "it is in the interest of women and men to help clean up their communities and protect them from killers. That it is in the domain of the Goddess to respond and help women to make their lives safe. That women have the psychic power to petition their own universal powerful force in their own behalf."

Traditional Versus New Age

All I have to say here is to each her/his own. Live and let live. We all choose the path we need for this moment in our spiritual evolution. If that path be of a more traditional level, wherein you study the ancient mysteries and go through a rigorous initiation process, then that is fine and wonderful. In more ways than one you will access powers rather than concepts, but it does not necessary mean that you become a more spiritual person for having studied such a tradition. Your spirituality is based on your consciousness, whether or not you can understand and accept. Likewise, if your path is that of the New Age, fine. Perhaps you will create a tradition that is very much needed, one that will guide us forward into the very balanced heart space we all seem to want to move into. But remember, you are not necessarily more advanced than the traditionalist, and calling on the "light" always and only is not balanced within itself. You must travel both sides of the spectrum and understand the variables contained within each aspect. "Lightism" has become a thing of the New Age and will not change everything.

In conclusion, both are equally valid and both must and need to exist. From each we learn and evolve in our understanding and awareness of life. What one lacks the other contains. Perhaps we can bring them together and find that balance, that here and now that is comprised of the past, present and future. After all, we are three dimensional.

Ending Persecution

It is never easy changing the consciousness of people who are afraid. To stop your own persecution, you must become learned in the terms that are applicable to your path. Understanding certain terminology and letting go of any negative connotations your mind may have in association with them is one of the first steps in altering possible accusations. You become stronger in your belief and can intelligently give a good representation of why the word is misunderstood. By researching your present path, understanding the history of it, you can also give guidance, directing individuals to resources that they too can read to gain a clear understanding. Theological discussions become fun and challenging instead of dreadful.

When you become learned in your tradition, you become a living example of all the positive qualities of your tradition's teachings. Your attitude shifts, your energy shifts and you simply are. You become a master, so to speak, and can speak intelligently about the misconstrued areas that still plague the minds of modern man.

So, to end the accusations that seem to naturally go hand in hand with any unorthodox religion and/or all spirituality (especially dealing with what has been termed the *occult*), become a scholar in your field and begin teaching. I believe the current religions call it "testimonials."

Living a Goddess life gives you power. At our finger tips are resources that can help us through every adverse situation that arises in our day-to-day life. We have but to remember that this power is available to us and call upon it.

It is not necessary to sit back and wade through the water as it floods around our ankles. We can take an active clean-up stance and prevent the flood from happening at the first onset of trouble.

For example, we constantly hear the term, "Be careful what you wish for; you may get it." This is more truthful than we care to believe. As we come into our power, we really do contain the energy and understanding to alter our reality, the physical. When we send up a prayer/blessing, we must be willing to accept the events that take place around us in order for Fate to give back to us the manifested version of the prayer/blessing. Sometimes the sacrifice we must make is more than we originally thought, but if we do not move with the changes required to receive the manifested prayer/blessing, an upset in our power will result, weakening us until our words are no longer heeded. Let me share an experience on this subject.

Just five nights ago (Thursday, March 1, 1990) I was leading a Wise Woman Circle at the Metaphysical Fellowship Church in Stanton, California. I was sharing the Roman celebration of Matronalia, the celebration of women and power. We were honoring Juno-Lucina, who is the protector of women and the family. Traditionally this celebration is for a prosperous and happy wedlock, as well as welcoming the new growth to the Earth. Bringing this tradition into current-day traditional use, I altered it and suggested that we perform a ceremony of Matronalia, honoring Juno-Lucina for her protection of women, with the added acknowledgement of taking back our power. The women who attended the circle were eager to undergo the ceremony.

After grounding/centering and purification, I invoked the quarters. We stood, holding hands and began raising the energy by chanting:

> *We are a circle, within a circle.*
> *With no beginning and never ending.*[4]

The Metaphysical Fellowship Church contains beautiful energy, and it took little time for the power to raise and alter our sacred space. I felt lightheaded and beautiful and proceeded to invoke Juno-Lucina.

Juno-Lucina, Queen of the Powers,
Bring me, bring me my own.
Let all that is needed be done well.
Let me sing of your glory under the Moon.
I am ready for my personal power.
I am the arm that does your work.
I am the mind of your thoughts.
I am the will of your achievements.
I am the conductor of your power.
Juno-Lucina,
I am the heart of your love.[5]

I continued with the Charge of the Star Goddess. The time had come to acknowledge women and our power. I picked up my magick mirror and held it to my face. I looked into the mirror and said, "Goddess is alive."

The women chanted back, "Magick is afoot."

I turned the mirror out to the women, reflecting my inner Goddess out to them, while mirroring back the sister goddesses that stood in circle with me. I said, "Juno-Luncina is alive!"

The women responded, "Magick is afoot!"

Again I turned the mirror back to me and smiled at my own face, acknowledging me as Goddess, and said, "Kisma is alive," to which the women immediately responded, "Magick is afoot."

I passed the mirror to the woman to my right. She repeated my actions. Around the circle the mirror went. Time after time the Goddess was acknowledged. When the mirror came back to me, I took us into the chant, saying it over and over and over again. It was great fun, and the women were really empowered performing this act.

When the chant ended and we stood swaying with the energy, we closed our eyes and went inside to touch upon the prayer each needed to individually offer to Juno-Lucina.

I was the first to kneel by the altar and pick up a white candle. I held the candle to my heart and prayed,

"Juno-Lucina, I offer this prayer up to you. Bring the 'time' I need that is required for me to finish the remaining chapters of *The Gaia Tradition*. Juno-Lucina, know that I am ready to make room for the 'time' you can give me for this accomplishment. Blessed Be."

I lowered the wick to an altar candle and lit it, then stood holding the flame before me. Each woman followed my guidance, offered her prayer, lit her candle and then stood holding out her flame.

I began chanting,

I am the old woman,
I am the new woman,
I am the same woman,
stronger than before.

The others joined in. We circled the altar three times and ended by bringing our flames into the center of the circle and merging them together, creating one large flame. With an inhalation, we blew out the flame together, releasing our prayers up to Juno-Lucina.

Our work was complete. I offered thanks to Juno-Lucina, dismissed the quarters and opened the circle, ending the rite.

The next morning (Friday, March 2) I was given two hours of free time at work in which to write. You can imagine my happiness over the fast manifestation of my prayer. However, I wasn't prepared for the biggest sacrifice required.

By Sunday, my most beautiful and intimate relationship was to change. Though the relationship did not end, through mutual agreement (and out of necessity for my sweet lover Jack who was feeling suffocated by the intensity of my love), we decided not to spend every night together. This change would allow us the space needed for "alone" time. Needless to say, I was quite saddened by this change and knew, within the crux of our four-hour conversation, that this was the sacrifice I would have to make because I had prayed for the "time" to write.

Monday morning I was rewarded with another three hours of free time at work in which I was able to write. Monday evening Rose Moon Tribe was to have a meeting. When I got home from work there were messages from each member of the coven. The majority would not be able to make the meeting. Again, I recognized this change as part of my prayer. I quickly called the women who could make it and cancelled the evening. I called Jack, who was on his way to play a game of basketball. We agreed we would not see each other that night. I hung up and gave my undivided attention to my writing. Today (Tuesday, March 6), I woke with a headache and depression. Without thinking I called in sick—presto magnifico—another day of "time" in which to write.

The moral of this story is simply: Be careful what you ask for; you just might receive it—and if you do receive it, be willing to make the sacrifice required to manifest your request.

So you see, the power behind my belief and the willingness to use the Goddess power at my finger tips allowed me to alter my reality in order to receive the time I need to write. As a result, in just five days I have been given the time required to finish one more chapter and possibly begin the last.

The taking of power and using it does not always result in a sacrifice. Calling upon the power for help is simply that, receiving the help needed and learning the lesson required so you will not have to call for help in that manner again. Let me be a little more specific.

Over the last seven years I have experienced many negative situations revolving around the management of money; i.e., credit cards and checking accounts. Five years ago I experienced the reality of the words *in debt* and had to borrow money to pay off credit cards. As a result of this financial crisis, I lost the privilege of being a cardholder of some credit cards, while others I simply destroyed. I won't go into the circumstances that led to this experience, but it was primarily due to living a wealthier lifestyle, deciding to leave and suddenly being on my own. However, instead of trimming my living style, I continued at the same materialistic level, which in a very short period of time became futile.

A year after the credit-card crisis, I had my checking account closed because of NSF items. Ugh. Well, I opened another and got the hang of keeping an average daily balance, and all was well.

Three years ago, my credit was back up there and I got a loan for a new car. I got a good job making decent money and I started spending again on a regular basis—not living above my means, mind you, but not denying myself anything if I wanted it. The momentum builds. You add cable T.V., daily newspapers, mandatory insurance, good food, new perfume, books etc. etc., and then the holiday seasons come along, you move into a new house and just have to buy all kinds of things you need in order to make this new house a home. As a result I started overdrawing my account again. For three months this went on until I got a letter informing me that my checking account was going to be closed. I panicked, realizing I would not be able to open another because of the credit checking system the banks now use. I went crazy because my rent check would bounce, and my car payment, which I had just bounced the previous month. I was frantic.

I dove into a mind disaster. Was I not supposed to have a checking account? Maybe I was supposed to circulate only the actual cash itself. Suddenly I felt very limited not having a checking account on top of already being very limited because I did not have credit cards.

Within two hours I was a menace to be around. I lost my cool. I blew up. I ranted and raved. I picked a fight with my lover. Then, as I sat holding back tears, while we (or he) watched a Lakers' game, I knew what I had to do. Quietly I got up and excused myself from the room. I went to his room and in the dark I prayed to Ishtar. I called on her power, asking for her assistance in this matter. I invoked her into me so that I could handle this matter and rectify it as a Goddess would. My chanting must have risen (I was really filling with power), because Jack opened the door, startling both of us.

The next morning I called the bank manager. The voice of a matronly woman answered. We discussed my account. I told her the circumstances revolving around it. She listened. After she confirmed the account was being closed, I mustered all my Goddess power and asked her not to close it but to allow me the opportunity to set it right.

In the moment of silence that followed my request, I felt the presence of the Mother flow in. She said to me through the bank manager's voice, "I hear the sincerity in your voice, and I know you mean well. I won't close it this time, but understand that if you bounce one more check I'll have no other course of action to take." Whether the woman actually spoke the next words or not, I knew they came from the Mother. She said very clearly, "You are my daughter and you must learn that if you want to play certain games, you must play by the rules."

It took six years and a last chance to learn that simple truth. I did want to play a social game, but I was refusing to play by the established rules. Today I understand how I had been revolting against the banking system. I know the inner attitude I had harbored toward this institution. Now, after filling with the powerful lesson of the Mother, I choose to play the game by the rules. Some rules are not meant to be broken, for, when we do try to break them, we bring more harm onto ourselves than anyone else.

If we learn to use Goddess power, we really can move forward. All it takes is the willingness to use it, accepting the strings that are sometimes attached, and the willingness to learn the lesson. After all, it really is quite simple. Action equals action equals action equals action.

Use the woman power, the Goddess power, the feminine power. It's our rightful heritage. Celebrate your goddesshood through the natural energy resources that are available to you. Walk your path, learning the lessons as they arise. Don't be afraid to ask for help in rectifying self-inflicted situations; that's how you're going to learn, through your own mistakes. Pray and invoke the powers of Fate, and, when your words become manifestations, be willing to make the sacrifice required. Be open to the changes that must accompany your prayers. Bend as the willow does. Be wise. Be free. Be empowered!

Rhiannon

Chapter Seven

CYCLES ——————————

Let the cycles of the Moon, the seasons and the wheel of life continue to carry you ever deeper, higher and more fully into your power, actualizing the ultimate potential of your goddesshood.

Journey onward. Learn and share, exploring the incredible experiences you undergo with your sisters, relations and community.

Create the richness in your life that you truly are capable of having. Set goals, for they are attainable if you but believe in them.

Use the power of the feminine to advance in your spirit evolution and to help you succeed in your day-to-day living.

Take the political stance of being a woman, an activist of the feminine, and support other women and our issues. Care for the children and welfare of Mother Earth.

Love deeply in your relationships, but above all be happy and know that below you is the powerful support of Goddess Gaia.

May peace prevail on Earth.
May peace prevail in your life.
May peace prevail in your mind.
May peace prevail in your heart.
May you know peace.
May your ancestors know peace.
May your children's children know peace, unto seven generations.
May peace prevail on Earth.[1]

Rick's living room was warm and full of warm bodies. We gathered to meditate. It was Thursday evening. I sat opposite Rick on an oversized pillow. I was bleeding. My womb center was swollen and tender, but when my body gets like this I always feel so much power from knowing that my sacred essence is flowing.

Pleasure. It is always a pleasure to attend Rick's meditations because he always seems to intuitively direct us into the inner realms where I need to work most—which is often the reason why I come to meditate. Too often my schedule is packed, and on free nights I want only to rest. On occasion when it is a Thursday and I am really working with something, I watch the clock and climb into my car at half past six. The short distance between my house and Rick's house, via the coast highway, always seems as if the view of the ocean begins the meditation process for me. Rick likes when I come. He is a good teacher and a good friend, someone whom I know will always be there.

On this particular Thursday night he chose to work with the Angel Cards and so passed a silk Chinese purse containing the cards around the circle. When I took the purse and slipped my fingers inside the soft lining, I focused on the discomfort I was experiencing in my mind. I withdrew the Angel Card Obligation. I smirked at the appropriateness of the card, as I had been feeling the pressure of teaching, and as of late I was feeling taken advantage of, a horrible feeling for a teacher to have.

I allowed Rick's soft guidance to take me in.

Plate 10—Wayne's Wash, Escalante, Utah

I went immediately to a high mesa overlooking the Valley of the Gods in Utah. There I sat on a red magic carpet which lifted and floated off. As the carpet lowered into the new landscape, I realized I was floating above the sand ledge in Wayne's Wash (Plate 10). Earlier this year I had hiked into the wash with my friend Kevin. During the night I was taken to the astral and given my first teaching assignment. I had graduated, in one sense, to a new dimension of teaching, for my pupils were silvery auras. I taught them that night about the connection and the star-seed, beginning their internal healing process. It had been an incredible experience, one that I knew would never be lost.

So here I was, floating on a red magic carpet above the sand ledge over the Medicine Wheel I had constructed during my backpacking trip. I spotted the same mugwort plant, and as

*if that was the cue someone or something had been waiting for,
the carpet lowered and touched down in the same spot where I
had slept.*

*Immediately I jumped off the carpet and ran down the ledge
to the giant cliff archway where the wash curved. Sunlight
sparkled on the water that pooled at the bend. I watched the
sparkles, absorbed in their dance.*

*Distracted by a feeling or a pulling of some type, I turned
and ran back to the sand ledge. The red granite wall of the cliff
towered above me and I moved to it. Red and strong it stood. I
placed my hands on it and tuned in. The heartbeat of Mother
Earth rose from deep within. To the right of my hands a black
stone rested on a small shelf. I picked the stone up and exam-
ined it. On its smooth surface there seemed to be a very light,
waning crescent scratched in.*

"Be constant," the stone told me.

*In that moment my Angel Card flashed through my mind:
Obligation. As if in response to my thoughts, the stone seemed
to reply.*

"Yes, constant as the Moon. For the Moon is constant in its
obligation *to cycle."*

I thought about this for a moment. Constant in its obligation
to cycle. *As I looked upon the surface of the stone it seemed to
appear liquid for a moment, watery. I broke the stone in half
and peered in both sides. They contained the Universe.* Constant
in its obligation.

*I became the Universe. The image of my body was outlined
against galaxies of stars and planets and moons.* Obligation.
*Clouds of gas floated in space, meterorites flared out and the
movement of planets and moons on their ecliptic courses took
place.* Its obligation to cycle.

*I closed my eyes, shutting out the vertigo effect the spinning
Universe had on my human mind.* Cycle.

*Without any warning the Universe disappeared and a loud
noise moved above me. I looked up and saw a winged shape
fluttering in place. A star being? A spirit? My higher self? An
angel? Angel Obligation? Constant in its obligation to cycle?*

"Will you come inside?" I asked.

The winds of its movement blew "yes" through me. My heart opened to allow the Being to enter. As it merged with me, each flutter of its wings tuned to the beat of my heart. Both movements became one. The separateness between us disappeared. There was only one. One constant in her obligation to cycle.

The cycle has always been our development. It is the element that takes us deeper and deeper into who we are and who we will become. In understanding the transformation I have undergone during the last 15 years, entries from my *Book of Shadows* highlight them most clearly. Let me share with you my transformation.

10-4-74

I have been drawn to the Great Goddess. Finally realizing the true spirit of my soul. Reading, reading and reading. Trying to consume all knowledge I can to open and direct me to the proper plane and consciousness of coming in contact with a coven of the Great Goddess and / or of the Faery Tradition.

I have found myself dancing to candlelight and music at the midnight hour and staring up into the sky. When the mists of the ocean float in, I want to go out and wander in them, possibly to cross that dimension between the two worlds of existence.

I feel my powers surge into my heart and mind. They come up from the ground into my feet. The feeling rushes through every particle of my being and explodes in a whirlwind in my brain. I feel a floating sensation and actually feel as if I could send all that power out into the universe. But then I lose it, and I'm back down again. I shall learn control!

10-9-74

My first casting of a circle and ritual to Mother. Amazing the emotions I felt. I sang, I danced, I asked upon her patience and guidance. I want companions to share this with. I felt charged. I felt the cool breeze of the air, the warmth of the Sun, the light of the Moon, the wetness of rain, the inner realm of living, that place between the worlds.

I still have a desire to run outdoors under the full bloom of the Moon. To be touched by her light. To drink it in and savor Goddess. I am goddess.

10-20-74

I have set up my first altar. I have not formally consecrated it as I am waiting for the New Moon to do so. I have come into contact with a new source, The Eye of the Cat located in Long Beach. I hope to join with someone to learn the Faery Tradition.

I went to my altar for the first time. This is my altar: a wicker trunk with a brown knit shawl draping it. The backdrop is a mirror. In the upper left corner of the mirror is a picture of the Mother and a girl-child; "learning" is the title of the picture. On my altar, in the center, is the picture of the Goddess ringed with yellow and purple little flowers I strung on a pink string. In front of the picture is a conch shell with a red rosebud in the opening or womb of the shell. To the right, or east of the picture, is a purple feather. Then my Book of Shadows, a censor and incense. A gold cord also lies in the east. On the right, or west side, is a white candle and a straw box. Inside the box are rose petals and a strand of my hair, braided and tied off at both ends with pink ribbon. Also a smooth piece of dark wood and a moon and stars I cut out of copper. On a piece of pink ribbon is a bell, a key charm, a heart charm and at the end a medallion of the Moon Goddess. On the corners of the altar I have different color scarfs tied through the brown knit shawl. I think it's a beautiful altar.

10-26-84

With each new phase I grow stronger. I become more tuned in, more aware. Halloween is approaching. A desire to unite and be with others is on fire inside me. The Goddess is flowing into my life. Feeling blessings. Love. Hope. Living for life and truth and light. At peace.

10-31-74
> *Happy Samhain,*
> *that time of year*
> *when the old ends*
> *and the new begins.*
> *Wiccan sisters*
> *in secret covens*
> *gather in the woods, or on beaches bare,*
> *to stand, thirteen strong,*
> *within the circle of magic.*
> *Ancient brand,*
> *Long before the morning hour*
> *touches light upon the Earth,*
> *the witches gather to dance and chant*
> *before the Prince of Shadows,*
> *the Lady, Goddess Diana's consort.*
> *Three times three,*
> *the spell is cast*
> *to light upon the world*
> *and touch the hearts of mortal men*
> *with Cupid's arrowed tips.*
> *And as the night time hour wanes*
> *into the midnight deep,*
> *the witching hour of long time past*
> *will flow justly.*
> *Trance and power,*
> *bright and strong*
> *springs forth into mind,*
> *and suddenly the eye*
> *can see beyond the veil*
> *the pure, ancient wisdom*
> *of goddesshood.*
> *Blessed be,*
> *'Tis All Hallow's Eve!*

These were some of the first entries I made in my first *Book of Shadows*. I was in high school then. But the wheel turned.

Ten years it turned. I worked solo, met a sister spirit, was introduced to a Celtic group and initiated into their coven. During
and after the initiation my awareness became heightened.

10-29-84

> *Ah, Sister,*
> *We have rejoiced in our union—*
> *A union from which we never really parted.*
> *For always do we linger*
> *within that same space of power,*
> *until we emerge to connect*
> *on this material plane once again.*

> *Yes, Sister,*
> *Forever do we hunger*
> *to return to the circle of wisdom,*
> *where ages long since dead,*
> *did we gather to glow in*
> *the universal law and bond of*
> *Goddess love and truth and*
> *life.*

10-30-84

> *Self realization, acceptance or rejection—each our own deci-
sion. Love and light, the inner essence of the heart. The heart so
very fragile, so very innocent. It gives of itself freely sometimes,
and no matter how much rationalization is done by the mind,
the heart has a will of its own, the will of intuition.*

10-30-84

> *I go to the night*
> *as a lover in waiting,*
> *holding on to the secrecy of the meeting.*
> *Stifling still the*
> *thrill of the essence*
> *that flows from the Moon*
> *to my veins.*

I go to the midnight hour
as a child in calling,
searching out the great wisdom of time.
Projecting forth and receiving all
substance of power the five points offer.

I go to the dawn
sleepy eyed and yawning,
crawling hungrily beneath the quilts,
to snuggle down with my visions
and to hold tight
to dreams come true.

11-2-84

Open wide to all that flows in, swallow the steam of life as it envelopes the soul—rebounding against the confines of the physical body.

Connections of the mind and psyche, revolving with silent whispers of visions of eyes penetrating into the heart, cages of the heart, bound eternally to a common space—once in contact no way of severing.

Denying sleep to learn and grow, conceiving the wisdom of old.

Ancient ones forever giving, forever flowing in and out, through the midnight hour, the dark of night.

New Moon
Full Moon
Dark Moon.

Flow within the designed path of light to accept the outcome of each idea, time between the worlds stopped in motion.

Endless.

Waiting upon the edge of dark.

Remembering, then dreaming—catching phrases here and there that connect us up with the short-lived past of life.

Connecting up with the ancient past.

Questions of the heart.

Questions of the night.

11-24-84
>   *Cycles.*
>   *Turning wheel of life.*
>   *Etchings in the night.*
>   *Shadow and light.*
>   *Onward spiraling and climbing.*
>   *Stages I have—*
>   *those of life,*
>   *down on level plane*
>   *where little girl still loves*
>   *to dance in the rain.*
>   *Cloudy days of gray,*
>   *water, water*
>   *live and wet,*
>   *sustaining moisture of life.*
>   *Cycles.*
>   *Here—there.*
>   *Always springing up*
>   *to say, "Learn. Know. Become!"*
>   *Flights, out into the side of life*
>   *that never shows itself visible,*
>   *but only gives us quick snatches*
>   *of wisdom*
>   *and the direction to follow.*

Then the cycle took me in. My Medicine Woman was birthed and I worked with herbs and flower essences, honing my skills of healing, healing of self first before I was ready to help others heal themselves.

2-17-85
>   *The ancient ones speak to me,*
>   *softly, subtlety.*
>   *I hear, listen and react.*
>   *Information of old*
>   *flows through the line.*
>   *Realigning me*

heart, body and mind.
Essences of flowers
melt in my mouth,
releasing, reopening,
lessons of love.
Simple foods are eaten,
flower water is taken,
prevention is promoted.
I cannot be whole
until I am cleansed—
purging of illness tucked deep in my mind.
Speak, wise one,
out in the dark,
outer world.
Come, force of Earth,
to revitalize and heal,
strengthen my will.
Flow down, warmth
from above—
gift from the Goddess
gift of love.
I am preparing to be taken
into your care—
a tool for healing—
a line for teaching—
a reaper for harvesting
all children home.

4-18-85

The essence comes in many forms;
when it appears it is as light as a feather,
thunderous as a storm.
Pureness, soft, soft gentleness,
bitter, bitter sadness.
In twos it comes, giving fully,
soft and secretly, pick up, pick up or control.
Receive or give.

The seeds need to be planted
  for the gathering is a twinkling of a light.

5-4-85
  How little faith we have—
    how is it we can try something once or twice
    and say we cannot do it?
  For did we expect to get behind the wheel of a car
    and drive it perfectly on the first try?
    Or a bike, ice skates or the cooking of a gourmet dinner?
  Did we not study and persevere with practice?
  Ah, sometimes I feel shame over how little we try
    in the spiritual.

Cycles. I moved into my power. Strong and dedicated to the Goddess and my path as a Priestess. Becoming constant in my obligation to cycle, I was brought into contact with Masters and Shamans of different traditions. In a whirlwind it seemed everywhere I turned I was connecting up with a teacher. I worked with Akuete Durchbach, an African herbal shaman and Virgiolo D. Gutierrez, a healer from the Philippines. Rolling Thunder, a Shoshone medicine man, called me one day and invited me to come meet him. Then there were Lynn Andrews, Black Wolf, Norma Cordell and finally Wallace Black Elk, a Lakota medicine man. Through them I experienced new levels of awareness, new levels of communication. With some I experienced initiation into their tradition; with the others I received valuable tools, tools which allowed me to go even further into my power.

I woke this morning in the dreamtime of Spirit. I was flying over land, through corridors, down streets, past buildings. Color was subtle, but there. I did not try to control anything: my speed, the scenes. I just went with the experience.
  I understood what Black Wolf spoke of yesterday. She said, "There are two dreamtimes: one of the mind, one of the Spirit World." We worked with the dreamtime of the mind then. She

took me into my power place and brought forward my power totem. But now I was in the Spirit World, realms of my inner being, realm of all realities and non-realities.

Before me was destruction. Erupting power of golden light. Women stood bound in chains, with black blindfolds over their eyes. Men were fighting, killing one another. I was witnessing the wars of the internal reality. I was witnessing the manifestation of the dreamtime of the mind, the journey Black Wolf had taken me on over the last three days. The journey which dealt with the realizing of self-bondage, the breaking apart of the blockages of the mind by usage of the golden light.

At first when I saw these scenes, I worried why I was in the middle of such destruction, such horrors. Why was I experiencing the Spirt World in such a hostile manner?

In that moment I became aware of someone holding my hand. I was being led through this world, past buildings raging with fire, children frightened and crying, the Earth screaming and expanding.

Then, through the self-realization we all hope to undergo in times such as this, I understood. I had to pass through these areas that were my closed gateways to the realm of realities and non-realities. I had to pass through this destruction to witness the drama which I created internally. By passing through, I would break apart, opening the doorway, the access which led to the dreamtime of Spirit.

Light erupted around me. Orange. Red. Purple. Gold. My mind reeled and scenes from the past day replayed. The people I had spoke with through psychic dialogue appeared: Father, Mother, Sister, Brother, Lover, Confidant, Friend. A warm rush of emotion spread through me. My body seemed to expand. The light subsided. Release came. The release of forgiveness I had worked on became real, completed. I was no longer holding on. The blockage which had prevented this process from completing itself had just blown open, and all the emotions of resentment and anger and expectations poured out, washing the destruction away, disolving the shattered scenes.

As the scene dissolved and shifted around me, I found that true freedom crept into the inner sanctum of my heart and mind. Through effort, through the belief behind the power of my words as I sang my Power Song, *through the affirmation that I would succeed, I did.*

The words from my Power Song *echoed around me. The world around me shifted and I was in a corridor of bluish-white light trimmed with sparkling gold. I walked down this corridor and became aware of birds singing. Birds in the trees outside my bedroom window. It was in this split second of conscious and subconscious awareness that all of the above took place. I was in two dimensions at the same time, both as equally as real as the next, only altered, different from each other in subtle ways.*

It was during this split second (of actually being split between two worlds, perhaps three), that I was acutely aware of being fully awake and surrounded by three women. They stood over me chanting, almost screaming their words. A ferocious man pushed them aside. He was painted and adorned the way I imagined a warrior shaman to be. His eyes bore down into mine, piercing me. Then he stepped back.

The women came down on me in a rush. With their fingers and teeth, they ripped me open. I was screaming. The pain was too great. My own blood clogged my throat, choking me. I was being torn apart. These three women were killing me.

The hand of the shaman came into sight. He reached down and yanked me up. As I lifted, a crackling, popping sound followed. He turned me to face the scene of my body being shredded and devoured. A bloody pulp of flesh lay sprawled beneath the frantic movements of the women.

I became aware of the sensation of lightness. There was no longer pain. I turned to face the shaman, my heart still beating from the terror I had just undergone. As I turned to face him, he held a red, spiraling whirlwind in his hands. The space in the center of the whirlwind was black, and white sparks of light flew from the red spiral. Gathering momentum, the spiral rose from the palm of his hand, growing in size. The momentum propelled the whirlwind from his hand to where my now unidentifiable body lay, knocking the three women out of sight.

I blinked with amazement and fear, trying to locate the women, afraid they would come for me again. Yet I was drawn to the whirlwind that hovered above the bloody pulp. It spiraled to a height of six feet. Its centrifugal force pulled bits of flesh and bone up into its spiral, splattering blood everywhere. As blood splashed over me, I gagged and threw up. At the same time I threw up, the spiral sunk into the pulp, reforming the body, pulling me back into the new form.

I was sucked in and, as I felt my feet enter the burning hot coldness of the flesh, I frantically searched for the shaman, who now stood poised, arms raised over his head, eyes closed. He was chanting. It was then I knew, he was responsible for all action that had taken place and was now taking place.

Excruciating pain shot through every part of me. I was blinded by this pain. I throbbed with this pain. All senses were totally absorbed with this pain.

As I opened my eyes, I was in the bluish-white corridor moving back to the world where I took physical form. The shaman stood in the distance. His voice shot down the corridor, but his mouth did not move. He told me that to control my movement in the dreamtime of Spirit I must not only sing my Power Song *but call on my* Power Totem *to prepare the way. He said it would be wise to evoke Medicine Woman or Aranda to walk by my side and lead me deeper, that they were the link I would require to solidness if ever I needed help. I stood there, unsure what to do or say.*

Sensing this, the shaman raised his right hand. A glow of golden light shot down the corridor and connected with my third-eye chakra.

"Shamaness," he said, "to walk alone in this dreamtime is not always good. To have your medicine with you is very wise."

I reached up to where his golden light entered my mind. As I touched my forehead, the light stopped. His image wavered and disappeared. As it did so, he said, "This is your shaman's eye, the corridor through which you have now been given access to travel into this dimension of reality. Choose well when the time to walk in this dreamtime will be."

The birds were singing outside my window. Whether I had my eyes open or not, I'll never know, but in that split second when all these events took place simultaneously, I saw the white mosquito net hanging above me, and yet the room was different. It was similar, but softer. Bluish-white veils hung everywhere. The covers and pillows of my bed were fluffy and white as clouds. A writing table made out of an almost transparent material sat off to the right; a bookshelf full of golden-bound books sat next to the table.

I blinked, and as I did so the morning light shifted and the items of my physical room became superimposed with those of the previous room in the dreamtime. Both worlds were combined for that split second.

Then I blinked again, and the physical world took solid form.

For some of us, the path continually winds up and down the mountain of learning while for others the path goes straight. Now I have settled into my own wisdom and that of Gaia. I no longer search for the answers, but sit quietly in my garden and watch the tender sprouts as they stretch just above the soil, the Earth still cracked and split apart where they pushed through. I contemplate the meaning of my navel and try to find humor. I have been far too serious for too long. I work quietly and, through my organization, Women Spirit Rising, I notify the women of my community when I will be performing ceremony. The door is always open; however, few walk through.

I dream of the sisterhood, women joining together in ritual, forming a bond, growing stronger, creating a support system, a network through which to work, but in reality this is still only a dream. The world is still plagued with the mind, the ego. We resent those whose names have become known, bicker between ourselves as to who is right and who is wrong or are simply still a child needing so much attention and reassurance—taking direction from others personally, rather than collectively. But this is part of the cycle.

Today, I underwent my power circle. For two years I have been gathering and constructing my power quarter tools. The sky threatened rain and a cold north wind howled through the sky, causing the blinds (the Temple walls) to flap excitedly.

I felt sad as I walked out to the Temple, and I wondered where all the sisters were. We have so much mending to do between ourselves.

I built a fire in the hearth, spread out my blankets, smudged and invoked the elements, placing my power tools in their proper quarters. I sang my power chant using my power rattle. I invoked the Goddess, and then I pulled the medicine blanket over my head, partially for warmth but mostly for inner focus. With the deer medicine rattle, I invited the gentle medicine I so badly need to guide me on my journey.

In my left hand, I held a sphere of lepidolite. With my right hand I shook my power rattle. (Rattling alters my consciousness quickly. It creates the same effect shamanic drumming does; it forces you to be right there with it, paying attention to that moment of awareness.)

As the heaviness slipped away from my shoulders and my jaw loosened so I was no longer clenching my teeth, I focused on my breath. I felt rushed. I wanted to go away. I wanted to fly and leave. Black wings spread out before me and I was beckoned to come, but the memory of the Death Goddess and the warning she gave me during the Winter season flashed into mind. I am not quite ready to leave this world behind. Even in my present state, I know it is important to work through this time of sorrow, of confusion.

I took a deep breath, tried to still my mind again. A mouse formed on the vision screen. I laughed. The medicine of the mouse comforted me. In my scrutiny of detail and reality, I must remember to look at the bigger picture. In that tone, I dived inside.

I invoke the Goddess eternal wisdom,
come forward into the physical,
come bring your wisdom forth into the light of my mind,
my life, my understanding.

I invoke the Goddess of air.
I invoke the Goddess of fire.
I invoke the Goddess of water.
I invoke the Goddess of earth.

I invoke the Goddess of above.
I invoke the Goddess of below.
I invoke the Goddess internal.
I invoke the Goddess external.

Spiraling, spiraling around me,
spiraling inside me.
Spiraling, spiraling around me,
spiraling inside me.

Inside the spiral I stand,
around the spiral I stand.
I am, I am, I am.
Goddess.

The dialogue of my mind continued. There was no denying it, the sisterhood was not completely formed. My heart bled. My sorrow was because I felt loneliness, misunderstood by other women who feared me, feared my position, feared my power.

Black Wolf once told me that the path of the teacher is rocky. She said, "Often you are brought into contact with those who truly hunger after their own power, but those who really choose to work at reclaiming that power are few."

She told me that to be a teacher meant being alone and that, if I had one true student, I was blessed. I guess I never thought that I would be so lonely. I guess I wanted to believe that women were so close to bonding that her words belonged to the teachers of the past or other belief systems, but not to the Goddess sisterhood.

When she told me that more often than not I would find myself working alone, performing ceremony alone, experiencing the magickal beauty of life alone and that it would be primarily through my stories that I would share my sacred journey with others, I didn't really believe her. I didn't understand the lesson she was actually giving, or that she was trying to teach me, the expectations she was trying to save me from having. The sorrow that I now feel is over the realization that her words are true. All she forewarned me about is true.

And so during my power circle I came to know that (as is consistent with all cycles) the phase I am entering has to be experienced. It is imperative I let go of my dire need to have the comfort and security of the sisterhood around me. I have to let go. I need to listen. I need to hear the feelings of others who walk around me. I have to let go. I need to be who I am. I have to let go. I need to allow others to experience and come to understand their problem of wanting to be me, resenting me because they aren't.

Clearly I learned that the women who live in my community close at hand would never be drawn to me. The old saying, "We take for granted that which we have" applies even to spiritual teachers and, unfortunately, to the sisterhood.

But then I was reassured. I received confirmation that my words and the sincerity of my spiritual journey would be received and shared by spirit sisters around the country, and I knew—suddenly I knew—that this was part of my power. My power would reach the sisters who really were working on their own Goddess, their own sisterhood, their own awakening, albeit privately.

Next, I was shown a golden-threaded web spreading underground, connecting up with sister spirits everywhere, a matrix of woman power. All would be okay. I would be okay.

"Be at rest in your home space," I was told. "Circle when it is important for you to do so. Those who join you should always feel welcome. Honor Gaia through the celebration of her seasonal cycles and continue to work with the energy shifts so that you are better attuned to the flowing current of life.

"Travel to where you are needed. Write your experiences. Send forth blessings and love to all sisters, all women, all men, all children, all life. And let go."

I took a deep breath, let out a deep sigh. Tears slipped from my eyes. The medicine blanket over my head fell back, and the cold wind gently brushed across my face. I sat there, looking up at the gray, cloudy sky.

I smiled.

The path of the teacher is a rocky one. It is a path that is filled with loneliness. Many will come who truly desire and hunger after their power, but few will choose to really work to attain that wisdom. If you have one real student, then you are blessed. More often than not, you will work alone, perform ceremony alone, and experience the magickal beauty of life alone. The path of the teacher is a lonely path, but the rewards are far greater than most will ever know.

To the Goddess of life, the ever-flowing wisdom of feminine power. We all come from your great body, and to you we shall return like a drop of rain flowing to the ocean.

To the Goddess, Mother of life, sister, friend, lover of feminine power. You are alive and magick is afoot.

To the Goddess in her many aspects of personality, shine above us, flow below us. Through the visible phases of your face as reflected through the small white orb that Moon's your body, mirror back your image to our awareness.

To the Goddess, whose wisdom and energy is the center of all women, awaken us to this strength. Stimulate our minds so that we are motivated to participate in your dance, weaving the web of creation, forming the circle of the continuing exchange of life. Form us anew, into the ultimate, powerful appendages of your power that we are capable of becoming.

To you we can then pay homage, honoring fully this female energy by being fully female. Let us take back the power, the right to manage our own bodies, minds and spirit. In turn we shall birth forth the balance of the eternal dance of life. By balancing the female with the male, we will reform the structures of civilized consciousness and teach a new way. Through a partnershipping of life, caretaking life, we will walk through the golden arches of time, cross the threshold between the old and the new, the past and the future. We will enter the sanctum of present, of now, of heaven, of living, of balance, of creation, of the heart space.

To the Goddess that dwells within, I give thanks for all the realizations that flow up from your well of wisdom. My heart is full. Blessed be.

Power of air that flows from the east, it is your life that passes through my body as the intake and release of breath. You are the power which carries the currents of movement of life, stirring the mind awake, stimulating the Mental Body to birth forth with inspiration.

Power that flows from the east, it is your birthing light that reveals the path we must individually travel. It is your light that clarifies the decisions we need to make.

I give thanks for your power of light-inspired breath. In beauty and strength, may your power continue to live. Blessed be.

Power of fire, the power of my inner life spark, it is your essence that flares within and activates my body into action. Your power burns into my cells, the passion of living, of dancing, of singing, of loving.

Power of south, the power of innocence and creativity, it is in your house that the inner child runs wild, the sacred place of experience.

I give thanks to your passion that has sparked my inner child into action, for it is your fire that burns wildly inside my heart, pushing me forward to reach out and play with other sis-

ters. *May you continue to dance with power and compassion. Blessed be.*

Great power of water, life blood, substenance which fills my body with the wells of love and feelings. It is your power that pools and overflows the inner knowing into my heart. It is your flowing force that magickally enlists my consciousness into the act of giving and receiving.

The place of woman power, the west, the great womb of female energy. It is your sacred place where life wanes, where the great experience of mystery of death resides, death of the physical, death of the ego. It is in your cauldron of regeneration where I scry upon the wisdom of the life/death cycle, deepest mystery of all.

I give thanks for this knowing, this sharing of wisdom. It is from you that I have gained the awareness surrounding the honoring of the womb, the flowing of the woman power, the mystery of life. It is through your essence I have learned the meaning of sisterhood. May your power continue to flow in honor and humility. Blessed be.

Power of Earth, the foundation, life-support system upon which all life dwells. It is your rich structure that perpetuates the abundance from which we live. The food of your body satisfies our hungry. You are the substance which forms the bones of our bodies. To you, I give back my physicalness when the day of transformation arrives.

You are the power of the north, the place of repose and regeneration. It is your power that teaches the still point before the cycles of life begins to turn once more. In your silence I have come to the place of the true acceptance required to fully integrate the lessons of wisdom that were experienced through the knowledge gained through living.

I give thanks to your power of solidness. I give thanks to you, the teacher of the physical. May your power continue to stand strong in times of mirth and reverence. Blessed be.

To the powers that reside above, the umbrella of protection that shields us from the powerful rays that fall down upon us from the Universes, the powerful rays that we are not yet evolved enough to receive, I give thanks. May your rainbow rise forever over us. Blessed be.

To the power that resides below, the hammock of support that holds us in suspended rest, not allowing us to fall away and sink beneath into the deepness of the dark that we are not yet evolved enough to delve into, I give thanks. May your reflection forever remind us of your depths. Blessed be.

The circle is open but ever unbroken. May the love and the peace of the Goddess go in your hearts. Merry meet, and merry part, and merry meet again.
Blessed be.
This rite has ended.

Notes ——————————————————————

Chapter I

1. Genesis 2:7, *Holy Bible*, King James Version
2. *Exploring the Cosmos*, Berman & Evans
3. *Thinking Like a Mountain*, Seed, Macy, Fleming & Naess.

Chapter II

1. *Lost Goddesses of Early Greece*, Spretnak
2. *Spiritual Value of Gemstones*, Richardson & Huett

Chapter III

1. *Natural Magic*, Valiente
2. *The Power of Love*, Frankie Goes To Hollywood
   (1984, Welcome to the Pleasuredome LP)
3. Saint Germain Foundation, 1120 Stonehedge Drive,
   Schaumburg, ILL 60194 (800/662-2800)
4. *Candle Power*, Mella

Chapter IV

1. *Magical Rites From the Crystal Well*, Fitch & Renee
2. *Harvest Dance*, Angie Remedi, 1984
3. Journal Entry, Lisa Hill, 1987

Chapter V

1. *Medicine Woman*, Andrews
2. *Dreams: Their Mysteries Revealed*, Dudley
3. Andrews, *Ibid.*
4. *The Complete Crystal Guidebook*, Silbey
5. *Jitterbug Perfume*, Robbins
6. *Magical Herbalism*, Cunningham
7. *Medicine Cards*, Sams & Carson
8. *Creative Visualization*, Gawain
9. *Nukespeake: The Selling of Nuclear Technology in America*, Hilgartner, Bell & O'Connor
10. *Speaking Up & Speaking Out*, Verdon-Roe
11. Children's Defense Fund 1991 Report after UN Summit, Marian Wright Edelman (President) and James D. Weill (General Counsel of)
12. *A Children's Defense Budget*: An Analysis of the President's FY 1986 Budget and Children by the Children's Defense Fund
13. Council on Economic Realities
14. *Women for America, for The World*, Verdon-Roe
15. Andrews, *Ibid.*

Chapter VI

1. *The Initiation of the World*, Alder
2. *Initiation: Human and Solar*, Bailey
3. Elsbeth and Thora (Cauldron of Cerridwen Coven, 1986 Candlemas Ritual)
4. *Welcome to Annwfn*, Rick Hamouris (1986, audiocassette, Nemeton)
5. *The Grandmother of Time*, Budapest

Chapter VII

1. Ochazania Klarich

Bibliography

Alder, Vera Stanley, *The Initiation of the World*, (1939, Rider & Co.).

Anderson, Mary, *Colour Healing* (1975, The Aquarian Press).

Andrews, Lynn V., *Medicine Woman* (1981, Harper & Row).

Bailey, Alice B., *Initiation: Human and Solar*, (1922, Lucis Publishing Company).

Berman, L., and J.C. Evans, *Exploring the Cosmos* (1983, Little Brown and Company).

Bolen, Jean Shinoda, *Goddesses In Every Woman* (1984, Harper & Row).

Budapest, Z., *The Holy Book of Women's Mysteries, Part I & II*, (1979, Susan B. Anthony Coven No. 1).

Budapest, Zsuzsanna E., *The Grandmother of Time*, (1989, Harper & Row, Publisher, Inc.).

Campbell, Joseph, *The Hero With a Thousand Faces* (1949, Princeton University Press).

Cunningham, Scott, *Magical Herbalism*, (1982, Llewellyn Publications).

Dudley, G. A., *Dreams: Their Mysteries Revealed*, (1969, Aquarian Press).

Eisler, Riane, *The Chalice and the Blade: Our History, Our Future* (1987, Harper & Row).

Farrar, Janet & Stewart, *The Witches' Goddess* (1987, Phoenix Publishing Inc.).

Fitch, Ed, and Janine Renee, *Magical Rites From the Crystal Well* (1984, Llewellyn Publications).

Frazer, Sir James George, *The Golden Bough* (1922, Collier Books).

Gawain, Shakti, *Creative Visualization*, (1987, Bantam Books, Inc.).

Goodman, Linda, *Sun Signs* (1968, Taplinger Publishing Company, Inc.).

Graves, Robert, *The White Goddess* (1948, Farrar, Straus & Giroux).

Harding, M. Esther, *Women's Mysteries* (1971, Harper & Row).

Keyes, Jr., Ken, *The Hundredth Monkey*, (1986, Vision Books).

King James Version, *Holy Bible*.

Leland, Charles Godfrey, *Aradia, the Gospel of the Witches* (1899).

Magickal Days, (1985, Castle Rising).

March, M.D., and J. McEvers, *The Only Way to Learn Astrology* (1980, ACS Publicators, Inc.).

Mariechild, Diane, *Crystal Visions* (1985, The Crossing Press).

Masters, Robert, *The Goddess Sekhmet* (1988, Amity House).

Maynards, Jim, *Pocket Astrologer* (1989, Llewellyn Publications).

Mella, Dorothee L., *Candle Power* (1978, A Domel Artbook).

Noble, Vicki, *The Shakti Woman* (in press, Harper & Row).

Richardson, Wally, and Lenora Huett, *Spiritual Value of Gemstones* (1980, DeVorss).

Robbins, Tom, *Jitterbug Perfume*, (1984, Bantam Books, Inc.).

Rush, Anne Kent, *Moon, Moon* (1976, Random House).

Sams, Jamie, & David Carson, *Medicine Cards: The Discovery of Power Through the Ways of Animals*, (1988, Bear & Co.).

Seed, J., J. Macy, P. Fleming and A. Naess, *Thinking Like a Mountain: Towards a Council of All Beings* (1988, New Society Publishers).

Silbey, Uma, *The Complete Crystal Guidebook* (1986, U-Read Publications).

Spretnak, Charlene, *Lost Goddesses of Early Greece: A Collection of Pre-Hellenic Myths* (1978, Beacon Press).

Starhawk, *The Spiral Dance* (1978, Harper & Row).

Stepanich, Kisma K., *An Act of Woman Power* (1989, Schiffer Publishing, Ltd.).

Stone, Merlin, *Ancient Mirrors of Womanhood* (1979, Beacon Press).

Valiente, Doreen, *Natural Magic* (1975, Phoenix Publishing, Inc.).

Verdon-Roe, Vivienne, *Women For America, For the World*, (1986, The Educational Film & Video Project).

——*Speaking Up & Speaking Out*, (1988, The Educational Film & Video Project).

Walker, Barbara G., *The Women's Encyclopedia of Myths and Secrets* (1983, Harper & Row).

Walker, Dael, *The Crystal Book* (1983, The Crystal Co.).

Weier, T.E., C.R. Stocking, M.G. Barbour, T.L. Rost, *Botany: An Introduction to Plant Biology* (1982, John Wiley and Sons, Publishing).

Zukav, Gary, *The Dancing Wu Li Masters* (1979, William Morrow and Company, Inc.).

Index ───────────────────────────────

A Pledge to Spirituality 7
A Winter Meditation 217-18
Acca Larentia 106, 221
Achaeans 51
Achna 173
Addiction 216
Affirmation 58, 93, 97-8, 198, 215, 241, 264, 288
Alchemical goddess 115
Amazon 59, 212
Amaterasu-O-Mi-Kami 117, 130
Ancient key 173
Anglo-Saxon 154
Anna Perenna 72, 130
Anthropocentrism 33
Aphrodite 60, 72, 76, 104, 106
Apical meristem 5
April 23, 25, 73
Aquarius 45
Aranda 184, 289
Ares 51
Aries 20
Artemis 49, 60, 66, 72, 92, 170, 212
Ash 195
Astarte 72, 106, 221
Astral Body 198-201
Athame 90, 246
Athena 60, 66, 72, 73, 117, 221
Atlas 18
Attica 188
Attitude 40, 82, 216, 220, 253, 266

August 23, 145, 151-61
Autumn 18, 20, 26, 36, 58, 105, 119-76
    Correspendences 140-44
    Element 144-51
    Phases 151-76
    Goddess 130-37
    Equinox 20, 23-6, 30, 32, 154, 167-70

Bast 60, 117
Bay Laurel 195, 210
Bear 211-12
Becoming Relative 99-104
Becoming Sisters Ceremony 101-04, 116
Beingness 215-16
Belief Statement 9,10
Beltane 23, 25, 26, 29, 31, 86, 88-92
Bendis 92, 106, 130
Bible 6, 18
Big Bang 5
Big Dipper 99
Black Wolf 95-6, 121, 184, 286-90, 292-94
Bonna Dea 92, 131, 221
Brain-Wave Machine 193
Bridget 49, 227, 254-58

Calliope 61, 104
Cancer 105
Candles 84-7, 93, 219-20, 252, 257
    magick 85, 93, 96, 268
    colors 93-5
Candlemas 23, 28, 29, 33, 49, 237, 250-58
Capricorn 222
Caristia 22, 61
Carmentalia 107, 225
Carna 104, 131, 227
Carnelian 184
Cattails 195
Cauldron 32, 115, 172, 226, 254-58, 296
Cedar 69
Celestial Equator 20, 25-7

Celtic 25, 259, 282
Ceres 76, 92, 107, 161
Ceremonial Magician 259
Cerridwen 107, 115, 116, 226
Chakra 81, 94-5, 192
   Base 81, 94, 246
   Womb 81, 94, 206
   Solar Plexus 81, 94, 179, 182
   Heart 81, 94, 192, 206, 208, 246
   Throat 81, 94
   Third Eye 75, 81, 94, 206, 208, 246, 289
   Crown 81, 94, 206
Charge of the Star Goddess 244-45
Cherokee Dance of Life 70, 128
Chicomecoatl 107, 169
Children 13, 16, 82, 88, 189, 216, 221, 232, 237, 260, 275
Christ 15, 188, 259
Christian 25, 70, 188, 259
Christmas 187
Cinquefoil 195, 210
Clairvoyant Brew 210-11
Clio 61, 104
Cloves 195
Copper 185
Corn Goddess 92, 169, 251-58
Cornmeal 2, 101, 180, 196, 197
Costmary 195
Cotton 195, 244
Coven Charge 243, 247-48
Coyote Woman 46-48
Creative Visualization 213-16
Creatrix 13-31
Crocidolite 73
Crone 14, 32, 49, 120, 130-39, 170-76, 222-25, 226, 255-58
Crystals 2, 70, 79, 179, 182, 186, 195, 196, 198-201
Cybele 72, 76, 227

Dancing Wu Li Master 15, 139, 238
Death 11, 17, 27, 30, 32, 119-20, 172, 182, 186-88, 193, 211, 217,
   222-25, 231, 245, 253, 255, 296

Death Goddess 222-25, 291
December 20, 23, 27, 213-21
Decreeing 93
Demeter 14, 51, 107, 171, 176, 221
Deosil 254-58
Deva 164
Devil 188
Diamonds 184, 227
Diana 107, 161
Dianic 259
Divination 85
Doingness 215-16
Dorians 51
Dragon's Blood 244
Dreaming 172, 187, 193-201, 223-25
    lodge 211
    pillows 195-96
    catcher 196-98
    web 196-98
    chant 197
    with crystals 198-201
Dreamtime 95, 185, 201, 203, 286-90

Eagle 39, 41-44, 102, 181
Earth Elemental Journey 189
Earth Healer 19
Earth Tradition, The 4, 260
Easter 70
Eight Energy Shifts 20, 23
Electroencephalograph 193
Elements
    Air 39, 41-5, 56, 295
    Earth 6-9, 11, 16, 18, 20, 56, 179, 182, 185, 187-92, 222, 296
    Fire 56, 84-6, 114, 252, 295 (philosophers) 85, (chant) 254
    Water 56, 119, 140, 144-51, 296
Elfin 259
Emotional Body 25-8, 105, 144
Eostre 61, 70, 73
Epona 104, 108
Erato 61, 105, 108

Eucaryotic 6
Europe 25, 108
Eurus 42
Eurydice 105
Euterpe 61, 104

Faery 25, 250
Fates 105, 197, 247, 263, 272
Father Sky 2, 5, 71, 81, 180, 186
February 23, 28, 45, 237, 251-58
Femi-Patriarch 207, 261
Fertility Bed 251-58
First Harvest 23, 153-61, 167
Five-fold Kiss 243
Flora 61, 76
Fors Fortuna 105, 108
Fortuna Redux 176
Four Seasons 20, 23
Friday 86, 196
    the 13th 86-7

Gaia 212, 227, 237, 275, 290, 294
Gaia Tradition, The 4, 7-8, 17, 260
Gardenia 29
Gardnerian 259
Gemini 87, 92
Gnomes 187, 189-92
God 6, 138, 251-58
    green wood 188
Gold 185
Grain Maiden 51
Grain Mother 51, 168
Great Goddess 218, 222-33
Great Spirit 180-86, 212
Great Water Gourd 99-104
Greece 51
Greetings Brightness Chant 43
Guedra 201-10
Guttate 6

Half-mas 154
Hall of Learning 238
Hallows Eve 23, 170-76
Harmonic Convergence 145
Harvest 26-7, 32, 153
Hathor 76, 228
Havingness 215-16
Healing 81, 205, 277, 284-86
Hecate 128, 132, 161, 172-76, 212
Hell 132, 171
Heliotrope 195
Hera 108, 225
Herkimer Diamond 195, 199
Hesiod 51
Hestia 66, 108, 221
Hexing 258, 263-65
Hilaria 73
Hiroshima 232
Holy Matrimony 29
Homer 51
Hygeia 50, 62
Hypatia 72, 132

Iacchos 132, 171
I AM 92, 167
Igne Natura Renovatur Integra 85
Imbolg 23, 28-9, 33, 49, 251-58
Initiation 237-50
    ceremony 242-50, 265
Inanna 109, 225, 228
Intellect 41, 44
Intuition 50
Ionians 51
Ishtar 70, 76, 89-91, 228, 244, 271
Isis 16, 72, 92, 109, 117, 161, 212
Ixchel 221
January 1, 222-25
Jasmine 29
Judaeo 25
July 26, 105-17

June 20, 23, 26, 92-105
Juno 50, 117
   Lucina 72, 110, 221, 267-69
   Regina 104
Jupiter 213
Juturna 132, 161

Kali 133, 137-38
Kami 133, 212
Karma 10, 101
Kinnikiniik 163
Knowledge 13, 238-40, 259
Kore 14, 51-9, 62, 171, 176, 225
   Kore Chant 57
Kundalini 192, 228, 249
Kwannon 63, 76
Kwan Yin 62, 76

Lakshmi 63, 170
Lammas 23, 26, 29, 32, 116, 153-60
Lapis 70
Lavender 69, 244
Law of the Goddess 139
Lemon Balm 195
Leo 151, 154
Libra 20, 110, 171
Life and Death Prayer Arrows 121-29
Litha 105, 110
Little Sister 99-104
Lord of the Green Wood 29, 31, 154
Luna 63, 73, 245
Luna Sea Coven 9
Lunar Calendar 22

Ma-Nu 148
Mabon 167
Maiden 31, 59, 254-58
March 20, 23, 25, 50
Marigold 195
Mars 73

Mask 171-76
Mater Matuta 104, 110
Matronalia 267-70
May 23, 25, 86
   May Day 88-92
   May Pole 89
Medicine Wheel 170, 179-86, 277
Medicine Woman 116, 151-53, 179-86, 235-37, 284, 289
Meditation 46, 116, 155, 162, 195, 201, 215, 216-18, 241, 264, 276
Melpomene 63, 104
Menstruation 22, 91, 119
Mental Body 25-8, 44, 253, 295
Mercury 92, 161
Midsummer 23, 26
Mimosa 195
Minerva 63, 73, 197
Mint 195
Mirror Magic 50
Mnemosyne 63, 104, 111
Moerae 63, 197
Monday 195
Moon 12, 22-3, 31, 105, 119, 188, 195, 275, 278
   Crescent 22, 41, 69
   New 22, 45, 58, 69, 196
   Dark 22, 187
   Full 22, 50, 58, 84, 87, 96, 196, 244, 250
   Waning 22, 140, 195, 196, 225
Mother 6-10, 14, 32, 105-15, 226, 255-58, 272, 279
Mother Earth 2, 5, 6, 23, 36, 39, 56, 71, 79, 154, 180, 186-92,
   255-58, 260, 275
Mugwort 163, 172, 195, 210, 277
Muses 63, 104
Myth 18
Mythology 6, 18, 28, 188

Native American 4, 102, 196, 211-12
Necna 144
Neptune 50
Nez Perce Indian 98, 102
November 27, 192-212

Nuclear War 232
Nutmeg 195
 oil 195

Obsidian 184-85
October 23, 27, 170-76
Olympian goddesses 66-188
Ops 111, 161, 221
Our Lady of Fatima 117
Owl Goddess 222-24

Pan 92, 188
Pandora 64, 139
Patriarch 9, 51, 87, 93, 114, 137-8
Pax 64, 104, 225
Pennyroyal 164
Persephone 51-59, 64
Phloem 6
Physical Body 26, 28, 198-201, 224
Pisces 20, 50
Planting of seeds 45, 56, 58
Pluto 192
Polyhmnia 64, 105
Poppy 54, 195
Poseidon 148
Power Song 95-6, 181, 288-90
Pre-Hellenic 51
Procaryotic 6
Proserpine 64, 92, 134
Pyromancy 85

Quarters
 East 41, 56, 181, 295
 South 20, 26, 56, 79, 84, 181, 198, 295
 West 56, 119, 140, 181, 296
 North 20, 26, 56, 179, 182, 187, 217, 296
Radha 64, 170
Radicle cells 5-6
Rai 165
Rapid Eye Movement (REM) 194

Raspberry 172
Religion 12, 18, 189, 258, 259, 266
Rhiannon 72, 112
Rosalia 104
Rose 195
Rosemary 244
Ruby 184

Sacred Hoop 99-104
Sacred Kiss 5, 31
Sage 69, 101, 172
Sagittarius 213
Saint Germain 92-3
Salamanders 84, 252
Samhain 23, 27, 30, 32, 171-76, 281
Sandalwood 195-218
Saturday 9, 196
Saturn 222
Saxon 259
Scorpio 183, 192
Scry 85
Sekhmet 117, 135
Selene 49, 112
September 20, 23, 26, 161-70
Seven Sisters 99-104
Shadow Dance 162-67, 171-76
Shakti 114, 230
Shaman's Eye 75, 81, 96, 116, 289
Sheila Na Gig 65, 92
Silver 69, 185
Sister Chant 103
Sisterhood 4, 82, 114, 210, 237, 250, 260, 290-94
Sisterhood of the Shields 95
Snake 211-12
Sophia 175, 230
Sparta 188
Spider Woman 135, 197, 230
Spirit Body 27-8
Spirit Sister 1-5, 99-104, 196, 293
Spirit Woman Agate 116

Spring 1, 18, 20, 23, 25, 28, 32, 33, 36, 39-76, 82, 119, 154, 161, 183,
    187, 215, 216, 235-73
    Correspondences 41-5
    Element 42-5
    Phases 45-76
    Goddess 59-71
    Vernal Equinox 20, 23, 25, 28-9, 31, 51-9
Stat Mater 135, 161
Stinkweed 163-67, 172
Stomates 6
Summer 18, 20, 31, 32, 36, 39, 50, 79-117, 119, 154, 161, 255
    Correspondences 84-5
    Element 85-6
    Phases 86-92
    Goddess 105-15
    Solstice 20, 23, 26, 29, 31, 98-104, 154
Sun 1, 12, 17, 20, 23, 25, 33, 41, 79, 81, 84-5, 151, 186, 188, 216-18,
    251, 279
Sunday 195
Sweet Grass 29
Sylphs 41, 43

Tao 92, 230
Tarot Cards 2, 145
Taurus 25, 86
Temperance 171, 264
Temple Dancing 85
Terpsichore 65, 104
Thanksgiving 26, 32, 167-70, 212
Thalia 65, 104
The Wheel of the Year 20
    Factual 20
    Mythological 28
    Esoteric Spirit Wheel 28
    Esoteric Physical Wheel 28, 31
Theban Three 173
Themis 113, 225
Threefold Law 139, 214, 263
Thursday 196
Tiger-eye 73, 195
    Journey 74

Tobacco 163
Tonantzin 113, 221
Topaz 184
Trance 162, 195, 201-10, 215
Triple Goddess 92, 226, 245, 252-58
Trumpet Flower 172
Trust and Experience 16
Truth 12, 171-76, 222-25
Tuesday 195
Turquoise 184

U'ma 113, 136, 173
Unconditional Love 12, 13
Understanding 238-40, 259
Undine 140, 144, 148
Urania 65, 105

Venus 65, 76, 86-7, 143, 149, 170-71
Vesta 73, 104, 113, 221
Vestal Virgins 257-58
Victoria 50, 136
Virgin 31, 59, 226, 254-58
Virgin Mary 49, 92, 104, 161, 170, 221, 230
Virgo 20, 65, 161
Visualization 213-16, 256

Wednesday 196
Welsh 259
Wicca 4, 9, 243, 246, 250, 259, 281
Winter 9, 18, 20, 26, 32-3, 36, 39, 154, 179-233, 255, 291
    Correspondences 187
    Element 187-92
    Phases 192-225
    Goddess 226-33
    Solstice 20, 23, 27-8, 33, 216-21
Wisdom 13, 238-40, 259
Witchcraft 243, 259
Women Spirit Rising 4
World War II 232
Wormwood 163, 172, 195

Xylem 6

Yemaya Olokun 66, 105
Yule 23, 216-21

Zeus 51
Zodiacal Celestial Sphere 20, 25

STAY IN TOUCH

On the following pages you will find listed, with their current prices, some of the books now available on related subjects. Your book dealer stocks most of these, and will stock new titles in the Llewellyn series as they become available. We urge your patronage.

However, to obtain our full catalog, to keep informed of new titles as they are released and to benefit from informative articles and helpful news, you are invited to write for our bi-monthly news magazine/catalog. A sample copy is free, and it will continue coming to you at no cost as long as you are an active mail customer. Or you may keep it coming for a full year with a donation of just $2.00 in U.S.A. ($7.00 for Canada & Mexico, $20.00 overseas, first class mail). Many bookstores also have *The Llewellyn New Times* available to their customers. Ask for it.

Stay in touch! In *The Llewellyn New Times'* pages you will find news and reviews of new books, tapes and services, announcements of meetings and seminars, articles helpful to our readers, news of authors, advertising of products and services, special money-making opportunities, and much more.

The Llewellyn New Times
P.O. Box 64383-Dept. 766, St. Paul, MN 55164-0383, U.S.A.
• • •
TO ORDER BOOKS AND TAPES

If your book dealer does not have the books described on the following pages readily available, you may order them direct from the publisher by sending full price in U.S. funds, plus $1.50 for postage and handling for orders *under* $10.00; $3.00 for orders *over* $10.00. There are no postage and handling charges for orders over $50. UPS Delivery: We ship UPS whenever possible. Delivery guaranteed. Provide your street address as UPS does not deliver to P.O. Boxes. UPS to Canada requires a $50 minimum order. Allow 4–6 weeks for delivery. Orders outside the U.S.A. and Canada: Airmail—add retail price of book; add $5 for each non-book item (tapes, etc.); add $1 per item for surface mail.

FOR GROUP STUDY AND PURCHASE

Because there is a great deal of interest in group discussion and study of the subject matter of this book, we feel that we should encourage the adoption and use of this particular book by such groups by offering a special "quantity" price to group leaders or "agents."

Our Special Quantity Price for a minimum order of five copies of *The Gaia Tradition* is $38.85 cash-with-order. This price includes postage and handling within the United States. Minnesota residents must add 6% sales tax. For additional quantities, please order in multiples of five. For Canadian and foreign orders, add postage and handling charges as above. Credit card (VISA, Master Card, American Express) orders are accepted. Charge card orders only may be phoned free ($15.00 minimum order) within the U.S.A. or Canada by dialing 1-800-THE-MOON. Customer service calls dial 1-612-291-1970. Mail Orders to:

LLEWELLYN PUBLICATIONS
P.O. Box 64383-Dept. 766 / St. Paul, MN 55164-0383, U.S.A.

THE BOOK OF GODDESSES & HEROINES
by Patrician Monaghan

The Book of Goddesses & Heroines is an historical landmark, a must for everyone interested in Goddesses and Goddess worship. It is not an effort to trivialize the beliefs of matriarchal cultures. It is not a collection of Goddess descriptions penned by biased male historians throughout the ages. It is the complete, non-biased account of Goddesses of every cultural and geographic area, including African, Japanese, Korean, Persian, Australian, Pacific, Latin American, British, Irish, Scottish, Welsh, Chinese, Greek, Icelandic, Italian, Finnish, German, Scandinavian, Indian, Tibetan, Mesopotamian, North American, Semitic and Slavic Goddesses!

Unlike some of the male historians before her, Patricia Monaghan eliminates as much bias as possible from her Goddess stories. Envisioning herself as a woman who might have revered each of these Goddesses, she has done away with language that referred to the deities in relation to their male counterparts, as well as with culturally relative terms such as "married" or "fertility cult." The beliefs of the cultures and the attributes of the Goddesses have been left intact.

Plus, this book has a new, complete index. If you are more concerned about finding a Goddess of war than you are a Goddess of a given country, this index will lead you to the right page. This is especially useful for anyone seeking to do Goddess rituals. Your work will be twice as efficient and effective with this detailed and easy-to-use book.

0-87542-573-9, 421 pgs., 6 x 9, illus.   **$17.95**

THE GODDESS BOOK OF DAYS
by Diane Stein

Diane Stein has created this wonderful guide to the Goddesses and festivals for every day of the year! This beautifully illustrated perpetual datebook will give you a listing for every day of the special Goddesses associated with that date along with plenty of room for writing in your appointments. It is a hardbound book for longevity, and has over 100 illustrations of Goddesses from around the world and from every culture. This is sure to have a special place on your desk.

None other like it!

0–87542–758–8, 300 pgs., 5 1/4 x 8, hardbound, illus.   **$12.95**

EARTH POWER:
TECHNIQUES OF NATURAL MAGIC
by Scott Cunningham

Magick is the art of working with the forces of Nature to bring about necessary, and desired, changes. The forces of Nature—expressed through Earth, Air, Fire and Water—are our "spiritual ancestors" who paved the way for our emergence from the prehistoric seas of creation. Attuning to, and working with these energies in magick not only lends you the power to affect changes in your life, it also allows you to sense your own place in the larger scheme of Nature. Using the "Old Ways" enables you to live a better life, and to deepen your understanding of the world about you. The tools and powers of magick are around you, waiting to be grasped and utilized. This book gives you the means to put Magick into your life, shows you how to make and use the tools, and gives you spells for every purpose.

0-87542-121-0, 176 pgs., 51/4 x 8, illus., softcover   **$6.95**

CUNNINGHAM'S ENCYCLOPEDIA OF MAGICAL HERBS
by Scott Cunningham

This is an expansion on the material presented in his first Llewellyn book, *Magical Herbalism*. This is not just another herbal for medicinal uses of herbs—*this is the most comprehensive source of herbal data for magical uses ever printed!* Almost every one of the more than 400 herbs are illustrated, making this a great source for herb identification. For each herb you will also find: magical properties, planetary rulerships, genders, associated deities, folk and Latin names and much more. To make this book even easier to use you will also find a folk name cross reference, and all of the herbs are fully indexed. There is also a large annotated bibliography, and a list of mail order suppliers so you can find the books and herbs you need.

Like all of Scott's books, this one does not require you to use complicated rituals or expensive magical paraphernalia. Instead, it shares with you the intrinsic powers of the herbs. Thus, you will be able to discover which herbs, by their very nature, can be used for luck, love, success, money, divination, astral projection, safety, psychic self-defense and much more. Besides being interesting and educational it is also fun, and fully illustrated with unusual woodcuts from old herbals. This book has rapidly become the classic in its field. It enhances books such as *777* and is a must for all Wiccans.

0-87542-122-9, 352 pgs., 6 x 9, illus., softcover   **$12.95**